THE WORLD'S CLASSICS

ZASTROZZI AND ST IRVYNE

PERCY BYSSHE SHELLEY (1792–1822), born at Field Place, near Horsham, Sussex, was the son of a member of Parliament (Timothy Shelley) and grandson of a wealthy landowner (Bysshe Shelley). After studying at Syon House Academy and Eton, he entered Oxford University but was quickly expelled over the authorship of a pamphlet called *The Necessity of Atheism*. Soon afterwards he eloped with Harriet Westbrook, settling briefly in Keswick (where he met Robert Southey), then going on to Dublin (where he involved himself with politics), and finally returning to England. In 1814 Shelley met the political philosopher and novelist William Godwin and his daughter Mary Wollstonecraft Godwin, with whom Shelley fell in love. In July 1814 he and Mary eloped to the Continent. During the summer of 1816 they became well acquainted with Lord Byron, who was their neighbour in Switzerland. Following Harriet's suicide in November 1816 Shelley and Mary were married. After settling permanently in Italy, Shelley began in 1818 to compose and publish his greatest works. Self-exiled from his homeland, he remained in Italy, although his publications were routinely condemned by most English journals except his liberal friend Leigh Hunt's *Examiner*. A confirmed reformer, Shelley devoted his energies to the causes he espoused until his early death in 1822, when his sailboat was destroyed in a storm. Both the range and the skill of his compositions in poetry and prose attest to Shelley's great literary sophistication and his powerfully humanitarian principles.

STEPHEN C. BEHRENDT is Associate Professor of English at the University of Nebraska, where he is a specialist in British Romanticism. He is author of *The Moment of Explosion: Blake and the Illustration of Milton* (1983) and of numerous articles on Blake, Shelley, and on relations among the arts. His poetry has been widely published.

THE WORLD'S CLASSICS

PERCY BYSSHE SHELLEY

Zastrozzi and St Irvyne

Edited with an Introduction by

STEPHEN C. BEHRENDT

Oxford New York

OXFORD UNIVERSITY PRESS

1986

Oxford University Press, Walton Street, Oxford OX2 6DP

Oxford New York Toronto
Delhi Bombay Calcutta Madras Karachi
Kuala Lumpur Singapore Hong Kong Tokyo
Nairobi Dar es Salaam Cape Town
Melbourne Auckland

and associated companies in
Beirut Berlin Ibadan Nicosia

Oxford is a trade mark of Oxford University Press

First published as a World's Classics paperback 1986

British Library Cataloguing in Publication Data

Shelley, Percy Bysshe
Percy Bysshe Shelley: Zastrozzi and St. Irvyne.—
(World's classics)
I. Title II. Behrendt, Stephen C. III. Shelley,
Percy Bysshe. St. Irvyne IV. Series
823'.7[F] PR5422.Z3

ISBN 0-19-281724-8

Library of Congress Cataloging in Publication Data

Shelley, Percy Bysshe, 1792–1822.
Zastrozzi; and, St. Irvyne.
(The World's classics)
Bibliography: p.
1. Horror tales, English. I. Behrendt, Stephen C.,
1947– . II. Shelley, Percy Bysshe, 1792–1822.
St. Irvyne. 1986. III. Title: Zastrozzi. IV. Title:
St. Irvyne.
PR5422.Z3 1986 823'.7 85-21500

ISBN 0-19-281724-8 (pbk.)

Printed in Great Britain by
Hazell Watson & Viney Limited
Aylesbury, Bucks

CONTENTS

INTRODUCTION

I

When Percy Bysshe Shelley arrived in Oxford in October 1810 to begin his university studies at the age of eighteen, no one could have foreseen the brief and tempestuous life that lay ahead for him. The young author who would die in the wreck of his sailboat in the Bay of Spezia, near Leghorn, Italy, on 8 July 1822 arrived in Oxford fully expecting to be the heir of his father, Timothy Shelley, and to assume his father's seat in Parliament upon attaining his majority. His plans quickly disintegrated after he was expelled from Oxford in March 1811 for his part in the publication of *The Necessity of Atheism*, a pamphlet he had written with his friend at University College, Thomas Jefferson Hogg. Soon his father had virtually disowned him, plunging the newly-married Shelley into a long and painful succession of difficulties. Before any of these storm clouds had ever formed, however, Shelley's father had generously indulged his son's interests in reading, story-telling, and publishing, so much so that when he took Bysshe—as Shelley was usually called—to Oxford he introduced him to Henry Slatter, Oxford's leading bookseller, with the comment that 'my son here has a literary turn; he is already an author, and do pray indulge him in his printing freaks.'[1]

Two of these 'freaks' were the Gothic novels (or 'romances', as Shelley called them, in keeping with the customary Gothic nomenclature) *Zastrozzi* (1810) and *St Irvyne, or, The Rosicrucian* (1810–11), though it was not Slatter who published them. Written by an energetic and ambitious young author not yet twenty, these novels appeared near the high-water mark of the first tide of enthusiasm in England for Gothic fiction. Indeed, before this first flowering ceased, Shelley's second wife, Mary

[1] Richard Holmes, *Shelley: The Pursuit* (New York: E. P. Dutton and Co., 1975), p. 36.

Wollstonecraft Godwin Shelley, would compose and publish her *Frankenstein* (1818) and Shelley would himself appear, only thinly disguised, as the impetuous Scythrop in his friend Thomas Love Peacock's delightful Gothic satire, *Nightmare Abbey* (1818). Shelley's own two novels are calculated attempts to capitalize on the wave of Gothic fiction that crested in his youth as an English public already weary of a protracted war against Revolutionary and Napoleonic France diverted itself with the sensational works of Ann Radcliffe, Charlotte Dacre ('Rosa Matilda'), and Matthew G. ('Monk') Lewis. Both works are clearly attempts to gain not only the immediate gratification of quick fame but also, more importantly, access to an audience for the purpose of delivering the liberal political, social, moral, and intellectual views that would grow ever stronger in Shelley's brief career as author and activist.

Gothic fiction was a logical product of eighteenth-century interest in the Sublime, an interest that also produced the more genteel—and certainly more tear-drenched—tradition of sentimental fiction with its extraordinary new variety of narrative that concerns itself less with what happens in the stories than with how people *feel* about what happens. Like Gothic fiction, sentimental fiction stresses *interiority*: the emotions and intuitive responses of character and reader alike. Both Gothic and sentimental fiction reject the generalizing tendencies and the studied moderation (or 'decorum') of Neoclassicism. Gothic fiction, in particular, opts instead for a highly particularized, dynamic narrative set in remote or mysterious surroundings, informed by a genuine psychological realism, and coloured with a strong eroticism.

Horace Walpole had established the Gothic genre in England in *The Castle of Otranto* (1764) with its crumbling castle, its relentless villain Manfred, its innocent 'damsel in distress' Isabella, and its taboo sexual relationships. By the time Shelley came to compose his novels, the conventions were firmly in place, so much so that Shelley was in fact able—even while writing with a serious moral purpose—to have some good-natured fun with this venerable machinery, simultaneously both exposing and exploiting the formulaic trappings of sentimental Gothic fiction. Hence, for instance, *St Irvyne* includes a gap in which two chapters appear to be 'missing', a device for entrapping the reader that we find also in non-Gothic works like Laurence Sterne's *Tristram Shandy* (1760–7) and Henry Mackenzie's *The Man of Feeling* (1771). Shelley's handling of formulaic settings and details, too, is often arguably tongue-in-cheek. In *St Irvyne*, for instance, the shadowy Ginotti appears to die more than once; Shelley's characters tend to hurl themselves to the ground—or to fall senseless there in exaggerated sentimental 'swoons'—with alarming frequency; and more than once a character falls a second or even a third time without ever being reported to have risen!

Yet while Shelley thus toys with the Gothic genre, he is also beginning in these two works to develop what would become a considerable skill at audience-manipulation. Shelley critics routinely note that the novels are addressed in large measure to their young author's desire for quick fame, which is certainly the case. Yet we need to recognize that more was at stake than mere vanity: Shelley was already deliberately advocating unconventional, generally liberal causes here, purposefully embedding subversive, 'anti-Establishment' propaganda in his tales while appearing to be writing conventional, conservative Gothic romances. In short, Shelley is an early example of the author who employs a popular genre as a vehicle for conveying radical social, political, and intellectual opinions and messages, much as authors as diverse as Dashiell Hammett and 'Amanda Cross' (Carolyn Heilbrun) have in the twentieth century employed detective fiction.

As literary texts, the novels are inherently interesting. Both are shorter than the more typical Gothic novels of the period, which often ran to several exhausting volumes, yet both incorporate the complex, often metaphysical apparatus of their longer relatives. Both are, in fact, essays in the 'literary Sublime', although each takes a different stylistic route, *Zastrozzi* being a breathlessly-paced, short-paragraph narrative full of spectacular events, and *St Irvyne* a more rhetorically complex, long-paragraph, internalized narrative punctuated by passages of questionable poetry. Both novels indicate clearly that early in his career Shelley had formulated and embraced themes that his critics have tended to attribute almost exclusively to the later or 'more mature' Shelley—who, after all, lived barely ten years after finishing *St Irvyne*. They exhibit the same principled concern with the themes of individual liberty, intellectual independence, social integration, and the pernicious effects of revenge that characterize the poems and essays upon which Shelley's reputation is customarily seen to rest.

Despite their relative immaturity, their lack of high surface polish, and their reliance upon the formulas of a literary sub-genre that critics tend to treat with a mixture of suspicion and contempt, *Zastrozzi* and *St Irvyne* none the less exhibit in vital, germinal form Shelley's considerable talent for audience-manipulation, for seductive presentation of subversion disguised as entertainment, and for making art serve the highest ideals of love and humanity—talents which Shelley would develop and refine in the great works of his later years. That he completed no other Gothic novels may appear at first to indicate that Shelley rejected the Gothic mode; yet elements of the Gothic persisted into his later works, appearing tellingly, for instance, in his tragedy *The Cenci* (1819). Perhaps the greatest testimony to the success with which Shelley embedded in these two early works the themes and techniques that would preoccupy him throughout his brief career lies in the fact that it has taken his critics so long to notice and appreciate them, and to recognize them for what they are.

II

Some initial sense of their plots may help us better to understand both the nature and the relationship between Shelley's two novels. In *Zastrozzi* the virtuous and innocent lovers Verezzi and Julia fall prey to the designs of the jealous Matilda, whose violent and unreciprocated passion for Verezzi leads her to plot Julia's murder. Having convinced him that Julia has died, she seduces and gradually wins over the susceptible Verezzi. Her scheme is undone, however, when in Venice Verezzi recognizes the still very much alive Julia, renounces Matilda, and, distraught, commits suicide. Enraged, Matilda plucks the dagger from Verezzi's bleeding breast, kills Julia, and mutilates her corpse. In most of her schemes, excepting the actual murder of Julia, Matilda is aided and abetted by the aloof and ominous Zastrozzi. Zastrozzi's motives are not revealed until the end, just before he is executed by the Inquisition, which has arrested him and Matilda. Zastrozzi's mother had, we learn, been seduced and then abandoned by Verezzi's father, Zastrozzi subsequently swearing revenge on Verezzi's family. Hence the brutality and the conniving of both Matilda and Zastrozzi are shown to stem from wounded, inflated pride (the standard tragic flaw of *hubris*) that takes the form of an overarching, irrational obsession with revenge for real or imagined offences.

St Irvyne, or, The Rosicrucian is a more elaborate variation on the same theme of self-destructive passions, ornamented with echoes of William Godwin's *St Leon*, Schiller's *The Robbers*, and the Faust stories. Here the outcast Wolfstein joins a band of robbers and eventually poisons its leader, Cavigni, in order to secure for himself Cavigni's captive, the beautiful and dangerous Megalena. The mysterious Ginotti sees Wolfstein poison Cavigni's wine, facilitates his escape from the angry robbers, and subsequently dogs his steps, extorting from Wolfstein the promise that at some future date he will accept a duty Ginotti will place upon him. Wolfstein soon begins to tire of the insatiable and jealously possessive Megalena, with whom he has settled in Genoa and who eventually contrives to have him murder her rival, Olympia. He never commits the crime, however, for when he refuses Olympia's romantic overtures she commits suicide with his dagger. Wolfstein and Megalena flee to a Bohemian castle Wolfstein has inherited, where Ginotti reappears to pass on to Wolfstein the secret of immortality (the 'elixir'), in exchange for which it appears Ginotti has at some time past sold himself to the devil. Interested, Wolfstein none the less resists the requirement that he deny God. Before he can act conclusively, the devil seizes Ginotti and Wolfstein appears to die of shock.

Meanwhile, in a subplot Wolfstein's innocent sister Eloise de St Irvyne is left a vulnerable orphan by the death of her saintly mother. Seduced by the unscrupulous Frederic de Nempere (who, it develops, is none other than Ginotti), she is freed by Nempere's colleague Mountfort and befriended by the sensitive, free-thinking, and very Shelleyan poet Fitzeustace. They fall in love, of course, and marry, Fitzeustace subsequently adopting Nempere's illegitimate child by Eloise. The conclusion of *St Irvyne* is impossibly hasty and inconclusive, its 'answers' tossed to the reader in a great rush. Shelley had apparently intended the novel as a 'three decker'—the typical three-volume format of much popular fiction—but when he abruptly lost interest in the project he tied the loose ends together (in the most careless of knots) and handed the manuscript over to its publisher, refusing even to deal with correcting the proof copy. Both novels were reviewed without enthusiasm by the English literary periodicals, though not without some alarm at their contents. Both found their way into circulating libraries, the customary abode of popular Gothic fiction, and *St Irvyne* was eventually reissued in 1822 by its publisher, J. J. Stockdale, though this was undoubtedly more a matter of using up his remaining copies (with a new title-page substituted for the old) than of actually reprinting the volume.

Modern critical response to Shelley's earliest works is perhaps epitomized by Kenneth Neill Cameron's summation in *The Young Shelley*:

> All in all, as we look on Shelley's 'votary of romance' period it is a dreary spectacle in spite of glimmerings, here and there, of the Shelley to come; and as we view his macabre collection of avenging demons, sinister Rosicrucians, and seductions by the brace, we cannot but heave a sigh of relief that he finally (via Godwin or any one else) found that he had social 'duties to perform' which would, henceforth, form the basis for his thinking and writing.[2]

It is easy to concur in Cameron's judgement and to prefer Shelley's later works like *Prometheus Unbound*, *The Cenci*, and

[2] Kenneth Neill Cameron, *The Young Shelley: Genesis of a Radical* (1950; rpt. New York: Collier Books, 1962), p. 51.

Adonais. But it is important to recognize in a complex character like Beatrice Cenci the mature culmination of a line of beautiful 'avenging demons' whose lineage can be traced directly back to the dangerous Matilda of *Zastrozzi*. However much the external *forms* of Shelley's work changed as his skill as a stylist in prose and poetry increased, if we look back at early works like *Zastrozzi* and *St Irvyne* we discover in them many of the themes we associate with the later Shelley.

Shelley's strong interest in Gothic fiction developed early. He writes to James Tisdall from his family home at Field Place, Sussex, in January of 1808 that he 'read[s] Novels & romances all day, till in the Evening I fancy myself a Character.'[3] Presumably he is reading not only bits and pieces of the seemingly endless run of cheap blue-covered thrillers put out by the Minerva Press but also earlier Gothic works like Ann Radcliffe's novels, whose chaste heroines escape the clutches of countless sinister villains, generally to find peace and fulfilment in blissful marriages. Shelley would have appreciated the psychological acuteness of Radcliffe's novels; works like *The Mysteries of Udolpho* (1794) and *The Italian* (1797), for instance, draw subtle distinctions between horror and terror, both in their effects upon the characters and in the literary and psychological stimuli by which the author produces those effects for the reader. One of the most important features of the Gothic fiction of Radcliffe and others is the characteristic tension they create by revealing the presence (or imminent presence) of real evil in the midst of—or in the guise of—apparent good (or beauty). Like many of his Romantic contemporaries, Coleridge had employed much the same sort of device in *Christabel*. It is a device that Shelley, too, employs in much of his writing, including his Gothic studies.

But *Zastrozzi* suggests that Shelley has also been reading stronger stuff than Mrs Radcliffe's novels. According to Thomas Medwin, the long production by Charlotte Dacre ('Rosa Matilda') called *Zofloya, or, The Moor: A Romance of the Fifteenth*

[3] *The Letters of Percy Bysshe Shelley*, ed. Frederick L. Jones (2 vols., Oxford: Clarendon Press, 1964), I, 2.

Century (1806) 'enchanted him'.[4] It is no coincidence that the name of one of Dacre's villainesses, Megalena Strozzi, is echoed both in the title of *Zastrozzi* and in the character of the scheming Megalena in *St Irvyne*. There is in Shelley's novels also a strong strain of Matthew Lewis, not only in the appropriation of the name Matilda (the sorceress-nun in Lewis's *The Monk* [1796]) as a passing tribute both to Lewis and to Rosa *Matilda*,[5] but in other resemblances as well. Lewis's lustful monk Ambrosio, and his demonic nun Matilda, for instance, would have appealed to Shelley, whose antipathy to orthodox Christianity generally was strong. These perverted figures who, like Shakespeare's Iago, 'are not what they are' find their successors in Shelley's Zastrozzi and Matilda, and in Wolfstein, Megalena, and Ginotti-Nempere, to cite the most obvious cases. They carry over from the tradition of Christian typology the representation of the 'subtile' Serpent that disrupts the serenity of Eden in an orgy of duplicity and deceit made possible by that most delicate trigger to human gullibility: pride.

Indeed the Gothic tradition replays with almost infinite variations the myths both of the temptation and fall in Eden and of the perilous experience of the post-lapsarian wilderness. The fruit consumed in Eden turns to poison, withering humanity's world into one of suffering and death rather than opening it into the bloom of divine infinity Satan had promised. So, too, do both real and metaphorical poisons operate in Gothic fiction. The poison by which Wolfstein frees himself and Megalena from the bandit chief Cavigni in *St Irvyne*, for instance, effectively poisons their relationship as well and brings the shadowy Ginotti, who had witnessed the crime, into the picture to dog Wolfstein's steps, much as the misbegotten Creature does Victor Frankenstein's a few years later in Mary Shelley's novel. The dark and threatening natural environments of Gothic fiction, the frequent storms, the

[4] Thomas Medwin, *The Life of Percy Bysshe Shelley*, ed. H. Buxton Forman (London: Oxford University Press, 1913), p. 25.

[5] The name has a venerable history. Introduced by Horace Walpole in *The Castle of Otranto* (1764), generally regarded as the first Gothic novel, 'Matilda' appears repeatedly in Gothic fiction.

multiple violent deaths, the decaying and collapsing castles with their perpetually twisting passageways and secret chambers—all these bespeak a world in decline, an ominous world that everywhere threatens its inhabitants, none of whom, it seems, can ever entirely be trusted to be what she or he appears.

Like many of the narrators who had preceded him, Shelley often appears to step in to help the reader recognize the evil that lurks behind the seductive façades erected by the moral and spiritual misfits who propel these novels to their generally violent conclusions. In a particularly nasty scene in *Zastrozzi* in which the pact is arranged to murder Matilda's rival Julia, Zastrozzi delivers a heretical argument against the orthodox Christian notion of the soul's immortality. Lest the reader be tempted to blame Shelley for Zastrozzi's heresy (as Dr Johnson had chastized Milton for Satan's), Shelley's narrator brackets Zastrozzi's opinions with properly censorious language that satisfies the immediate need to counsel the reader and distance the narrator (and presumably the author) from those opinions. But Shelley is employing a propagandizing technique here that is not unlike that used by the courtroom lawyer who makes inflammatory and damning remarks knowing full well that the judge will instruct the jury to 'disregard' them. Once out, though, they are not easily obliterated: the mind cannot simply be erased.

And here we come to a central feature of Shelley's work, a feature that characterizes not just the two Gothic novels but indeed all of his major prose and poetry: his calculated subversions. For Shelley is far more sympathetic to Zastrozzi than he allows his narrator to be. The warnings and admonitions to the reader, couched as they are in the language of moral disapprobation, *seem* geared to reinforcing the reader's own moral disapproval: it is apparently 'safe' for the reader to hear Zastrozzi's blasphemies, since Shelley has set up a sort of moral and psychological 'buffer' in the person of the narrator. But despite this rhetorical insulation in the *surface* of the narrative, the reader is still forced to confront what Zastrozzi has to say. It is a rhetorical manœuvre Shelley would employ on many occasions. Entrapping the unsuspecting reader through the apparent form of a work, he saturates that reader with subversions of all sorts, forcing on her or him active consideration rather than mere passive observation. One of Shelley's favourite rhetorical modes was that of the sceptical debate, a form in which *each* side argues so effectively that the other is demolished, leaving it for the audience to construct a third, more tenable position. As early as *Zastrozzi* and *St Irvyne* Shelley was attempting to involve his reader in just such a process of evaluating, choosing, and creating.

It is no mere coincidence that Zastrozzi's view of religion ('false, foolish, and vulgar prejudices') so nearly approximates Shelley's own in 1810; nor is it coincidental that Zastrozzi in many ways prefigures the flawed Satan-Prometheus figure Shelley would later 'redeem' in the perfected, benevolent Prometheus of his *Prometheus Unbound*. (Prometheus was of central importance to Shelley and his circle, as we see in his friend Lord Byron's 'Prometheus' and *Manfred* and in Mary's *Frankenstein*, which bore the subtitle 'The Modern Prometheus'.) In fact, Zastrozzi undoubtedly reflects an aspect of Shelley's own personality. Likewise, when Ginotti recounts his own history in Chapter 10 of *St Irvyne*, it sounds curiously like Shelley's, even down to his age at the time when he 'dived into the depths of metaphysical speculations' (p. 181): like Shelley, he is seventeen, and just beginning to learn that there is more to heaven and earth than is dreamed of in his nature-based philosophy. Like Zastrozzi, Ginotti faced a crucial decision: he stood at seventeen at much the same crossroads as had his Faustian predecessors, and he had to choose, essentially, between a bond with humanity (represented in an acceptance of natural, bodily mortality) and a breach with them in the form of the opening abyss of speculative science (represented by the elixir). The former is selfless, the latter selfish; the first is social and integrative, leading to the fullness of shared human experience, the latter self-centred and isolating, leading to the physical and psychological horrors of alienation experienced by moral and social deviants like Cain and by both the Creature and his creator in Mary's *Frankenstein*. Like so much of Shelley's writing, both these novels are profoundly autobiographical, either of real external incidents or, as is more often the case, of internal psychological states and crises.

Underlying all of Shelley's work—even the earliest—is a strong moral and social conscience, a commitment to an integrative, egalitarian love for one's fellow creatures and to a principled effort to improve the human condition. Hence both *Zastrozzi* and *St Irvyne* provide multiple object lessons about the Shelleyan cardinal sin of *vengeance*, perhaps the epitome of self-centredness. Yet while Zastrozzi is the most completely Satanic manipulator of others, his *physical* immensity, which Shelley stresses repeatedly, symbolizes his spiritual immensity. Like Satan, Zastrozzi has been destroyed from within by an ego grown beyond all bounds of reason; in his role of self-appointed avenger he is not unlike the cruel and retributive God of the Old Testament whom Shelley rejected. But Zastrozzi's final scene is none the less an ambivalent one for the reader as Shelley presents it: the noble bearing of this dark giant as he faces death is strangely compelling, especially when contrasted to that of Matilda, who by the end has 'repented' and assumed the conventional visual trappings of innocence. Even in apparent defeat Zastrozzi's obduracy is more powerful than Matilda's conformity.

Shelley's point is not that Zastrozzi is a total villain; rather it is that Zastrozzi has fallen through a weakness of human character—essentially the traditional tragic flaw of *hubris*. To colour him entirely black would be to render him a farcical figure, a two-dimensional, cardboard Gothic silhouette. To empower him with the ability to choose—however wrongly—and to follow an inner necessity—however misguided—is to invest him with the properties of tragedy. The Gothic universe is, in fact, a tragic one,[6] and Zastrozzi is a tragic hero whose ancestry reaches back to the great fallen figures both of Aeschylus and, more recently, of Milton, who portrayed complex characters engaged in momentous psychological struggles. There is a creeping horror in *Zastrozzi*, and it is a moral and intellectual one, an internal erosion that the author clearly wishes his readers to perceive. Zastrozzi is

[6] See Peter L. Thorslev, Jr., *Romantic Contraries: Freedom versus Destiny* (New Haven and London: Yale University Press, 1984), esp. pp. 126–41.

the prime example of the character who embodies the *potential* for good, like Wolfstein, and to a lesser extent Ginotti, in *St Irvyne*. Zastrozzi lacks the melioristic socializing impulse that informs the words and actions of the virtuous friend of humanity: the Jesus Christ—or the Shelley. Despite his rejection of the *institution* of orthodox Christianity, Shelley admired Christ—as political reformer, as visionary prophet, and as the ideal of humanitarian self-sacrifice—and often linked himself, both implicitly and explicitly, with him. It is the lack of any such human sympathy (or empathy) that dooms Zastrozzi, for the power of imparting joy has given place in him to the joy of imparting pain: benevolence has become vengeance, poisoning the 'milk of human kindness' and making a hell of heaven. Convinced that 'Heaven' is a fiction of vulgar religious superstition invented to coerce the free into conformity, Shelley argues implicitly in both *Zastrozzi* and *St Irvyne*, as he was to do more explicitly elsewhere, for a secular heaven, a recreation of paradise specifically *on earth*, in the universe of human society.

Stylistically, *Zastrozzi* and *St Irvyne* are very different. The short, breathless paragraphs and crisp sentences of the former give place to the complex periodicity of sentences and paragraphs in the latter:

> It was at this dark and silent hour that Wolfstein, unheeding the surrounding objects,—objects which might have touched with awe, or heightened to devotion, any other breast,—wandered alone—pensively he wandered—dark images for futurity possessed his soul: he shuddered when he reflected upon what had passed; nor was his present situation calculated to satisfy a mind eagerly panting for liberty and independence. [p. 114]

The abrupt beginning of *Zastrozzi*, with Verezzi's unexplained dilemma thrust suddenly upon the reader in a series of rapidly-moving paragraphs, is markedly different from the slow, involuted paragraph that opens *St Irvyne*, a paragraph whose *visual* as well as verbal density creates a considerable obstacle for the reader. In *St Irvyne*, no matter how fast the plot may move, the language in which it is expressed forces the reader to slow down, to internalize the text in a different way. In many places the diction and syntax might almost be described as 'poetic', emphasizing internal repetitions, rhythms, and cadences. Indeed, Shelley even inserts several poems into the narrative.

There is also a greater and more sophisticated use of metaphor in *St Irvyne*, particularly in 'attention positions' at the beginnings or conclusions of chapters. At the end of the first chapter, for instance, this impulse is applied to Wolfstein:

> He longed again to try his fortune; he longed to re-enter that world which he had never tried but once, and that indeed for a short time; sufficiently long, however, to blast his blooming hopes, and to graft on the stock, which otherwise might have produced virtue, the fatal seeds of vice. [p.124]

Like Zastrozzi, Wolfstein (who is related to the powerful dark figure of Karl Moor from Schiller's *The Robbers* [1781], a play that likewise features a robber band and whose influence motivated no less than Wordsworth and Coleridge, among many others, to compose dramas[7]) is another figure whose potential for good has been misdirected, both by circumstance and by choice.

The narrator's voice in *St Irvyne* is often significantly different from those of the characters, who frequently speak a stilted and unnatural language. Such highly artificial diction, a staple of Gothic romance, is made the more noticeable because it *is* so different from the narrator's sensuous, often almost incantatory language, a difference not nearly so apparent in *Zastrozzi*, where the tale and its teller are less clearly differentiated. Finally, natural settings are handled differently in *St Irvyne*. Instead of the verbal shorthand of formulaic moonlit scenes and thunderstorms we find in *Zastrozzi*, Shelley paints a lusher, more particularized landscape, with his characters consciously musing upon or reacting to those settings.

Furthermore, both novels contain obvious invitations to the reader to participate actively in the process of creation. In *Zastrozzi*, for instance, after Matilda is first interrogated by the

[7] Schiller's popular play had been translated and published in England as early as 1792; by 1809 it was available in no less than fourteen English editions.

Inquisition, she is led to a cell where, the narrator tells us, 'Matilda's situation is better conceived than described' (p. 95). Likewise, after Wolfstein and Megalena escape the robber band in *St Irvyne*, they repair to a friendly inn, where the narrator remarks of their amorous evening that 'it is sufficient to conceive what cannot be so well described' (p. 132). Such comments, a stock device of late eighteenth-century fiction—perhaps epitomized in Tristram Shandy's genial invitation to the reader to use the blank page provided in the text for her or his own portrait of the widow Wadman—are also very much a part of Romantic notions of reader participation. In quite another context, for instance, when words fail Shelley at a crucial point in his 'Hymn to Intellectual Beauty' (1816), the poet turns that apparent failure into a rhetorical climax, implicitly inviting the reader to leap from the inadequacies of language to the fullness of pure Idea:

> . . . even now
> I call the phantoms of a thousand hours
> Each from his voiceless grave: they have in visioned bowers
> Of studious zeal or love's delight
> Outwatched with me the envious night—
> They know that never joy illumed my brow
> Unlinked with the hope that thou wouldst free
> This world from its dark slavery,
> That thou—O awful LOVELINESS,
> Wouldst give *whate'er these words cannot express*. [my italics][8]

Other such invitations abound, as for instance in the narrator's frequent addresses directly to the reader in the Eloise sections where, at one point, he lectures his readers: 'Reflect on *this*, ye libertines, and, in the full career of the lasciviousness which has unfitted your souls for enjoying the *slightest* real happiness here or hereafter, tremble! Tremble! I say; for the day of retribution will arrive.' [p. 176]

The Eloise sections provide a number of curiosities, in fact, not the least of which is the apparent absence of the fifth and sixth

[8] *Shelley: Poetical Works*, ed. Thomas Hutchinson, rev. G. M. Matthews (Oxford and New York: Oxford University Press, 1971), p. 531.

chapters, which chapters one might expect to supply a transition from the Wolfstein-Megalena story line. Sometimes regarded as 'a deliberate ploy to intensify the reader's consternation',[9] these two 'missing' chapters may simply be chapters Shelley left unwritten as he composed, intending to fill them in later, much as he often left gaps marked only by dashes in early drafts of his poems. But given Shelley's generally underestimated sense of fun, it is tempting to see in these chapters something of a joke upon the reader in the manner of Mackenzie's novel *The Man of Feeling* (which begins with Chapter 11) or Sterne's *Tristram Shandy* (where two chapters are omitted, only to be inserted in the middle of a subsequent chapter). Still, Chapter 7 of *St Irvyne* contains enough information to allow the reader to begin filling in the gap Shelley has left. Perhaps Shelley simply misnumbered his chapters; perhaps in his hasty and careless submission of the manuscript to its publisher he simply failed to renumber the chapters, just as he failed to correct other anomalies in the text. But the fact that *Zastrozzi*, too, has a 'missing' chapter (Chapter 7)—although there is no perceptible gap in the narrative between Chapters 6 and 8—makes one suspect Shelley's numbering may have been deliberate, a further indication of the sense of fun which is often only barely held in check in the novels.

A final word about *St Irvyne*. It appears Shelley originally intended to write a 'three decker', a novel in three volumes designed to capitalize upon the popularity with circulating libraries of novels of such ambitious dimensions: libraries could charge patrons by the volume, thereby tripling their revenue on borrowings. He wrote to Stockdale that 'I think . . . it is a thing which almost *mechanically* sells to circulating libraries.'[10] Unlike *Zastrozzi*, whose author was identified as 'P.B.S.', the author of *St Irvyne* was given as 'A Gentleman of the University of Oxford'. Shelley had attempted—apparently without success—to purchase favourable reviews of *Zastrozzi*; this time, it seems, he would trust the 'Oxford connection' and the subtitle, 'the Rosicrucian',

[9] Frederick S. Frank, Introduction to *Zastrozzi and St Irvyne* (New York: Arno Press, 1977), p. xiv.

[10] *Letters*, I, 20.

to arouse reader interest. He even complimented Stockdale on advance advertisements of the novel which he felt were 'likely to excite curiosity'.[11] For an author not yet twenty, Shelley demonstrates considerable shrewdness about marketing strategies as means of obtaining and manipulating audiences.

By this time, however, Shelley was becoming involved in other projects, both literary and non-literary. One of these was a manuscript he sounded Stockdale out about publishing. This may have been the never-seen *Hubert Cauvin*, a philosophical *novel* (Shelley had called his Gothic tales 'Romances') on the failure of the French Revolution, a subject that much interested Shelley and that eventually resulted in his longest poem, *Laon and Cythna*, published and withdrawn late in 1817, revised and released as *The Revolt of Islam* in January 1818. In any event, Shelley's immediate interest in Gothic fiction waned before *St Irvyne* was properly 'finished'. Rapid conclusions, in which all is explained, are common in Gothic fiction, of course, but *St Irvyne* does not really conclude: it simply stops, with a pair of brief paragraphs tossed to the reader, one at the end of each of the final two chapters. Despite the one at the end of Chapter 12, for instance, we never actually see the fruition of the central romantic relationship, the paradigmatic case of ideal and selfless love between the virtuous Eloisė and the distinctively Shelleyan poet Fitzeustace, whose views on love, marriage, and human aspiration so closely resemble the author's own. In its essentially unfinished state the manuscript was thus dispatched to Stockdale.

It is worth emphasizing, in conclusion, that already in these early works Shelley plants the seeds of liberal and humanitarian ideas that would reach their fruition in later, more famous works: notions of the necessity for selfless love and integration, of the poisonous nature of selfishness and revenge as motives for human activity, of liberty in opposition to the tyranny of Custom and received ideas. Shelley would return again and again in his brief but spectacular career to both the themes and the techniques with which we see him experimenting in *Zastrozzi* and *St Irvyne*.

[11] *Letters*, I, 24.

Though he turned away from the Gothic novel as he became involved in other, more ambitious literary, political, and social projects, Shelley never entirely abandoned the Gothic, as is evident from the powerful Gothicism of *The Cenci* (1819), probably the finest—and the most stageable—English Romantic play. Nor did he entirely lose interest in the novel form; at least two other (and probably more) novels were begun but never completed. Only fragments remain of *The Assassins* (1814) and *The Coliseum* (1818?–19); *Hubert Cauvin* was never seen. Had Shelley continued in the direction indicated by *Zastrozzi* and *St Irvyne*, he might have attained considerable eminence (or notoriety) as a novelist. While these are, after all, boisterous but immature works, they *are* intrinsically interesting, and the advances in both style and overall sophistication from the first to the second are striking. They are early indicators of a creative genius that would never tire of experimenting with genres, with conventions, and with audience manipulation.

NOTE ON THE TEXT

The present text reproduces that of the standard complete edition of Shelley's works, the 'Julian' edition of 1926–30, prepared by Roger Ingpen and Walter E. Peck. Ingpen and Peck were rather free in their alteration of Shelley's punctuation, particularly in the addition and omission of dashes and semi-colons, or the substitution of one for the other. Such alterations are far too numerous to itemize; as they do not affect the content of the novels, however, no attempt has been made here to list all these variations. Differences in language, however, have been noted where they are clearly not merely the result of misprinting. In one other respect there is a visual difference: the original printings of the novels used enlarged and highlighted initial letters at the start of each chapter, and all chapter designations were followed by periods. The Julian text has been carefully compared with original copies of the novels, and all significant variations and omissions are indicated in the Explanatory Notes. Both novels contain misnumbered or 'missing' chapters; these, too, are indicated in the Notes.

SELECT BIBLIOGRAPHY

EDITIONS

Zastrozzi, A Romance, by P.B.S. (London: G. Wilkie and J. Robinson, 1810). *St Irvyne, or, The Rosicrucian*, by A Gentleman of the University of Oxford (London: J. J. Stockdale, 1811). *The Complete Works of Percy Bysshe Shelley*, ed. Roger Ingpen and Walter E. Peck, 10 vols. (London: Ernest Benn, 1926–30) [the 'Julian Edition']. *Shelley: Poetical Works*, ed. Thomas Hutchinson, revised by G. M. Matthews (Oxford and New York: Oxford University Press, 1971). *Shelley's Poetry and Prose*, ed. Donald H. Reiman and Sharon B. Powers (New York: W. W. Norton, 1977). *The Letters of Percy Bysshe Shelley*, ed. Frederick L. Jones, 2 vols. (Oxford: Clarendon Press, 1964). *Shelley and His Circle: 1773–1822*, ed. Kenneth Neill Cameron and Donald H. Reiman, 6 vols. (Cambridge, Mass.: Harvard University Press, 1961–73). *The Letters of Mary Wollstonecraft Shelley*, ed. Betty T. Bennett, 3 vols. (Baltimore and London: Johns Hopkins University Press, 1980–). A new edition of Shelley's prose, edited by E. B. Murray and Timothy Webb, is in preparation.

CRITICAL BIOGRAPHIES

Edward Dowden, *The Life of Percy Bysshe Shelley*, 2 vols. (London: Kegan, Paul, Trench and Co., 1886 [revised, 1896]). Walter E. Peck, *Shelley: His Life and Work*, 2 vols. (Boston: Houghton Mifflin, 1927). Newman Ivey White, *Shelley*, 2 vols. (New York: Alfred A. Knopf, 1940). Kenneth Neill Cameron, *The Young Shelley: Genesis of a Radical* (New York: Macmillan, 1950). Kenneth Neill Cameron, *Shelley: The Golden Years* (Cambridge, Mass.: Harvard University Press, 1974). Richard Holmes, *Shelley: The Pursuit* (New York: E. P. Dutton, 1975).

MODERN CRITICAL STUDIES OF SHELLEY

Carlos Baker, *Shelley's Major Poetry: The Fabric of a Vision* (Princeton: Princeton University Press, 1948). C. E. Pulos, *The Deep Truth: A Study of Shelley's Skepticism* (Lincoln: University of Nebraska Press, 1954). Donald H. Reiman, *Percy Bysshe Shelley* (New York: Twayne, 1969). Earl R. Wasserman, *Shelley: A Critical Reading* (Baltimore and London: Johns

Hopkins University Press, 1971). Judith Chernaik, *The Lyrics of Shelley* (Cleveland and London: Press of Case Western Reserve University, 1972). Stuart Curran, *Shelley's Annus Mirabilis: The Maturing of an Epic Vision* (San Marino, CA: Huntington Library, 1975). Timothy Webb, *Shelley: A Voice Not Understood* (Atlantic Highlands, NJ: Humanities Press, 1977). P. M. S. Dawson, *The Unacknowledged Legislator: Shelley and Politics* Oxford: Clarendon Press, 1980). Stephen C. Behrendt, 'The Exoteric Species: The Popular Idiom in Shelley's Poetry', *Genre* 14 (1981), 473–92. Michael Henry Scrivener, *Radical Shelley: The Philosophical Anarchism and Utopian Thought of Percy Bysshe Shelley* (Princeton: Princeton University Press, 1982). William Keach, *Shelley's Style* (London: Methuen, 1984).

CRITICAL STUDIES RELEVANT TO 'ZASTROZZI' AND 'ST IRVYNE'

Devendra P. Varma, *The Gothic Flame* (New York: Russell and Russell, 1966). David G. Halliburton, 'Shelley's "Gothic" Novels', *Keats–Shelley Journal* 16 (1967), 39–49. James Rieger, *The Mutiny Within: The Heresies of Percy Bysshe Shelley* (New York: George Braziller, 1967). John V. Murphy, *The Dark Angel: Gothic Elements in Shelley's Works* (Lewisburg, PA: Bucknell University Press, 1975). *The Gothic Imagination: Essays in Dark Romanticism*, ed. G. R. Thompson (Pullman, WA: Washington State University Press, 1974). Percy Bysshe Shelley, *Zastrozzi: a Romance and St Irvyne, or The Rosicrucian: a Romance*, Foreword by A. J. Hartley, Introduction by Frederick S. Frank (New York: Arno Press, 1977). Ann B. Tracy, *The Gothic Novel, 1790–1830* (Lexington: University Press of Kentucky, 1981). Robert Donald Spector, *The English Gothic: A Bibliographic Guide to Writers from Horace Walpole to Mary Shelley* (Westport, CT and London: Greenwood Press, 1984).

SOME RELATED NOVELS

[Anonymous], *Fatal Vows, or, The False Monk. A Romance* (London: Thomas Tegg, 1810). Charlotte Dacre, *Zofloya, or, The Moor. A Romance of the Fifteenth Century* (London: Longman, Hurst, Rees, and Orme, 1806). William Godwin, *St Leon. A Tale of the Sixteenth Century* (London: G. G. and J. Robinson, 1799). Matthew G. Lewis, *The Monk. A Romance* (London: J. Bell, 1796). John Palmer, Jr., *The Mystery of the Black Tower. A Romance* (London: William Lane, 1796).

SELECT BIBLIOGRAPHY

Ann Radcliffe, *A Sicilian Romance* (London: T. Hookham, 1790). Ann Radcliffe, *The Mysteries of Udolpho* (London: G. G. and J. Robinson, 1794). Mary Shelley, *Frankenstein, or, The Modern Prometheus* (London: Lackington, Huges, Harding, Mavor, and Jones, 1818). Horace Walpole, *The Castle of Otranto* (London: Thomas Lownds, 1764).

A CHRONOLOGY OF PERCY BYSSHE SHELLEY

1792 4 August: Shelley born at Field Place, near Horsham, Sussex, the first of seven children of Timothy Shelley and the former Elizabeth Pilfold.

1798 Pursues studies with the Revd Evan Edwards.

1802–4 Attends Syon House Academy at Isleworth, near London.

1804–10 Attends Eton.

1810 Spring: *Zastrozzi* published by G. Wilkie and J. Robinson, London.

1810 Autumn: *Original Poetry by Victor and Cazire* published and withdrawn.

1810 October: Enters University College, Oxford. Meets Thomas Jefferson Hogg, who becomes his closest friend in this period.

1810 Winter: *Posthumous Fragments of Margaret Nicholson* (poems), written with Hogg and 'edited' by the fictitious 'John Fitzvictor', published in November; *St Irvyne, or, The Rosicrucian* published in December (though title page dated 1811).

1811 Meets Harriet Westbrook (January); *The Necessity of Atheism* published (February).

1811 25 March: Expelled from Oxford over *The Necessity of Atheism.*

1811 29 August: Marries Harriet Westbrook after eloping to Edinburgh. Subsequent falling-out with Hogg, who attempts to seduce Harriet (at York); the Shelleys move to Keswick.

1812 Political activities in Dublin: Shelley addresses at least one public meeting on Irish political liberty, publishes broadsides and pamphlets including *An Address to the Irish People.* Returns disillusioned, settling first in Wales, then at Lynmouth, Devon. Shelleys joined in July by Elizabeth Hitchener, schoolteacher and 'spiritual soulmate' of Shelley during this time, until actual acquaintance sours the relationship (she leaves, to mutual relief, in November).

CHRONOLOGY

1812 October: First meeting with William Godwin, political philosopher and novelist.

1813 After second trip to Ireland, returns to London, subsequently settles in Bracknell (July).

1813 May: *Queen Mab* issued privately.

1813 23 June: Ianthe Shelley born.

1814 27 July: Elopes to France with Mary Wollstonecraft Godwin (whom he had met while visiting Godwin in June) and her 'half-sister' Claire Clairmont; the three tour the Continent.

1814 30 November: Charles Shelley born to Harriet.

1815 5 January: Shelley's grandfather, Sir Bysshe Shelley, dies; subsequent estate arrangements give Shelley his first relative financial security since expulsion from Oxford: annual income of £1000, with £200 paid directly to Harriet.

1815 22 February: First child by Mary born, dies two weeks later.

1816 24 January: William Shelley born to Mary.

1816 *Alastor, and Other Poems* published (February); returning to the Continent, spends the summer in Switzerland, where he and Byron (whom he has now first met) are nearly daily companions.

1816 9 November: Harriet Shelley drowns herself in the Serpentine.

1816 30 December: Shelley and Mary married.

1817 27 March: Court of Chancery denies Shelley custody of his children by Harriet.

1817 March: Settles at Marlow; writes *A Proposal for Putting Reform to the Vote Throughout the Kingdom* and *An Address to the People on the Death of the Princess Charlotte*; develops friendship with liberal journalist Leigh Hunt, who will consistently support and praise his works in his journal, *The Examiner*.

1817 2 September: Clara Shelley born.

1817 December: *Laon and Cythna*, Shelley's longest poem, published and withdrawn; subsequently revised and reissued in January 1818 as *The Revolt of Islam*.

1818 Sails to the Continent, eventually settling at Naples in December.

CHRONOLOGY

1818 Composes *Rosalind and Helen* (published in Spring 1819) and *Prometheus Unbound*, Act I.

1819 Shelley's most remarkable literary year: completes *Prometheus Unbound* and *Julian and Maddalo*; writes *The Cenci*, *The Mask of Anarchy*, *Peter Bell the Third*, *A Philosophical View of Reform*, and 'Ode to the West Wind', among other works.

1819 7 June: William Shelley dies.

1819 12 November: Percy Florence Shelley born.

1820 26 January: Moves to Pisa.

1820 Writes, among other works, 'The Sensitive Plant', 'Ode to Liberty', 'To a Skylark', 'The Witch of Atlas', and the burlesque *Swellfoot the Tyrant*.

1821 January–February: Writes *Epipsychidion*, which relates to Emilia Viviani, whom Shelley, Mary, and Claire had met late in 1820.

1821 13 January: Meets Jane and Edward Ellerker Williams.

1821 Writes *A Defence of Poetry* in February and March, initially intending it as a response to his friend Thomas Love Peacock's 'The Four Ages of Poetry'.

1821 11 April: Receives news of Keats's death in Rome on 23 February; writes *Adonais* in May and June (published in July).

1821 October: Writes *Hellas*.

1822 30 April: The Shelleys and Williamses relocate at San Terenzo, where Shelley begins writing *The Triumph of Life* in May and June.

1822 12 May: Shelley takes delivery of his sailboat, the *Don Juan*.

1822 1 July: Shelley and Williams sail to Leghorn to meet Leigh Hunt.

1822 8 July: Shelley and Williams drowned during a storm on their return trip; their bodies are found washed ashore on 18 July.

1822 14 August: Shelley's body cremated on the shore near Viareggio.

1823 21 January: Shelley's remains buried in Rome.

ZASTROZZI

ZASTROZZI,

A ROMANCE.

BY

P. B. S.

——That their God
May prove their foe, and with repenting hand
Abolish his own works—This would surpass
Common revenge.*

PARADISE LOST.

LONDON:
PRINTED FOR G. WILKIE AND J. ROBINSON,
57, PATERNOSTER ROW.

1810.

ZASTROZZI,

A ROMANCE

CHAPTER I

Torn from the society of all he held dear on earth, the victim of secret enemies, and exiled from happiness, was the wretched Verezzi!

All was quiet; a pitchy darkness involved the face of things, when, urged by fiercest revenge, Zastrozzi placed himself at the door of the inn where, undisturbed, Verezzi slept.

Loudly he called the landlord. The landlord, to whom the bare name of Zastrozzi was terrible, trembling obeyed the summons.

"Thou knowest Verezzi the Italian? he lodges here." "He does," answered the landlord.

"Him, then, have I devoted to destruction," exclaimed Zastrozzi. "Let Ugo and Bernardo follow you to his apartment; I will be with you to prevent mischief."

Cautiously they ascended—successfully they executed their revengeful purpose, and bore the sleeping Verezzi to the place, where a chariot waited to convey the vindictive Zastrozzi's prey to the place of its destination.

Ugo and Bernardo lifted the still sleeping Verezzi into the chariot. Rapidly they travelled onwards for several hours. Verezzi was still wrapped in deep sleep, from which all the movements he had undergone had been insufficient to rouse him.

Zastrozzi and Ugo were masked, as was Bernardo, who acted as postilion.

It was still dark, when they stopped at a small inn, on a remote and desolate heath; and waiting but to change horses, again advanced. At last day appeared—still the slumbers of Verezzi remained unbroken.

Ugo fearfully questioned Zastrozzi as to the cause of his extraordinary sleep. Zastrozzi, who, however, was well acquainted with it, gloomily answered, "I know not."

Swiftly they travelled during the whole of the day, over which nature seemed to have drawn her most gloomy curtain.—They stopped occasionally at inns to change horses and obtain refreshments.

Night came on—they forsook the beaten track, and, entering an immense forest, made their way slowly through the rugged underwood.

At last they stopped—they lifted their victim from the chariot, and bore him to a cavern, which yawned in a dell close by.

Not long did the hapless victim of unmerited persecution enjoy an oblivion which deprived him of a knowledge of his horrible situation. He awoke—and overcome by excess of terror, started violently from the ruffians' arms.

They had now entered the cavern—Verezzi supported himself against a fragment of rock which jutted out.

"Resistance is useless," exclaimed Zastrozzi; "following us in submissive silence can alone procure the slightest mitigation of your punishment."

Verezzi followed as fast as his frame, weakened by unnatural sleep, and enfeebled by recent illness, would permit; yet, scarcely believing that he was awake, and not thoroughly convinced of the reality of the scene before him, he viewed every thing with that kind of inexplicable horror, which a terrible dream is wont to excite.

After winding down the rugged descent for some time, they arrived at an iron door, which at first sight appeared to be part of the rock itself. Every thing had till now been obscured by total darkness; and Verezzi, for the first time, saw the masked faces of his persecutors, which a torch brought by Bernardo rendered visible.

The massy door flew open.

The torches from without rendered the darkness which reigned within still more horrible; and Verezzi beheld the interior of this cavern as a place whence he was never again about to emerge—as his grave. Again he struggled with his persecutors, but his enfeebled frame was insufficient to support a conflict with the strong-nerved Ugo, and, subdued, he sank fainting into his arms.

His triumphant persecutor bore him into the damp cell, and chained him to the wall. An iron chain encircled his waist; his limbs, which not even a little straw kept from the rock, were fixed by immense staples to the flinty floor; and but one of his hands was left at liberty, to take the scanty pittance of bread and water which was daily allowed him.

Everything was denied him but thought, which, by comparing the present with the past, was his greatest torment.

Ugo entered the cell every morning and evening, to bring coarse bread, and a pitcher of water, seldom, yet sometimes, accompanied by Zastrozzi.

In vain did he implore mercy, pity, and even death: useless were all his enquiries concerning the cause of his barbarous imprisonment—a stern silence was maintained by his relentless gaoler.

Languishing in painful captivity, Verezzi pased days and nights seemingly countless, in the same monotonous uniformity of horror and despair. He scarcely now shuddered when the slimy lizard crossed his naked and motionless limbs. The large earth-worms, which twined* themselves in his long and matted hair, almost ceased to excite sensations of horror.

Days and nights were undistinguishable from each other; and the period which he had passed there, though in reality but a few weeks, was lengthened by his perturbed imagination into many years. Sometimes he scarcely supposed that his torments were earthly, but that Ugo, whose countenance bespoke him a demon, was the fury who blasted his reviving hopes. His mysterious removal from the inn near Munich also confused his ideas, and he never could bring his thoughts to any conclusion on the subject which occupied them.

One evening, overcome by long watching, he sank to sleep, for almost the first time since his confinement, when he was aroused by a loud crash, which seemed to burst over the cavern. Attentively he listened—he even hoped, though hope was almost dead within his breast. Again he listened—again the same noise was repeated—it was but a violent thunderstorm which shook the elements above.

Convinced of the folly of hope, he addressed a prayer to his

Creator—to Him who hears a suppliant from the bowels of the earth. His thoughts were elevated above terrestrial enjoyments—his sufferings sank into nothing on the comparison.

Whilst his thoughts were thus employed, a more violent crash shook the cavern. A scintillating flame darted from the ceiling to the floor. Almost at the same instant the roof fell in.

A large fragment of the rock was laid athwart the cavern; one end being grooved into the solid wall, the other having almost forced open the massy iron door.

Verezzi was chained to a piece of rock which remained immovable. The violence of the storm was past, but the hail descended rapidly, each stone of which wounded his naked limbs. Every flash of lightning, although now distant, dazzled his eyes, unaccustomed as they had been to the least ray of light.

The storm at last ceased, the pealing thunders died away in indistinct murmurs, and the lightning was too faint to be visible. Day appeared—no one had yet been to the cavern—Verezzi concluded that they either intended him to perish with hunger, or that some misfortune, by which themselves had suffered, had occurred. In the most solemn manner, therefore, he now prepared himself for death, which he was fully convinced within himself was rapidly approaching.

His pitcher of water was broken by the falling fragments, and a small crust of bread was all that now remained of his scanty allowance of provisions.

A burning fever raged through his veins; and, delirious with despairing illness, he cast from him the crust which alone could now retard the rapid advances of death.

Oh! what ravages did the united efforts of disease and suffering make on the manly and handsome figure of Verezzi! His bones had almost started through his skin; his eyes were sunken and hollow; and his hair, matted with the damps, hung in strings upon his faded cheek. The day passed as had the morning—death was every instant before his eyes—a lingering death by famine—he felt its approaches: night came, but with it brought no change. He was aroused by a noise against the iron door: it was the time when Ugo usually brought fresh provisions. The noise lessened, at last it totally ceased—with it ceased all hope of life in Verezzi's bosom. A cold tremor pervaded his limbs—his eyes but faintly presented to his imagination the ruined cavern—he sank, as far as the chains which encircled his waist would permit him, upon the flinty pavement; and, in the crisis of the fever which then occurred, his youth and good constitution prevailed.

CHAPTER II

In the meantime, Ugo, who had received orders from Zastrozzi not to allow Verezzi to die, came at the accustomed hour to bring provisions, but finding that, in the last night's storm, the rock had been struck by lightning, concluded that Verezzi had lost his life amid the ruins, and he went with this news to Zastrozzi.—Zastrozzi, who, for inexplicable reasons, wished not Verezzi's death, sent Ugo and Bernardo to search for him.

After a long scrutiny they discovered their hapless victim. He was chained to the rock where they had left him, but in that exhausted condition, which want of food, and a violent fever, had reduced him to.

They unchained him, and lifting him into a chariot, after four hours rapid travelling, brought the insensible Verezzi to a cottage, inhabited by an old woman alone. The cottage stood on an immense heath, lonely, desolate, and remote from other human habitation.

Zastrozzi waited their arrival with impatience: eagerly he flew to meet them, and, with a demoniac smile, surveyed the agonised features of his prey, who lay insensible and stretched on the shoulders of Ugo.

"His life must not be lost," exclaimed Zastrozzi; "I have need of it. Tell Bianca, therefore, to prepare a bed."

Ugo obeyed, and Bernardo followed, bearing the emaciated Verezzi. A physician was sent for, who declared, that the crisis of the fever which had attacked him being past, proper care might reinstate him; but that the disorder having attacked his brain, a tranquillity of mind was absolutely necessary for his recovery.

Zastrozzi, to whom the life, though not the happiness of Verezzi was requisite, saw that his too eager desire for revenge had carried him beyond his point. He saw that some deception was requisite; he accordingly instructed the old woman to inform him, when he recovered, that he was placed in this situation, because the physician had asserted that the air of this country was necessary for a recovery from a brain fever which attacked him.

It was long before Verezzi recovered—long did he languish in torpid insensibility, during which his soul seemed to have winged its way to happier regions.

At last, however, he recovered, and the first use he made of his senses was to inquire where he was.

The old woman told him the story which she had been instructed in by Zastrozzi.

"Who ordered me then* to be chained in that desolate and dark cavern?" inquired Verezzi, "where I have been for many years, and suffered most insupportable torments?"

"Lord bless me!" said the old woman; "why, baron, how strangely you talk! I begin to fear you will again lose your senses, at the very time when you ought to be thanking God for suffering them to return to you. What can you mean by being chained in a cavern? I declare I am frightened at the very thought: pray do compose yourself."

Verezzi was much perplexed by the old woman's assertions. That Julia should send him to a mean cottage, and desert him, was impossible.

The old woman's relation seemed so well connected, and told with such an air of characteristic simplicity, that he could not disbelieve her.

But to doubt the evidence of his own senses, and the strong proofs of his imprisonment, which the deep marks of the chains had left till now, was impossible.

Had not those marks still remained, he would have conceived the horrible events which had led him thither to have been but the dreams of his perturbed imagination. He, however, thought it better to yield, since, as Ugo and Bernardo attended him in the short walks he was able to take, an escape was impossible, and its attempt would but make his situation more unpleasant.

He often expressed a wish to write to Julia, but the old woman said she had orders neither to permit him to write nor receive letters—on pretence of not agitating his mind; and, to avoid the consequences of despair, knives were denied him.

As Verezzi recovered, and his mind obtained that firm tone which it was wont to possess, he perceived that it was but a device of his enemies that detained him at the cottage, and his whole thoughts were now bent upon the means for effecting his escape.

It was late one evening, when, tempted by the peculiar beauty of the weather, Verezzi wandered beyond the usual limits, attended by Ugo and Bernardo, who narrowly watched his every movement. Immersed in thought, he wandered onwards, till he came to a woody eminence, whose beauty tempted him to rest a little, in a seat carved in the side of an ancient oak. Forgetful of his unhappy and dependent situation, he sat there some time, until Ugo told him that it was time to return.

In their absence, Zastrozzi had arrived at the cottage. He had impatiently inquired for Verezzi.

"It is the baron's custom to walk every evening," said Bianca; "I soon expect him to return."

Verezzi at last arrived.

Not knowing Zastrozzi as he entered, he started back, overcome by the likeness he bore to one of the men he had seen in the cavern.

He was now convinced that all the sufferings he had undergone in that horrible abode of misery were not imaginary, and that he was at this instant in the power of his bitterest enemy.

Zastrozzi's eyes were fixed on him with an expression too manifest to be misunderstood; and, with an air in which he struggled to disguise the natural malevolence of his heart, he said, that he hoped Verezzi's health had not suffered from the evening air.

Enraged beyond measure at this hypocrisy, from a man whom he now no longer doubted to be the cause of all his misfortunes, he could not forbear inquiring for what purpose he had conveyed him hither, and told him instantly to release him.

Zastrozzi's cheeks turned pale with passion, his lips quivered, his eyes darted revengeful glances, as thus he spoke:—

"Retire to your chamber, young fool, which is the fittest place for you to reflect on, and repent of, the insolence shown to one so much your superior."

"I fear nothing," interrupted Verezzi, "from your vain threats and empty denunciations of vengeance: justice, Heaven! is on my side, and I must eventually triumph."

What can be a greater proof of the superiority of virtue, than that the terrible, the dauntless Zastrozzi trembled! for he did tremble; and, conquered by the emotions of the moment, paced the circumscribed apartment with unequal steps. For an instant he shrunk within himself: he thought of his past life, and his awakened conscience reflected images of horror. But again revenge drowned the voice of virtue—again passion obscured the light of reason, and his steeled soul persisted in its scheme.

Whilst he still thought, Ugo entered. Zastrozzi, smothering his stinging conscience, told Ugo to follow him to the heath.—Ugo obeyed.

CHAPTER III

Zastrozzi and Ugo proceeded along the heath, on the skirts of which stood the cottage. Verezzi leaned against the casement, when a low voice, which floated in indistinct murmurs on the silence of the evening, reached his ear.—He listened attentively. He looked into the darkness, and saw the towering form of Zastrozzi, and Ugo, whose awkward, ruffian-like gait could never be mistaken.—He could not hear their discourse, except a few detached words which reached his ears. They seemed to be denunciations of anger; a low tone afterwards succeeded, and it appeared as if a dispute, which had arisen between them, was settled: their voices at last died away in distance.

Bernardo now left the room. Bianca entered; but Verezzi plainly heard Bernardo lingering at the door.

The old woman continued sitting in silence at a remote corner of the chamber. It was Verezzi's hour for supper: he desired Bianca to bring it. She obeyed, and brought some dried raisins in a plate. He was surprised to see a knife was likewise brought; an indulgence he imputed to the inadvertency of the old woman. A thought started across his mind—it was now time to escape.

He seized the knife—he looked expressively at the old woman—she trembled. He advanced from the casement to the door: he called for Bernardo—Bernardo entered, and Verezzi, lifting his arm high, aimed the knife at the villain's heart. Bernardo started aside, and the knife was fixed firmly in the doorcase. Verezzi attempted by one effort to extricate it. The effort was vain. Bianca, as fast as her tottering limbs could carry her, hastened through the opposite door, calling loudly for Zastrozzi.

Verezzi attempted to rush through the open door, but Bernardo opposed himself to it. A long and violent contest ensued, and Bernardo's superior strength was on the point of overcoming Verezzi, when the latter, by a dexterous blow, precipitated him down the steep and narrow staircase.

Not waiting to see the event of his victory, he rushed through the opposite door, and meeting with no opposition, ran swiftly across the heath.

The moon, in tranquil majesty, hung high in air, and showed the immense extent of the plain before him. He continued rapidly advancing, and the cottage was soon out of sight. He thought that he heard Zastrozzi's voice in every gale. Turning round, he thought Zastrozzi's eye glanced over his shoulder. But even had Bianca taken the right road, and found Zastrozzi, Verezzi's speed would have mocked pursuit.

He ran several miles, still the dreary extent of the heath was before him; no cottage yet appeared, where he might take shelter. He cast himself for an instant on the bank of a rivulet, which stole slowly across the heath. The moonbeam played upon its surface—he started at his own reflected image—he thought that voices were wafted on the western gale, and, nerved anew, pursued his course across the plain.

The moon had gained the zenith before Verezzi rested again. Two pine-trees, of extraordinary size, stood on a small eminence: he climbed one, and found a convenient seat in its immense branches.

Fatigued, he sank to sleep.

Two hours he lay hushed in oblivion, when he was awakened by a noise. It is but the hooting of the night-raven, thought he.

Day had not yet appeared, but faint streaks in the east presaged the coming morn. Verezzi heard the clattering of hoofs. What was his horror to see that Zastrozzi, Bernardo, and Ugo, were the horsemen! Overcome by terror, he clung to the rugged branch. His persecutors advanced to the spot—they stopped under the tree wherein he was.

"Eternal curses," exclaimed Zastrozzi, "upon Verezzi! I swear never to rest until I find him, and then I will accomplish the purpose of my soul. But come, Ugo, Bernardo, let us proceed."

"Signor," said Ugo, "let us the rather stop here to refresh ourselves and our horses. You, perhaps, will not make this pine your couch, but I will get up, for I think I spy an excellent bed above there."

"No, no," answered Zastrozzi; "did not I resolve never to rest until I had found Verezzi? Mount, villain, or die."

Ugo sullenly obeyed. They galloped off, and were quickly out of sight.

Verezzi returned thanks to Heaven for his escape; for he thought that Ugo's eye, as the villain pointed to the branch where he reposed, met his.

It was now morning. Verezzi surveyed the heath, and thought he saw buildings at a distance. Could he gain a town or city, he might defy Zastrozzi's power.

He descended the pine-tree, and advanced as quickly as he could towards the distant buildings. He proceeded across the heath for half an hour, and perceived that, at last, he had arrived at its termination.

The country assumed a new aspect, and the number of cottages and villas showed him that he was in the neighbourhood of some city. A large road which he now entered confirmed his opinion. He saw two peasants, and asked them where the road led,—"To Passau," was the answer.

It was yet very early in the morning, when he walked through the principal street of Passau.* He felt very faint with his recent and unusual exertions; and, overcome by languor, sank on some lofty stone steps, which led to a magnificent mansion, and resting his head on his arm, soon fell asleep.

He had been there nearly an hour, when he was awakened by an old woman. She had a basket on her arm in which were flowers, which it was her custom to bring to Passau every market-day. Hardly knowing where he was, he answered the old woman's inquiries in a vague and unsatisfactory manner. By degrees, however, they became better acquainted; and, as Verezzi had no money, nor any means of procuring it, he accepted of an offer which Claudine (for that was the old woman's name) made him, to work for her, and share her cottage, which, together with a little garden, was all she could call her own. Claudine quickly disposed of her flowers, and, accompanied by Verezzi, soon arrived at a little cottage near Passau. It was situated on a pleasant and cultivated spot; at the foot of a small eminence, on which it was situated, flowed the majestic Danube, and on the opposite side was a forest belonging to the Baron of Schwepper, whose vassal Claudine was.

Her little cottage was kept extremely neat; and, by the charity of the Baron, wanted none of those little comforts which old age requires.

Verezzi thought that, in so retired a spot, he might at least pass his time tranquilly, and elude Zastrozzi.

"What induced you," said he to Claudine, as in the evening they sat before the cottage door, "what induced you to make that offer this morning to me?"

"Ah!" said the old woman, "it was but last week that I lost my dear son, who was everything to me: he died by a fever which he caught by his too great exertions in obtaining a livelihood for me; and I came to the market yesterday, for the first time since my son's death, hoping to find some peasant who would fill his place, when chance threw you in my way.

"I had hoped that he would have outlived me, as I am quickly hastening to the grave, to which I look forward as to the coming of a friend, who would relieve me from those cares which, alas! but increase with my years."

Verezzi's heart was touched with compassion for the forlorn situation of Claudine. He tenderly told her that he would not forsake her; but if any opportunity occurred for ameliorating her situation, she should no longer continue in poverty.

CHAPTER IV

BUT let us return to Zastrozzi.—He had walked with Ugo on the heath, and had returned late. He was surprised to see no light in the cottage. He advanced to the door—he rapped violently—no one answered. "Very strange!" exclaimed Zastrozzi, as he burst open the door with his foot. He entered the cottage—no one was there. He searched it, and at last saw Bernardo lying, seemingly lifeless, at the foot of the staircase. Zastrozzi advanced to him, and lifted him from the ground: he had been but in a trance, and immediately recovered.

As soon as his astonishment was dissipated, he told Zastrozzi what had happened.

"What!" exclaimed Zastrozzi, interrupting him, "Verezzi escaped! Hell and furies! Villain, you deserve instant death; but thy life is at present necessary to me. Arise, go instantly to Rosenheim, and bring three of my horses from the inn there—make haste! begone!"

Bernardo trembling arose, and obeying Zastrozzi's commands, crossed the heath quickly towards Rosenheim,* a village about half a league distant on the north.

Whilst he was gone, Zastrozzi, agitated by contending passions, knew scarcely what to do. With hurried strides he paced the cottage. He sometimes spoke lowly to himself. The feelings of his soul flashed from his eyes—his frown was terrible.

"Would I had his heart reeking on my dagger, Signor!" said Ugo. "Kill him when you catch him, which you soon will, I am sure."

"Ugo," said Zastrozzi, "you are my friend; you advise me well. —But no! he must not die.—Ah! by what horrible fetters am I chained—fool that I was—Ugo! he shall die—die by the most hellish torments. I give myself up to fate;—I will taste revenge, for revenge is sweeter than life: and even were I to die with him, and, as the punishment of my crime, be instantly plunged into eternal torments, I should taste superior joy in recollecting the sweet moment of his destruction. Oh! would that destruction could be eternal!"

The clattering of hoofs was heard, and Zastrozzi was now interrupted by the arrival of Bernardo—they instantly mounted, and the high-spirited steeds bore them swiftly across the heath.

Rapidly, for some time, were Zastrozzi and his companions borne across the plain. They took the same road as Verezzi had. They passed the pines where he reposed. They hurried on.

The fainting horses were scarce able to bear their guilty burthens. No one had spoken since they had left the clustered pines.

Bernardo's horse, overcome by excessive fatigue, sank on the ground; that of Zastrozzi scarce appeared in better condition.—They stopped.

"What!" exclaimed Zastrozzi, "must we give up the search? Ah! I am afraid we must; our horses can proceed no further—curse on the horses.

"But let us proceed on foot—Verezzi shall not escape me—nothing shall now retard the completion of my just revenge."

As he thus spoke, Zastrozzi's eye gleamed with impatient revenge; and with rapid steps he advanced towards the south of the heath.

Daylight at length appeared; still were the villains' efforts to find Verezzi insufficient. Hunger, thirst, and fatigue conspired to make them relinquish the pursuit—they lay at intervals upon the stony soil.

"This is but an uncomfortable couch, Signor," muttered Ugo.

Zastrozzi, whose whole thoughts were centred in revenge, heeded him not, but nerved anew by impatient vengeance, he started from the bosom of the earth, and muttering curses upon the innocent object of his hatred, proceeded onwards. The day passed as had the morning and preceding night. Their hunger was scantily allayed by the wild berries which grew amid the heathy shrubs; and their thirst but increased by the brackish pools of water which alone they met with. They perceived a wood at some distance. "That is a likely place for Verezzi to have retired to, for the day is hot, and he must want repose as well as ourselves," said Bernardo. "True," replied Zastrozzi, as he advanced towards it. They quickly arrived at its borders: it was not a wood, but an immense forest, which stretched southward as far as Schaffhausen.* They advanced into it.

The tall trees rising above their heads warded off the meridian sun; the mossy banks beneath invited repose; but Zastrozzi, little recking a scene so fair, hastily scrutinized every recess which might afford an asylum to Verezzi.

Useless were all his researches—fruitless his endeavours: still, however, though faint with hunger, and weary with exertion, he nearly sank upon the turf. His mind was superior to corporeal toil; for *that*, nerved by revenge, was indefatigable.

Ugo and Bernardo, overcome by the extreme fatigue which they had undergone, and strong as the assassins were, fell fainting on the earth.

The sun began to decline; at last it sank beneath the western mountain, and the forest-tops were tinged by its departing ray. The shades of night rapidly thickened.

Zastrozzi sat awhile upon the decayed trunk of a scathed oak.

The sky was serene; the blue ether was spangled with countless myriads of stars: the tops of the lofty forest-trees waved mournfully in the evening wind; and the moon-beam penetrating at intervals, as they moved, through the matted branches, threw dubious shades upon the dark underwood beneath.

Ugo and Bernardo, conquered by irresistible torpor, sank to rest upon the dewy turf.

A scene so fair—a scene so congenial to those who can reflect upon their past lives with pleasure, and anticipate the future with the enthusiasm of innocence, ill accorded with the ferocious soul of Zastrozzi, which at one time agitated by revenge, at another by agonising remorse, or contending passions, could derive no pleasure from the past—anticipate no happiness in futurity.

Zastrozzi sat for some time immersed in heart-rending contemplations; but though conscience for awhile reflected his past life in images of horror, again was his heart steeled by fiercest vengeance; and, aroused by images of insatiate revenge, he hastily arose, and, waking Ugo and Bernardo, pursued his course.

The night was calm and serene—not a cloud obscured the azure brilliancy of the spangled concave above—not a wind ruffled the tranquillity of the atmosphere below.

Zastrozzi, Ugo, and Bernardo, advanced into the forest. They had tasted no food, save the wild berries of the wood, for some time, and were anxious to arrive at some cottage, where they might procure refreshments. For some time the deep silence which reigned was uninterrupted.

"What is that?" exclaimed Zastrozzi, as he beheld a large and magnificent building, whose battlements rose above the lofty trees. It was built in the Gothic style of architecture, and appeared to be inhabited.

The building reared its pointed casements loftily to the sky; their treillaged ornaments were silvered by the clear moon-light, to which the dark shades of the arches beneath formed a striking contrast. A large portico jutted out: they advanced towards it, and Zastrozzi attempted to open the door.

An open window on one side of the casement arrested Zastrozzi's attention. "Let us enter that," said he.—They entered. It was a large saloon, with many windows. Everything within was arranged with princely magnificence. Four ancient and immense sofas in the apartment invited repose.

Near one of the windows stood a table, with an escritoire on it; a paper lay on the ground near it.

Zastrozzi, as he passed, heedlessly took up the paper. He advanced nearer to the window, thinking his senses had deceived him when he read, "La Contessa di Laurentini"; but they had not done so, for La Contessa di Laurentini still continued on the paper. He hastily opened it; and the letter, though of no importance, convinced him that this must have been the place to which Matilda said that she had removed.

Ugo and Bernardo lay sleeping on the sofas. Zastrozzi, leaving them as they were, opened an opposite door—it led into a vaulted hall—a large flight of stairs rose from the opposite side—he ascended them.—He advanced along a lengthened corridor—a female in white robes stood at the other end—a lamp burnt near her on the balustrade. She was in a reclining attitude, and had not observed his approach. Zastrozzi recognized her for Matilda. He approached her, and beholding Zastrozzi before her, she started back, with surprise. For awhile she gazed on him in silence, and at last exclaimed, "Zastrozzi! ah! are we revenged on Julia? am I happy? Answer me quickly. Well by your silence do I perceive that our plans have been put into execution. Excellent Zastrozzi! accept my most fervent thanks, my eternal gratitude."

"Matilda!" returned Zastrozzi, "would I could say that we were happy! but, alas! it is but misery and disappointment that cause this my so unexpected visit. I know nothing of the Marchesa de Strobazzo—less of Verezzi. I fear that I must wait till age has unstrung my now so fervent energies; and when time has damped your passion, perhaps you may gain Verezzi's love. Julia is returned to Italy—is even now in Naples; and, secure in the immensity of her possessions, laughs at our trifling vengeance. But it shall not be always thus," continued Zastrozzi, his eyes sparkling with inexpressible brilliancy; "I will accomplish my purpose; and, Matilda, thine shall likewise be effected. But, come, I have not tasted food for these two days."

"Oh! supper is prepared below," said Matilda. Seated at the supper-table, the conversation, enlivened by wine, took an animated turn. After some subjects, irrelevant to this history, being discussed, Matilda said, "Ha! but I forgot to tell you, that I have done some good. I have secured that diabolical Paulo, Julia's servant, who was of great service to her, and, by penetrating our schemes, might have even discomfited our grand design. I have lodged him in the lowest cavern of those dungeons which are under this building—will you go and see him?" Zastrozzi answered in the affirmative, and seizing a lamp which burnt in a recess of the apartment, followed Matilda.

The rays of the lamp but partially dissipated the darkness as they advanced through the antiquated passages. They arrived at a door: Matilda opened it, and they quickly crossed a grass-grown courtyard.

The grass which grew on the lofty battlements waved mournfully in the rising blast, as Matilda and Zastrozzi entered a dark and narrow casement.—Cautiously they descended the slippery and precipitous steps. The lamp, obscured by the vapours, burnt dimly as they advanced. They arrived at the foot of the staircase. "Zastrozzi!" exclaimed Matilda. Zastrozzi turned quickly, and, perceiving a door, obeyed Matilda's directions.

On some straw, chained to the wall, lay Paulo.

"O pity! stranger, pity!" exclaimed the miserable Paulo.

No answer, save a smile of most expressive scorn, was given by Zastrozzi. They again ascended the narrow staircase, and, passing the courtyard, arrived at the supper-room.

"But," said Zastrozzi, again taking his seat, "what use is that fellow Paulo in the dungeon? Why do you keep him there?"

"Oh!" answered Matilda, "I know not; but if you wish——"

She paused, but her eye expressively filled up the sentence.

Zastrozzi poured out an overflowing goblet of wine. He summoned Ugo and Bernardo—"Take that," said Matilda, presenting them a key. One of the villains took it, and in a few moments returned with the hapless Paulo.

"Paulo!" exclaimed Zastrozzi, loudly, "I have prevailed on La Contessa to restore your freedom: here," added he, "take this; I pledge to your future happiness."

Paulo bowed low—he drank the poisoned portion to the dregs, and, overcome by sudden and irresistible faintness, fell at Zastrozzi's feet. Sudden convulsions shook his frame, his lips trembled, his eyes rolled horribly, and, uttering an agonised and lengthened groan, he expired.

"Ugo! Bernardo! take that body and bury it immediately," cried Zastrozzi. "There, Matilda, by such means must Julia die: you see, that the poisons which I possess are quick in their effect."

A pause ensued, during which the eyes of Zastrozzi and Matilda spoke volumes to each guilty soul.

The silence was interrupted by Matilda. Not shocked at the dreadful outrage which had been committed, she told Zastrozzi to come out into the forest, for that she had something for his private ear.

"Matilda," said Zastrozzi, as they advanced along the forest. "I must not stay here, and waste moments in inactivity, which might be more usefully employed. I must quit you to-morrow—I must destroy Julia."

"Zastrozzi," returned Matilda, "I am so far from wishing you to spend your time here in ignoble listlessness, that I will myself join your search. You shall to Italy—to Naples—watch Julia's every movement, attend her every step, and in the guise of a friend destroy her : but beware, whilst you assume the softness of the dove, to forget not the cunning of the serpent. On you I depend for destroying her, my own exertions shall find Verezzi ; I myself will gain his love—Julia must die, and expiate the crime of daring to rival me, with her hated blood."

Whilst thus they conversed, whilst they planned these horrid schemes of destruction, the night wore away.

The moon-beam darting her oblique rays from under volumes of lowering vapour, threatened an approaching storm. The lurid sky was tinged with a yellowish lustre—the forest-tops rustled in the rising tempest—big drops fell—a flash of lightning, and, instantly after, a peal of bursting thunder, struck with sudden terror the bosom of Matilda. She, however, immediately overcame it, and, regarding the battling element with indifference, continued her discourse with Zastrozzi.

They wore out the night in many visionary plans for the future, and now and then a gleam of remorse assailed Matilda's heart. Heedless of the storm, they had remained in the forest late. Flushed with wickedness, they at last sought their respective couches, but sleep forsook their pillow.

In all the luxuriance of extravagant fancy, Matilda portrayed the symmetrical form, the expressive countenance, of Verezzi ; whilst Zastrozzi, who played a double part, anticipated, with ferocious exultation, the torments which he she loved was eventually fated to endure, and changed his plan, for a sublimer mode of vengeance was opened to his view.

Matilda passed a night of restlessness and agitation : her mind was harassed by contending passions, and her whole soul wound up to deeds of horror and wickedness. Zastrozzi's countenance, as she met him in the breakfast-parlour, wore a settled expression of determined revenge—"I almost shudder," exclaimed Matilda, "at the sea of wickedness on which I am about to embark! But still, Verezzi—ah! for him would I even lose my hopes of eternal happiness. In the sweet idea of calling him mine, no scrupulous delicacy, no mistaken superstitious fear, shall prevent me from deserving him by daring acts—No! I am resolved," continued Matilda, as, recollecting his graceful form, her soul was assailed by tenfold love.

"And I am likewise resolved," said Zastrozzi; "I am resolved on revenge—my revenge shall be gratified. Julia shall die, and Verezzi——"

Zastrozzi paused; his eye gleamed with a peculiar expression, and Matilda thought he meant more than he had said—she raised her eyes—they encountered his.

The guilt-bronzed cheek of Zastrozzi was tinged with a momentary blush, but it quickly passed away, and his countenance recovered its wonted firm and determined expression.

"Zastrozzi!" exclaimed Matilda. "Should you be false—should you seek to deceive me—— But no; it is impossible.—Pardon, my friend—I meant not what I said—my thoughts are crazed——"

"'Tis well," said Zastrozzi, haughtily.

"But you forgive my momentary, unmeaning doubt?" said Matilda, and fixed her unmeaning eyes on his countenance.

"It is not for us to dwell on vain, unmeaning expressions, which the soul dictates not," returned Zastrozzi; "and I sue for pardon from you, for having, by ambiguous expressions, caused the least agitation: but, believe me, Matilda, we will not forsake each other; your cause is mine; distrust between us is foolish.—But, farewell for the present; I must order Bernardo to go to Passau to purchase horses."

The day passed on; each waited with impatience for the arrival of Bernardo.—"Farewell, Matilda," exclaimed Zastrozzi, as he mounted the horses which Bernardo brought;* and, taking the route of Italy, galloped off.

CHAPTER V

HER whole soul wrapped up in one idea, the guilty Matilda threw herself into a chariot which waited at the door, and ordered the equipage to proceed towards Passau.

Left to indulge reflection in solitude, her mind recurred to the object nearest her heart—to Verezzi.

Her bosom was scorched by an ardent and unquenchable fire; and while she thought of him, she even shuddered at the intenseness of her own sensations.

"He shall love me—he shall be mine—mine for ever," mentally ejaculated Matilda.

The streets of Passau echoed to La Contessa di Laurentini's equipage, before, roused from her reverie, she found herself at the place of her destination; and she was seated in her hotel in that city, before she had well arranged her unsettled ideas. She summoned Ferdinand, a trusty servant, to whom she confided everything. "Ferdinand," said she, "you have many claims on my gratitude: I have never had cause to reproach you with infidelity in executing my purposes—add another debt to that which I already owe you: find Il Conte Verezzi within three days, and you are my best friend." Ferdinand bowed, and prepared to execute her commands. Two days passed, during which Matilda failed not to make every personal inquiry, even in the suburbs of Passau.

Alternately depressed by fear, and revived by hope, for three days was Matilda's mind in a state of disturbance and fluctuation. The evening of the third day, of the day on which Ferdinand was to return, arrived. Matilda's mind, wound up to the extreme of impatience, was the scene of conflicting passions.—She paced the room rapidly.

A servant entered, and announced supper.

"Is Ferdinand returned?" hastily inquired Matilda.

The domestic answered in the negative.—She sighed deeply, and struck her forehead.

Footsteps were heard in the antichamber without.

"There is Ferdinand!" exclaimed Matilda, exultingly, as he entered. "Well, well! have you found Verezzi? Ah! speak quickly! Ease me of this horrible suspense."

"Signora!" said Ferdinand, "it grieves me much to be obliged to declare that all my endeavours have been inefficient to find Il Conte Verezzi——"

"Oh, madness! madness!" exclaimed Matilda, "is it for this that I have plunged into the dark abyss of crime?—is it for this that I have despised the delicacy of my sex, and, braving consequences, have offered my love to one who despises me—who shuns me, as does the barbarous Verezzi? But if he is in Passau—if he is in the environs of the city, I will find him."

Thus saying, despising the remonstrances of her domestics, casting off all sense of decorum, she rushed into the streets of Passau. A gloomy silence reigned through the streets of the city; it was past midnight, and every inhabitant seemed to be sunk in sleep—sleep which Matilda was almost a stranger to. Her white robes floated on the night air—her shadowy and dishevelled hair flew over her form, which, as she passed the bridge, seemed to strike the boatmen below with the idea of some supernatural and ethereal form.

She hastily crossed the bridge—she entered the fields on the right—the Danube, whose placid stream was scarcely agitated by the wind, reflected her symmetrical form, as, scarcely knowing what direction she pursued, Matilda hastened along its banks. Sudden horror, resistless despair, seized her brain, maddened as it was by hopeless love.

"What have I to do in this world, my fairest prospect blighted, my fondest hope rendered futile?" exclaimed the frantic Matilda, as, wound up to the highest pitch of desperation, she attempted to plunge herself into the river.

But life fled; for Matilda, caught by a stranger's arm, was prevented from the desperate act.

Overcome by horror, she fainted.

Some time did she lie in a state of torpid insensibility, till the stranger, filling his cup with water, and sprinkling her pallid countenance with it, recalled to life the miserable Matilda.

What was her surprise, what was her mingled emotion of rapture and doubt, when the moon-beam disclosed to her view the countenance of Verezzi, as in anxious solicitude he bent over her elegantly-proportioned form!

"By what chance," exclaimed the surprised Verezzi, "do I see here La Contessa di Laurentini? Did not I leave you at your Italian castella? I had hoped you would have ceased to persecute me, when I told you that I was irrevocably another's."

"Oh, Verezzi!" exclaimed Matilda, casting herself at his feet, "I adore you to madness—I love you to distraction. If you have one mark of compassion, let me not sue in vain—reject not one who feels it impossible to overcome the fatal, resistless passion which consumes her."

"Rise, Signora," returned Verezzi—"rise; this discourse is improper—it is not suiting the dignity of your rank, or the delicacy of your sex: but suffer me to conduct you to yon cottage, where, perhaps, you may deign to refresh yourself, or pass the night."

The moonbeams played upon the tranquil waters of the Danube, as Verezzi silently conducted the beautiful Matilda to the humble dwelling where he resided.

Claudine waited at the door, and had begun to fear that some mischance had befallen Verezzi, as, when he arrived at the cottage-door, it was long past his usual hour of return.

It was his custom, during those hours when the twilight of evening cools the air, to wander through the adjacent rich scenery, though he seldom prolonged his walks till midnight.

He supported the fainting form of Matilda as he advanced towards Claudine. The old woman's eyes had lately failed her, from extreme age; and it was not until Verezzi called to her that she saw him, accompanied by La Contessa di Laurentini.

"Claudine," said Verezzi, "I have another claim upon your kindness; this lady, who has wandered beyond her knowledge, will honour our cottage so far as to pass the night here. If you would prepare the pallet which I usually occupy for her, I will repose this evening on the turf, and will now get supper ready. Signora," continued he, addressing Matilda, "some wine would, I think, refresh your spirits; permit me to fill you a glass of wine."

Matilda silently accepted his offer—their eyes met—those of Matilda were sparkling and full of meaning.

"Verezzi!" exclaimed Matilda, "I arrived but four days since at Passau—I have eagerly inquired for you—oh! how eagerly! Will you accompany me to-morrow to Passau?"

"Yes," said Verezzi, hesitatingly.

Claudine soon joined them. Matilda exulted in the success of her schemes, and Claudine being present, the conversation took a general turn. The lateness of the hour, at last, warned them to separate.

Verezzi, left to solitude and his own reflections, threw himself on the turf, which extended to the Danube below. Ideas of the most gloomy nature took possession of his soul; and, in the event of the evening, he saw the foundation of the most bitter misfortunes.

He could not love Matilda; and though he never had seen her but in the most amiable light, he found it impossible to feel any sentiment towards her, save cold esteem. Never had he beheld those dark shades in her character, which, if developed, could excite nothing but horror and detestation: he regarded her as a woman of strong passions, who, having resisted them to the utmost of her power, was at last borne away in the current—whose brilliant virtues one fault had obscured—as such he pitied her: but still he could not help observing a comparison between her and Julia, whose feminine delicacy shrunk from the slightest suspicion, even, of indecorum. Her fragile form, her mild, heavenly countenance, was contrasted with all the partiality of love, to the scintillating eye, the commanding countenance, the bold expressive gaze, of Matilda.

He must accompany her on the morrow to Passau.—During their walk, he determined to observe a strict silence; or, at all events, not to hazard one equivocal expression, which might be construed into what it was not meant for.

The night passed away—morning came, and the tops of the far-seen mountains were gilded by the rising sun.

Exulting in the success of her schemes, and scarcely able to disguise the vivid feelings of her heart, the wily Matilda, as early as she descended to the narrow parlour, where Claudine had prepared a simple breakfast, affected a gloom she was far from feeling.

An unequivocal expression of innocent and mild tenderness marked her manner towards Verezzi: her eyes were cast on the ground, and her every movement spoke meekness and sensibility.

At last, breakfast being finished, the time arrived when Matilda, accompanied by Verezzi, pursued the course of the river, to retrace her footsteps to Passau. A gloomy silence for some time prevailed —at last Matilda spoke:

"Unkind Verezzi! is it thus that you will ever slight me? is it for this that I have laid aside the delicacy of my sex, and owned to you a passion which was but too violent to be concealed?—Ah! at least pity me! I love you: oh! I adore you to madness!"

She paused—the peculiar expression which beamed in her dark eye, told the tumultuous wishes of her bosom.

"Distress not yourself and me, Signora," said Verezzi, "by these unavailing protestations. Is it for you—is it for Matilda," continued he, his countenance assuming a smile of bitterest scorn, "to talk of love to the lover of Julia?"

Rapid tears coursed down Matilda's cheek. She sighed—the sigh seemed to rend her inmost bosom.

So unexpected a reply conquered Verezzi. He had been prepared for reproaches, but his feelings could not withstand Matilda's tears.

"Ah! forgive me, Signora," exclaimed Verezzi, "if my brain, crazed by disappointments, dictated words which my heart intended not."

"Oh," replied Matilda, "it is I who am wrong: led on by the violence of my passion, I have uttered words, the bare recollection of which fills me with horror. Oh! forgive, forgive an unhappy woman, whose only fault is loving you too well."

As thus she spoke, they entered the crowded streets of Passau, and, proceeding rapidly onwards, soon arrived at La Contessa di Laurentini's hotel.

CHAPTER VI

The character of Matilda has been already so far revealed, as to render it unnecessary to expatiate upon it farther. Suffice it to say, that her syren illusions and well-timed blandishments, obtained so great a power over the imagination of Verezzi, that his resolution to return to Claudine's cottage before sunset became every instant fainter and fainter.

"And will you thus leave me?" exclaimed Matilda, in accents of the bitterest anguish, as Verezzi prepared to depart—"will you thus leave unnoticed, her who, for your sake alone, casting aside the pride of high birth, has wandered, unknown, through foreign climes? Oh! if I have (led away by love for you) outstepped the bounds of modesty, let me not, oh! let me not be injured by others with impunity. Stay I entreat thee, Verezzi, if yet one spark of compassion lingers in your breast—stay and defend me from those who vainly seek one who is irrevocably thine."

With words such as these did the wily*Matilda work upon the generous passions of Verezzi. Emotions of pity, of compassion, for one whose only fault he supposed to be love for him, conquered Verezzi's softened soul.

"Oh! Matilda," said he, "though I cannot love thee—though my soul is irrevocably another's—yet, believe me, I esteem, I admire thee; and it grieves me that a heart, fraught with so many and so brilliant virtues, has fixed itself on one who is incapable of appreciating its value."

The time passed away, and each returning sun beheld Verezzi still at Passau—still under Matilda's roof. That softness, that melting tenderness, which she knew so well how to assume, began to convince Verezzi of the injustice of the involuntary hatred which had filled his soul towards her. Her conversation was fraught with sense and elegant ideas. She played to him in the cool of the evening; and often, after sunset, they rambled together into the rich scenery and luxuriant meadows which are washed by the Danube.

Claudine was not forgotten: indeed, Matilda first recollected her, and, by placing her in an independent situation, added a new claim to the gratitude of Verezzi.

In this manner three weeks passed away. Every day did Matilda practise new arts, employ new blandishments, to detain under her roof the fascinated Verezzi.

The most select parties in Passau, flitted in varied movements to exquisite harmony, when Matilda perceived Verezzi's spirits to be ruffled by recollection.

When he seemed to prefer solitude, a moonlight walk by the Danube was proposed by Matilda; or, with skilful fingers, she drew from her harp sounds of the most heart-touching, most enchanting melody. Her behaviour towards him was soft, tender and quiet, and might rather have characterised the mild, serene love of a friend or sister, than the ardent, unquenchable fire, which burnt, though concealed, within Matilda's bosom.

It was one calm evening that Matilda and Verezzi sat in a back saloon, which overlooked the gliding Danube. Verezzi was listening, with all the enthusiasm of silent rapture, to a favourite soft air which Matilda sang, when a loud rap at the hall-door startled them. A domestic entered, and told Matilda that a stranger, on particular business, waited to speak with her.

"Oh!" exclaimed Matilda, "I cannot attend to him now; bid him wait."

The stranger was impatient, and would not be denied.

"Desire him to come in, then," said Matilda.

The domestic hastened to obey her commands.

Verezzi had arisen to leave the room. "No," cried Matilda, "sit still; I shall soon dismiss the fellow; besides, I have no secrets from you." Verezzi took his seat.

The wide folding-doors which led into the passage were open.

Verezzi observed Matilda, as she gazed fixedly through them, to grow pale.

He could not see the cause, as he was seated on a sofa at the other end of the saloon.

Suddenly she started from her seat; her whole frame seemed convulsed by agitation, as she rushed through the door.

Verezzi heard an agitated voice exclaim, "Go! go!—to-morrow morning!"

Matilda returned.—She seated herself again at the harp which she had quitted, and essayed to compose herself; but it was in vain—she was too much agitated.

Her voice, as she again attempted to sing, refused to perform its office; and her humid hands, as they swept the strings of the harp, violently trembled.

"Matilda," said Verezzi, in a sympathising tone, "what has agitated you? Make me a repository of your sorrows: I would, if possible, alleviate them."

"Oh, no," said Matilda, affecting unconcern, "nothing—nothing has happened. I was even myself unconscious that I appeared agitated."

Verezzi affected to believe her, and assumed a composure which he felt not. The conversation changed, and Matilda assumed her wonted mien. The lateness of the hour at last warned them to separate.

The more Verezzi thought upon the evening's occurrence, the more did a conviction in his mind, inexplicable even to himself, strengthen, that Matilda's agitation originated in something of consequence. He knew her mind to be superior to common circumstance, and fortuitous casualty, which might have ruffled an inferior soul. Besides, the words which he had heard her utter—"Go! go!—to-morrow morning!"—and though he resolved to disguise his real sentiments, and seem to let the subject drop, he determined narrowly to scrutinise Matilda's conduct; and particularly to know what took place on the following morning.—An indefinable presentiment that something horrible was about to occur, filled Verezzi's mind. A long chain of retrospection ensued—he could not forget the happy hours he had passed with Julia; her interesting softness, her ethereal form, pressed on his aching sense.

Still did he feel his soul irresistibly softened towards Matilda—her love for him flattered his vanity; and though he could not feel reciprocal affection towards her, yet her kindness in rescuing him from his former degraded situation, her altered manner towards him, and her unremitting endeavours to please, to humour him in everything, called for his warmest, his sincerest gratitude.

The morning came—Verezzi arose from a sleepless couch, and descending into the breakfast-parlour, there found Matilda.

He endeavoured to appear the same as usual, but in vain; for an expression of reserve and scrutiny was apparent on his features.

Matilda perceived it, and shrunk abashed from his keen gaze.

The meal passed away in silence.

"Excuse me for an hour or two," at last stammered out Matilda —"my steward has accounts to settle;" and she left the apartment.

Verezzi had now no doubt but that the stranger, who had caused Matilda's agitation the day before, was now returned to finish his business.

He moved towards the door to follow her—he stopped.

"What right have I to pry into the secrets of another?" thought Verezzi; "besides, the business which this stranger has with Matilda cannot possibly concern me."

Still was he compelled, by an irresistible fascination, as it were, to unravel what appeared to him so mysterious an affair. He endeavoured to believe it to be as she affirmed; he endeavoured to compose himself: he took a book, but his eyes wandered insensibly.

Thrice he hesitated—thrice he shut the door of the apartment; till at last, a curiosity, unaccountable even to himself, propelled him to seek Matilda.

Mechanically he moved along the passage. He met one of the domestics—he inquired where Matilda was.

"In the grand saloon," was the reply.

With trembling steps he advanced towards it.—The folding-doors were open.—He saw Matilda and the stranger standing at the remote end of the apartment.

The stranger's figure, which was towering and majestic, was rendered more peculiarly striking, by the elegantly proportioned form of Matilda, who leant on a marble table near her; and her gestures, as she conversed with him, manifested the most eager impatience, the deepest interest.

At so great a distance, Verezzi could not hear their conversation; but, by the low murmurs which occasionally reached his ear, he perceived that whatever it might be, they were both equally interested in the subject.

For some time he contemplated them with mingled surprise and curiosity—he tried to arrange the confused murmurs of their voices, which floated along the immense and vaulted apartment, but no articulate sound reached his ear.

At last Matilda took the stranger's hand: she pressed it to her lips with an eager and impassioned gesture, and led him to the opposite door of the saloon.

Suddenly the stranger turned, but as quickly regained his former position, as he retreated through the door; not quickly enough, however, but, in the stranger's fire-darting eye, Verezzi recognised him who had declared eternal enmity at the cottage on the heath.

Scarcely knowing where he was, or what to believe, for a few moments Verezzi stood bewildered, and unable to arrange the confusion of ideas which floated in his brain, and assailed his terror-struck imagination. He knew not what to believe—what phantom it could be that, in the shape of Zastrozzi, blasted his straining eye-balls.—Could it really be Zastrozzi? Could his most rancorous, his bitterest enemy, be thus beloved, thus confided in, by the perfidious Matilda?

For several moments he stood doubting what he should resolve upon. At one while he determined to reproach Matilda with treachery and baseness, and overwhelm her in the mid career of wickedness; but at last concluding it to be more politic to dissemble and subdue his emotions, he went into the breakfast-parlour which he had left, and seated himself as if nothing had happened, at a drawing which he had left incomplete.

Besides, perhaps Matilda might not be guilty—perhaps she was deceived; and though some scheme of villainy and destruction to himself was preparing, she might be the dupe, and not the coadjutor, of Zastrozzi. The idea that she was innocent soothed him; for he was anxious to make up, in his own mind, for the injustice which he had been guilty of towards her: and though he could not conquer the disgusting ideas, the unaccountable detestations, which often, in spite of himself, filled his soul towards her, he was willing to overcome what he considered but as an illusion of the imagination, and to pay that just tribute of esteem to her virtues which they demanded.

Whilst these ideas, although confused and unconnected, passed in Verezzi's brain, Matilda again entered the apartment.

Her countenance exhibited the strongest marks of agitation, and full of inexpressible and confused meaning was her dark eye, as she addressed some trifling question to Verezzi, in a hurried accent, and threw herself into a chair beside him.

"Verezzi!" exclaimed Matilda, after a pause equally painful to both—"Verezzi! I am deeply grieved to be the messenger of bad news—willingly would I withhold the fatal truth from you; yet, by some other means, it may meet your unprepared ear. I have something dreadful, shocking, to relate; can you bear the recital?"

The nerveless fingers of Verezzi dropped the pencil—he seized Matilda's hand, and, in accents almost inarticulate from terror, conjured her to explain her horrid surmises.

"Oh! my friend! my sister!" exclaimed Matilda, as well-feigned tears coursed down her cheeks,—"oh! she is——"

"What! what!" interrupted Verezzi, as the idea of something having befallen his adored Julia filled his maddened brain with tenfold horror: for often had Matilda declared that since she could not become his wife, she would willingly be his friend, and had even called Julia her sister.

"Oh!" exclaimed Matilda, hiding her face in her hands, "Julia—Julia—whom you love, is dead."

Unable to withhold his fleeting faculties from a sudden and chilly horror which seized them, Verezzi sank forward, and, fainting, fell at Matilda's feet.

In vain, for some time, was every effort to recover him. Every restorative which was administered, for a long time, was unavailing; at last his lips unclosed—he seemed to take his breath easier—he moved—he slowly opened his eyes.

CHAPTER VIII*

His head reposed upon Matilda's bosom; he started from it violently, as if stung by a scorpion, and fell upon the floor. His eyes rolled horribly, and seemed as if starting from their sockets.

"Is she then dead?—is Julia dead?" in accents scarcely articulate exclaimed Verezzi. "Ah, Matilda! was it you then who destroyed her? was it by thy jealous hand that she sank to an untimely grave?—Ah, Matilda! Matilda! say that she yet lives! Alas! what have I to do in the world without Julia?—an empty, uninteresting void!"

Every word uttered by the hapless Verezzi spoke daggers to the agitated Matilda.

Again overpowered by the acuteness of his sensations, he sank on the floor, and, in violent convulsions, he remained bereft of sense.

Matilda again raised him—again laid his throbbing head upon her bosom.—Again, as, recovering, the wretched Verezzi perceived his situation—overcome by agonising reflection, he relapsed into insensibility.

One fit rapidly followed another, and at last, in a state of the wildest delirium, he was conveyed to bed.

Matilda found that a too eager impatience had carried her too far. She had prepared herself for violent grief, but not for the paroxysms of madness which now seemed really to have seized the brain of the devoted Verezzi.

She sent for a physician—he arrived, and his opinion of Verezzi's danger almost drove the wretched Matilda to desperation.

Exhausted by contending passions, she threw herself on a sofa: she thought of the deeds which she had perpetrated to gain Verezzi's love; she considered that should her purpose be defeated, at the very instant which her heated imagination had portrayed as the commencement of her triumph; should all the wickedness, all the crimes, into which she had plunged herself, be of no avail—this idea, more than remorse for her enormities, affected her.

She sat for a time absorbed in a confusion of contending thought: her mind was the scene of anarchy and horror: at last, exhausted by their own violence, a deep, a desperate calm, took possession of her faculties. She started from the sofa, and, maddened by the idea of Verezzi's danger, sought his apartment.

On a bed lay Verezzi.

A thick film overspread his eye, and he seemed sunk in insensibility.

Matilda approached him—she pressed her burning lips to his.—She took his hand—it was cold, and at intervals slightly agitated by convulsions.

A deep sigh at this instant burst from his lips—a momentary hectic flushed his cheek, as the miserable Verezzi attempted to rise.

Matilda, though almost too much agitated to command her emotions, threw herself into a chair behind the curtain, and prepared to watch his movements.

"Julia! Julia!" exclaimed he, starting from the bed, as his flaming eye-balls were unconsciously fixed upon the agitated Matilda, "where art thou? Ah! thy fair form now moulders in the dark sepulchre! would I were laid beside thee! thou art now an ethereal spirit!" And then, in a seemingly triumphant accent, he added, "But, ere long, I will seek thy unspotted soul—ere long I will again clasp my lost Julia!" Overcome by resistless delirium, he was for an instant silent—his starting eyes seemed to follow some form, which imagination had portrayed in vacuity. He dashed his head against the wall, and sank, overpowered by insensibility, on the floor.

Accustomed as she was to scenes of horror, and firm and dauntless as was Matilda's soul, yet this was too much to behold with composure. She rushed towards him, and lifted him from the floor. In a delirium of terror, she wildly called for help. Unconscious of everything around her, she feared Verezzi had destroyed himself. She clasped him to her bosom, and called on his name, in an ecstasy of terror.

The domestics, alarmed by her exclamations, rushed in. Once again they lifted the insensible Verezzi into the bed. Every spark of life seemed now to have been extinguished; for the transport of horror which had torn his soul was almost too much to be sustained. A physician was again sent for—Matilda, maddened by desperation, in accents almost inarticulate from terror, demanded hope or despair from the physician.

He, who was a man of sense, declared his opinion, that Verezzi would speedily recover, though he knew not the event which might take place in the crisis of the disorder, which now rapidly approached.

The remonstrances of those around her were unavailing, to draw Matilda from the bedside of Verezzi.

She sat there, a prey to disappointed passion, silent, and watching every turn of the hapless Verezzi's countenance, as, bereft of sense, he lay extended on the bed before her.

The animation which was wont to illumine his sparkling eye was fled: the roseate colour which had tinged his cheek had given way to an ashy paleness—he was insensible to all around him. Matilda sat there the whole day, and silently administered medicines to the unconscious Verezzi, as occasion required.

Towards night the physician again came. Matilda's head thoughtfully leant upon her arm as he entered the apartment.

"Ah! what hope? what hope?" wildly she exclaimed.

The physician calmed her, and bid her not despair: then, observing her pallid countenance, he said, he believed she required his skill as much as his patient.

"Oh! heed me not," she exclaimed; "but how is Verezzi? will he live or die?"

The physician advanced towards the emaciated Verezzi—he took his hand.

A burning fever raged through his veins.

"Oh, how is he?" exclaimed Matilda, as, anxiously watching the humane physician's countenance, she thought a shade of sorrow spread itself over his features—"but tell me my fate quickly," continued she: "I am prepared to hear the worst—prepared to hear that he is even dead already."

As she spoke this, a sort of desperate serenity overspread her features—she seized the physician's arm, and looked steadfastly on his countenance, and then, as if overcome by unwonted exertions, she sank fainting at his feet.

The physician raised her, and soon succeeded in recalling her fleeted*faculties.

Overcome by its own violence, Matilda's despair became softened, and the words of the physician operated as a balm upon her soul, and bid her feel hope.

She again resumed her seat, and waited with smothered impatience for the event of the decisive crisis, which the physician could now no longer conceal.

She pressed his burning hand in hers, and waited, with apparent composure, for eleven o'clock.

Slowly the hours passed—the clock of Passau tolled each lingering quarter as they rolled away, and hastened towards the appointed time, when the chamber-door of Verezzi was slowly opened by Ferdinand.

"Ha! why do you disturb me now?" exclaimed Matilda, whom the entrance of Ferdinand had roused from a profound reverie.

"Signora!" whispered Ferdinand—"Signor Zastrozzi waits below: he wishes to see you there."

"Ah!" said Matilda, thoughtfully, "conduct him here."

Ferdinand departed to obey her; footsteps were heard in the passage, and immediately afterwards Zastrozzi stood before Matilda.

"Matilda!" exclaimed he, "why do I see you here? What accident has happened which confines you to this chamber?"

"Ah!" replied Matilda, in an undervoice, "look in that bed—behold Verezzi! emaciated and insensible—in a quarter of an hour, perhaps, all animation will be fled—fled for ever!" continued she, as a deeper expression of despair shaded her beautiful features.

Zastrozzi advanced to the foot of the bed—Verezzi lay, as if dead, before his eyes; for the ashy hue of his lips, and his sunken inexpressive eye, almost declared that his spirit was fled.

Zastrozzi gazed upon him with an indefinable expression of insatiated vengeance—indefinable to Matilda, as she gazed upon the expressive countenance of her coadjutor in crime.

"Matilda! I want you: come to the lower saloon; I have something to speak to you of," said Zastrozzi.

"Oh! if it concerned my soul's eternal happiness, I could not now attend," exclaimed Matilda, energetically; "in less than a quarter of an hour, perhaps, all I hold dear on earth will be dead; with him, every hope, every wish, every tie which binds me to earth. Oh!" exclaimed she, her voice assuming a tone of extreme horror, "see how pale he looks!"

Zastrozzi bade Matilda farewell, and went away.

The physician yet continued watching in silence the countenance of Verezzi: it still retained its unchanging expression of fixed despair.

Matilda gazed upon it, and waited with the most eager, yet subdued impatience, for the expiration of the few minutes which yet remained—she still gazed.

The features of Verezzi's countenance were slightly convulsed.

The clock struck eleven.

His lips unclosed—Matilda turned pale with terror; yet mute, and absorbed by expectation, remained rooted to her seat.

She raised her eyes, and hope again returned, as she beheld the countenance of the humane physician lighted up with a beam of pleasure.

She could no longer contain herself, but, in an ecstasy of pleasure, as excessive as her grief and horror before had been violent, in rapid and hurried accents questioned the physician. The physician, with an expressive smile, pressed his finger on his lip. She understood the movement; and though her heart was dilated with sudden and excessive delight, she smothered her joy, as she had before her grief, and gazed with rapturous emotion on the countenance of Verezzi, as, to her expectant eyes, a blush of animation tinged his before-pallid countenance.

Matilda took his hand—the pulses yet beat with feverish violence. She gazed upon his countenance—the film, which before had overspread his eye, disappeared: returning expression pervaded its orbit, but it was the expression of deep, of rooted grief.

The physician made a sign to Matilda to withdraw.

She drew the curtain before her, and in anxious expectation, awaited the event.

A deep, a long-drawn sigh, at last burst from Verezzi's bosom. He raised himself—his eyes seemed to follow some form, which imagination had portrayed in the remote obscurity of the apartment, for the shades of night were but partially dissipated by a lamp which burnt on a table behind. He raised his almost nerveless arm, and passed it across his eyes, as if to convince himself, that what he saw was not an illusion of the imagination.

He looked at the physician, who sat near to and silent by the bedside, and patiently awaited whatever event that might occur.

Verezzi slowly arose, and violently exclaimed, "Julia! Julia! my long-lost Julia, come!" And then, more collected, he added, in a mournful tone, "Ah, no! you are dead; lost, lost for ever!"

He turned round, and saw the physician, but Matilda was still concealed.

"Where am I?" inquired Verezzi, addressing the physician. "Safe, safe," answered he, "compose yourself; all will be well."

"Ah, but Julia?" inquired Verezzi, with a tone so expressive of despair, as threatened returning delirium.

"Oh! compose yourself," said the humane physician: "you have been very ill; this is but an illusion of the imagination; and even now, I fear, that you labour under that delirium which attends a brain-fever."

Verezzi's nerveless frame again sunk upon the bed—still his eyes were open, and fixed upon vacancy; he seemed to be endeavouring to arrange the confusion of ideas which pressed upon his brain.

Matilda undrew the curtain; but, as her eye met the physician's, his glance told her to place it in its original situation.

As she thought of the events of the day, her heart was dilated by tumultuous, yet pleasurable emotions. She conjectured that were Verezzi to recover, of which she now entertained but little doubt, she might easily erase from his heart the boyish passion which before had possessed it; might convince him of the folly of supposing that a first attachment is fated to endure for ever; and, by unremitting assiduity in pleasing him—by soft, quiet attentions, and an affected sensibility, might at last acquire the attainment of that object, for which her bosom had so long and so ardently panted.

Soothed by these ideas, and willing to hear from the physician's mouth a more explicit affirmation of Verezzi's safety than his looks had given, Matilda rose, for the first time since his illness, and, unseen by Verezzi, approached the physician—"Follow me to the saloon," said Matilda.

The physician obeyed, and, by his fervent assurances of Verezzi's safety and speedy recovery, confirmed Matilda's fluctuating hopes. "But," added the physician, "though my patient will recover if his mind be unruffled, I will not answer for his re-establishment should he see you, as his disorder, being wholly on the mind, may be possibly augmented by——"

The physician paused, and left Matilda to finish the sentence; for he was a man of penetration and judgment, and conjectured that some sudden and violent emotion, of which she was the cause, occasioned his patient's illness. This conjecture became certainty, as, when he concluded, he observed Matilda's face change to an ashy paleness.

"May I not watch him—attend him?" inquired Matilda, imploringly.

"No," answered the physician: "in the weakened state in which he now is, the sight of you might cause immediate dissolution."

Matilda started, as if overcome by horror at the bare idea, and promised to obey his commands.

The morning came—Matilda arose from a sleepless couch, and with hopes yet unconfirmed sought Verezzi's apartment.

She stood near the door listening.—Her heart palpitated with tremendous violence as she listened to Verezzi's breathing—every sound from within alarmed her. At last she slowly opened the door, and, though adhering to the physician's directions in not suffering Verezzi to see her, she could not deny herself the pleasure of watching him, and busying herself in little offices about his apartment.

She could hear Verezzi question the attendant collectedly, yet as a person who was ignorant where he was, and knew not the events which had immediately preceded his present state.

At last he sank into a deep sleep.—Matilda now dared to gaze on him: the hectic colour which had flushed his cheek was fled, but the ashy hue of his lips had given place to a brilliant vermilion. —She gazed intently on his countenance.

A heavenly, yet faint smile, diffused itself over his countenance —his hand slightly moved.

Matilda, fearing that he would awake, again concealed herself. She was mistaken, for, on looking again, he still slept.

She still gazed upon his countenance. The visions of his sleep were changed, for tears came fast from under his eyelids, and a deep sigh burst from his bosom.

Thus passed several days: Matilda still watched, with most affectionate assiduity, by the bedside of the unconscious Verezzi.

The physician declared that his patient's mind was yet in too irritable a state to permit him to see Matilda, but that he was convalescent.

One evening she sat by his bedside, and gazing upon the features of the sleeping Verezzi, felt unusual softness take possession of her soul—an indefinable and tumultuous emotion shook her bosom—her whole frame thrilled with rapturous ecstasy, and seizing the hand, which lay motionless beside her, she imprinted on it a thousand burning kisses.

"Ah, Julia! Julia! is it you?" exclaimed Verezzi, as he raised his enfeebled frame; but perceiving his mistake, as he cast his eyes on Matilda, sank back, and fainted.

Matilda hastened with restoratives, and soon succeeded in recalling to life Verezzi's fleeted faculties.

CHAPTER IX

Art thou afraid
To be the same in thine own act and valour
As thou art in desire? Wouldst thou have that
Which thou esteemest the ornament of life,
Or live a coward in thine own esteem,
Letting *I dare not* wait upon *I would?*

MACBETH.

For love is heaven, and heaven is love.

LAY OF THE LAST MINSTREL.

THE soul of Verezzi was filled with irresistible disgust, as, recovering, he found himself in Matilda's arms. His whole frame trembled with chilly horror, and he could scarcely withhold himself from again fainting. He fixed his eyes upon the countenance—they met hers—an ardent fire, mingled with a touching softness, filled their orbits.

In a hurried and almost inarticulate accent, he reproached Matilda with perfidy, baseness, and even murder. The roseate colour which had tinged Matilda's cheek, gave place to an ashy hue—the animation which had sparkled in her eye, yielded to a confused expression of apprehension, as the almost delirious Verezzi uttered accusations he knew not the meaning of; for his brain, maddened by the idea of Julia's death, was whirled round in an ecstasy of terror.

Matilda seemed to have composed every passion; a forced serenity overspread her features, as, in a sympathising and tender tone, she entreated him to calm his emotions, and giving him a composing* medicine, left him.

She descended to the saloon.

"Ah! he yet despises me—he even hates me," ejaculated Matilda. "An irresistible antipathy—irresistible, I fear, as my love for him is ardent, has taken possession of his soul towards me. Ah! miserable, hapless being that I am! doomed to have my fondest hope, my brightest prospect, blighted."

Alive alike to the tortures of despair and the illusions of hope, Matilda, now in an agony of desperation, impatiently paced the saloon.

Her mind was inflamed by a more violent emotion of hate towards Julia, as she recollected Verezzi's fond expressions: she determined, however, that were Verezzi not to be hers, he should never be Julia's.

Whilst thus she thought, Zastrozzi entered.

The conversation was concerning Verezzi.

"How shall I gain his love, Zastrozzi?" exclaimed Matilda. "Oh! I will renew every tender office—I will watch by him day and night, and, by unremitting attentions, I will try to soften his flinty soul. But, alas! it was but now that he started from my arms in horror, and, in accents of desperation, accused me of perfidy—of murder. Could I be perfidious to Verezzi, my heart, which burns with so fervent a fire, declares I could not, and murder——"

Matilda paused.

"Would thou could say thou wert guilty, or even accessary to *that*," exclaimed Zastrozzi, his eye gleaming with disappointed ferocity. "Would Julia of Strobazzo's heart was reeking on my dagger!"

"Fervently do I join in that wish, my best Zastrozzi," returned Matilda: "but, alas! what avail wishes—what avail useless protestations of revenge, whilst Julia yet lives?—yet lives, perhaps, again to obtain Verezzi—to clasp him constant to her bosom—and perhaps—oh, horror! perhaps to——"

Stung to madness by the picture which her fancy had portrayed, Matilda paused.

Her bosom heaved with throbbing palpitations; and, whilst describing the success of her rival, her warring soul shone apparent from her scintillating eyes.

Zastrozzi, meanwhile, stood collected in himself; and, scarcely heeding the violence of Matilda, awaited the issue of her speech.

He besought her to calm herself, nor, by those violent emotions, unfit herself for prosecuting the attainment of her fondest hope.

"Are you firm?" inquired Zastrozzi.

"Yes!"

"Are you resolved? Does fear, amid the other passions, shake your soul?"

"No, no—this heart knows not to fear—this breast knows not to shrink," exclaimed Matilda eagerly.

"Then be cool—be collected," returned Zastrozzi, "and thy purpose is effected."

Though little was in these words which might warrant hope, yet Matilda's susceptible soul, as Zastrozzi spoke, thrilled with anticipated delight.

"My maxim, therefore," said Zastrozzi, "through life has been, wherever I am, whatever passions shake my inmost soul, at least to *appear* collected. I generally am; for, by suffering no common events, no fortuitous casualty to disturb me, my soul becomes steeled to more interesting trials. I have a spirit, ardent, impetuous as thine; but acquaintance with the world has induced me to veil it, though it still continues to burn within my bosom. Believe me, I am far from wishing to persuade you from your purpose. No—any purpose undertaken with ardour, and prosecuted with perseverance, must eventually be crowned with success. Love is worthy of any risque—I felt it once, but revenge has now swallowed up every other feeling of my soul—I am alive to nothing but revenge. But even did I desire to persuade you from the purpose on which your heart is fixed, I should not say it was wrong to attempt it; for whatever procures pleasure is right, and consonant to the dignity of man, who was created for no other purpose but to obtain happiness; else, why were passions given us? why were those emotions which agitate my breast and madden my brain implanted in us by nature? As for the confused hope of a future state, why should we debar ourselves of the delights of this, even though purchased by what the misguided multitude calls immorality?"

Thus sophistically argued Zastrozzi.—His soul, deadened by crime, could only entertain confused ideas of immortal happiness; for in proportion as human nature departs from virtue, so far are they also from being able clearly to contemplate the wonderful operations, the mysterious ways of Providence.

Coolly and collectedly argued Zastrozzi: he delivered his sentiments with the air of one who was wholly convinced of the truth of the doctrines he uttered,—a conviction to be dissipated by shunning proof.

Whilst Zastrozzi thus spoke, Matilda remained silent,—she

paused. Zastrozzi must have strong powers of reflection; he must be convinced of the truth of his own reasoning, thought Matilda, as eagerly she yet gazed on his countenance. Its unchanging expression of firmness and conviction still continued.

"Ah!" said Matilda, "Zastrozzi, thy words are a balm to my soul. I never yet knew thy real sentiments on this subject; but answer me, do you believe that the soul decays with the body, or if you do not, when this perishable form mingles with its parent earth, where goes the soul which now actuates its movements? perhaps, it wastes its fervent energies in tasteless apathy, or lingering torments."

"Matilda," returned Zastrozzi, "think not so; rather suppose that by its own innate and energetical exertions, this soul must endure for ever, that no fortuitous occurrences, no incidental events, can affect its happiness; but by daring boldly, by striving to verge from the beaten path, whilst yet trammelled in the chains of mortality, it will gain superior advantages in a future state."

"But religion! oh, Zastrozzi!"—

"I thought thy soul was daring," replied Zastrozzi; "I thought thy mind was towering; and did I then err in the different estimate I had formed of thy character?—O yield not yourself, Matilda, thus to false, foolish, and vulgar prejudices—for the present, farewell."

Saying this, Zastrozzi departed.

Thus, by an artful appeal to her passions, did Zastrozzi extinguish the faint spark of religion which yet gleamed in Matilda's bosom.

In proportion as her belief of an Omnipotent Power, and consequently her hopes of eternal salvation declined, her ardent and unquenchable passion for Verezzi increased, and a delirium of guilty love filled her soul.—

"Shall I then call him mine for ever?" mentally inquired Matilda; "will the passion which now consumes me, possess my soul to all eternity? Ah! well I know it will; and when emancipated from this terrestrial form, my soul departs; still its fervent energies unrepressed, will remain; and in the union of soul to soul, it will taste celestial transports." An ecstasy of tumultuous and confused delight rushed through her veins; she stood for some time immersed in thought.—Agitated by the emotions of her soul, her every limb trembled—she thought upon Zastrozzi's sentiments, she almost shuddered as she reflected; yet was convinced, by the cool and collected manner in which he had delivered them.—She thought on his advice, and steeling her soul, repressing every emotion, she now acquired that coolness so necessary to the attainment of her desire.

Thinking of nothing else, alive to no idea but Verezzi, Matilda's countenance assumed a placid serenity—she even calmed her soul, she bid it restrain its emotions, and the passions which so lately had battled fiercely in her bosom, were calmed.

She again went to Verezzi's apartment, but, as she approached, vague fears lest he should have penetrated her schemes confused her: but his mildly beaming eyes, as she gazed upon them, convinced her, that the horrid expressions which he had before uttered were merely the effect of temporary delirium.

"Ah, Matilda!" exclaimed Verezzi, "where have you been?"

Matilda's soul, alive alike to despair and hope, was filled with momentary delight as he addressed her; but bitter hate, and disappointed love, again tortured her bosom, as he exclaimed in accents of heart-felt agony: "Oh! Julia, my long-lost Julia!"

"Matilda," said he, "my friend, farewell; I feel that I am dying, but I feel pleasure,—oh! transporting pleasure, in the idea that I shall soon meet my Julia. Matilda," added he, in a softened accent, "farewell for ever." Scarcely able to contain the emotions which the idea alone of Verezzi's death excited, Matilda, though the crisis of the disorder, she knew, had been favourable, shuddered—bitter hate, even more rancorous than ever, kindled in her bosom against Julia, for to hear Verezzi talk of her with soul-subduing tenderness, but wound up her soul to the highest pitch of uncontrollable vengeance. Her breast heaved violently, her dark eye, in expressive glances, told the fierce passions of her soul; yet, sensible of the necessity of controlling her emotions, she leaned her head upon her hand, and when she answered Verezzi, a calmness, a melting expression of grief, overspread her features. She conjured him, in the most tender, the most soothing terms, to compose himself, and though Julia was gone for ever, to remember that there was yet one in the world, one tender friend who would render the burden of life less insupportable.

"Oh! Matilda," exclaimed Verezzi, "talk not to me of comfort, talk not of happiness. All that constituted my comfort, all to which I looked forward with rapturous anticipation of happiness, is fled—fled for ever."

Ceaselessly did Matilda watch by the bed-side of Verezzi; the melting tenderness of his voice, the melancholy, interesting expression of his countenance, but added fuel to the flame which consumed her: her soul was engrossed by one idea; every extraneous passion was conquered, and nerved for the execution of its fondest purpose; a seeming tranquillity overspread her mind, not that tranquillity which results from conscious innocence and mild delights, but that which calms every tumultuous emotion for a time; when firm in a settled purpose, the passions but pause, to break out with more resistless violence. In the meantime, the strength of Verezzi's constitution overcame the malignity of his disorder, returning strength again braced his nerves, and he was able to descend to the saloon.

The violent grief of Verezzi had subsided into a deep and settled melancholy; he could now talk of his Julia, indeed it was his constant theme; he spoke of her virtues, her celestial form, her sensibility, and by his ardent professions of eternal fidelity to her memory, unconsciously almost drove Matilda to desperation.—Once he asked Matilda how she died, for on the day when the intelligence first turned his brain, he waited not to hear the particulars, the bare fact drove him to instant madness.

Matilda was startled at the question, yet ready invention supplied the place of a premeditated story.

"Oh! my friend," said she, tenderly, "unwillingly do I tell you, that for you she died; disappointed love, like a worm in the bud, destroyed the unhappy Julia; fruitless were all her endeavours to find you; till at last, concluding that you were lost to her for ever, a deep melancholy by degrees consumed her, and gently led to the grave—she sank into the arms of death without a groan."

"And there shall I soon follow her," exclaimed Verezzi, as a severer pang of anguish and regret darted through his soul. "I caused her death, whose life was far, far dearer to me than my own. But now it is all over, my hopes of happiness in this world are blasted, blasted for ever."

As he said this, a convulsive sigh heaved his breast, and the tears silently rolled down his cheeks; for some time, in vain were Matilda's endeavours to calm him, till at last, mellowed by time, and overcome by reflection, his violent and fierce sorrow was softened into a fixed melancholy.

Unremittingly Matilda attended him, and gratified his every wish: she, conjecturing that solitude might be detrimental to him, often entertained parties, and endeavoured by gaiety to drive away his dejection; but if Verezzi's spirits were elevated by company and merriment, in solitude again they sank, and a deeper melancholy, a severer regret possessed his bosom, for having allowed himself to be momentarily interested by any thing but the remembrance of his Julia; for he felt a soft, a tender and ecstatic emotion of regret, when retrospection portrayed the blissful time long since gone by, while, happy in the society of her whom he idolised, he thought he could never be otherwise than then, enjoying the sweet, the serene delights of association with a congenial mind, he often now amused himself in retracing with his pencil, from memory, scenes which, though in his Julia's society he had beheld unnoticed, yet were now hallowed by the remembrance of her: for he always associated the idea of Julia with the remembrance of those scenes which she had so often admired, and where, accompanied by her, he had so often wandered.

Matilda, meanwhile, firm in the purpose of her soul, unremittingly persevered: she calmed her mind, and though, at intervals, shook by almost superhuman emotions, before Verezzi a fixed serenity, a well-feigned sensibility, and a downcast tenderness, marked her manner. Grief, melancholy, a fixed, a quiet depression of spirits, seemed to have calmed every fiercer feeling when she talked with Verezzi of his lost Julia: but, though subdued for the present, revenge, hate, and the fervour of disappointed love, burned her soul.

Often, when she had retired from Verezzi, when he had talked with tenderness, as he was wont, of Julia, and sworn everlasting fidelity to her memory, would Matilda's soul be tortured by fiercest desperation.

One day, when conversing with him of Julia, she ventured to hint, though remotely, at her own faithful and ardent attachment.

"Think you," replied Verezzi, "that because my Julia's spirit is no longer enshrined in its earthly form, that I am the less devotedly, the less irrevocably hers?—No! no! I was hers, I am hers, and to all eternity shall be hers: and when my soul, divested of mortality, departs into another world, even amid the universal wreck of nature, attracted by congeniality of sentiment, it will seek the unspotted spirit of my idolised Julia.—Oh, Matilda! thy attention, thy kindness, calls for my warmest gratitude—thy virtue demands my sincerest esteem; but, devoted to the memory of Julia,* I can *love* none but her."

Matilda's whole frame trembled with unconquerable emotion, as thus determinedly he rejected her; but, calming the more violent passions, a flood of tears rushed from her eyes; and, as she leant over the back of a sofa on which she reclined, her sobs were audible.

Verezzi's soul was softened towards her—he raised the humbled Matilda, and bid her be comforted, for he was conscious that her tenderness towards him deserved not an unkind return.

"Oh! forgive, forgive me!" exclaimed Matilda, with well-feigned humility: "I knew not what I said."—She then abruptly left the saloon.

Reaching her own apartment, Matilda threw herself on the floor, in an agony of mind too great to be described. Those infuriate passions, restrained as they had been in the presence of Verezzi, now agitated her soul with inconceivable terror. Shook by sudden and irresistible emotions, she gave vent to her despair.

"Where, then, is the boasted mercy of God," exclaimed the frantic Matilda, "if he suffer his creatures to endure such agony as this? or where his wisdom, if he implant in the heart passions furious—uncontrollable—as mine, doomed to destroy their happiness?"

Outraged pride, disappointed love, and infuriate revenge, revelled through her bosom. Revenge, which called for innocent blood—the blood of the hapless Julia.

Her passions were now wound up to the highest pitch of desperation. In indescribable agony of mind, she dashed her head against the floor—she imprecated a thousand curses upon Julia, and swore eternal revenge.

At last, exhausted by their own violence, the warring passions subsided—a calm took possession of her soul—she thought again upon Zastrozzi's advice.—Was she now cool? was she now collected?

She was now immersed in a chain of thought; unaccountable, even to herself, was the serenity which had succeeded.

CHAPTER X

PERSEVERING in the prosecution of her design, the time passed away slowly to Matilda; for Verezzi's frame, becoming every day more emaciated, threatened, to her alarmed imagination, approaching dissolution.—Slowly to Verezzi, for he waited with impatience for the arrival of death, since nothing but misery was his in this world.

Useless would it be to enumerate the conflicts in Matilda's soul: suffice it to say, that they were many, and that their violence progressively increased.

Verezzi's illness at last assumed so dangerous an appearance that Matilda, alarmed, sent for a physician.

The humane man, who had attended Verezzi before, was from home, but one, skilful in his profession, arrived, who declared that a warmer climate could alone restore Verezzi's health.

Matilda proposed to him to remove to a retired and picturesque spot which she possessed in the Venetian territory. Verezzi, expecting speedy dissolution, and conceiving it to be immaterial where he died, consented; and, indeed, he was unwilling to pain one so kind as Matilda by a refusal.

The following morning was fixed for the journey.

The morning arrived, and Verezzi was lifted into the chariot, being yet extremely weak and emaciated.

Matilda, during the journey, by every care, every kind and sympathising attention, tried to drive away Verezzi's melancholy; sensible that, could the weight which pressed upon his spirits be removed, he would speedily regain health. But no! it was impossible. Though he was grateful for Matilda's attention, a still deeper shade of melancholy overspread his features; a more heartfelt inanity and languor sapped his life. He was sensible of a total distaste of former objects—objects which, perhaps, had formerly forcibly interested him. The terrific grandeur of the Alps, the dashing cataract, as it foamed beneath their feet, ceased to excite those feelings of awe which formerly they were wont to inspire.

The lofty pine-groves inspired no additional melancholy, nor did the blooming valleys of Piedmont, or the odoriferous orangeries which scented the air, gladden his deadened soul.

They travelled on—they soon entered the Venetian territory, where, in a gloomy and remote spot, stood the Castella di Laurentini.

It was situated in a dark forest—lofty mountains around lifted their aspiring and craggy summits to the skies.

The mountains were clothed half up by ancient pines and plane-trees, whose immense branches stretched far; and above, bare granite rocks, on which might be seen, occasionally a scathed larch, lifted their gigantic and misshapen forms.*

In the centre of an amphitheatre, formed by these mountains, surrounded by wood, stood the Castella di Laurentini, whose grey turrets and time-worn battlements, overtopped the giants of the forest.

Into this gloomy mansion was Verezzi conducted by Matilda. The only sentiment he felt was surprise at the prolongation of his existence. As he advanced, supported by Matilda and a domestic, into the castella, Matilda's soul, engrossed by one idea, confused by its own unquenchable passions, felt not that ecstatic, that calm and serene delight, only experienced by the innocent, and which is excited by a return to the place where we have spent our days of infancy.

No—she felt not this; the only pleasurable emotion which her return to this remote castella afforded, was the hope that, disengaged from the tumult of, and proximity to the world, she might be the less interrupted in the prosecution of her madly-planned schemes.

Though Verezzi's melancholy seemed rather increased than diminished by the journey, yet his health was visibly improved by the progressive change of air and variation of scenery, which must, at times, momentarily alleviate the most deep-rooted grief; yet, again in a fixed spot—again left to solitude and his own torturing reflections, Verezzi's mind returned to his lost, his still adored Julia. He thought of her ever; unconsciously he spoke of her; and, by his rapturous exclamations, sometimes almost drove Matilda to desperation.

Several days thus passed away. Matilda's passion, which, mellowed by time, and diverted by the variety of objects, and the hurry of the journey, had relaxed its violence, now, like a stream pent up, burst all bounds.

But one evening, maddened by the tender protestations of eternal fidelity to Julia's memory which Verezzi uttered, her brain was almost turned.

Her tumultuous soul, agitated by contending emotions, flashed from her eyes. Unable to disguise the extreme violence of her sensations, in an ecstasy of despairing love, she rushed from the apartment where she had left Verezzi, and, unaccompanied, wandered into the forest, to calm her emotions, and concert some better plans of revenge; for, in Verezzi's presence, she scarcely dared to think.

Her infuriated soul burned with fiercest revenge: she wandered into the trackless forest, and, conscious that she was unobserved, gave vent to her feelings in wild exclamations.

"Oh, Julia! hated Julia! words are not able to express my detestation of thee. Thou hast destroyed Verezzi. Thy cursed image, revelling in his heart, has blasted my happiness for ever; but, ere I die, I will taste revenge—oh! exquisite revenge!" She paused—she thought of the passion which consumed her.—"Perhaps one no less violent has induced Julia to rival me," said she. Again the idea of Verezzi's illness—perhaps his death—infuriated her soul. Pity, chased away by vengeance and disappointed passion, fled.—"Did I say that I pitied thee? Detested Julia, much did my words belie the feelings of my soul. No—no—thou shalt not escape me.—Pity thee!"

Again immersed in corroding thought, she heeded not the hour, till looking up, she saw the shades of night were gaining fast upon the earth. The evening was calm and serene: gently agitated by the evening zephyr, the lofty pines sighed mournfully. Far to the west appeared the evening star, which faintly glittered in the twilight. The scene was solemnly calm, but not in unison with Matilda's soul. Softest, most melancholy music, seemed to float upon the southern gale. Matilda listened—it was the nuns at a convent, chanting the requiem for the soul of a departed sister.

"Perhaps gone to heaven!" exclaimed Matilda, as, affected by the contrast, her guilty soul trembled. A chain of horrible racking thoughts pressed upon her soul; and, unable to bear the acuteness of her sensations, she hastily returned to the castella.

Thus, marked only by the varying paroxysms of the passions which consumed her, Matilda passed the time: her brain was confused, her mind agitated by the ill success of her schemes, and her spirits, once so light and buoyant, were now depressed by disappointed hope.

"What shall I next concert?" was the mental inquiry of Matilda. "Ah! I know not."

She suddenly started—she thought of Zastrozzi.

"Oh! that I should have till now forgotten Zastrozzi," exclaimed Matilda, as a new ray of hope darted through her soul. "But he is now at Naples, and some time must necessarily elapse before I can see him."

"Oh, Zastrozzi, Zastrozzi! would that you were here!"

No sooner had she well arranged her resolutions, which before had been confused by eagerness, than she summoned Ferdinand, on whose fidelity she dared to depend, and bid him speed to Naples, and bear a letter, with which he was entrusted, to Zastrozzi.

Meanwhile Verezzi's health, as the physician had predicted, was so much improved by the warm climate and pure air of the Castella di Laurentini, that, though yet extremely weak and emaciated, he was able, as the weather was fine, and the summer evenings tranquil, to wander, accompanied by Matilda, through the surrounding scenery.

In this gloomy solitude, where, except the occasional and infrequent visits of a father confessor, nothing occurred to disturb the uniform tenour of their life, Verezzi was everything to Matilda—she thought of him ever: at night, in dreams, his image was present to her enraptured imagination. She was uneasy, except in his presence; and her soul, shook by contending paroxysms of the passion which consumed her, was transported by unutterable ecstasies of delirious and maddening love.

Her taste for music was exquisite; her voice of celestial sweetness; and her skill, as she drew sounds of soul-touching melody from the harp, enraptured the mind to melancholy pleasure.

The affecting expression of her voice, mellowed as it was by the tenderness which at times stole over her soul, softened Verezzi's listening ear to ecstasy.

Yet, again recovering from the temporary delight which her seductive blandishments had excited, he thought of Julia. As he remembered her ethereal form, her retiring modesty, and unaffected sweetness, a more violent, a deeper pang of regret and sorrow assailed his bosom, for having suffered himself to be even momentarily interested by Matilda.

Hours, days passed lingering away. They walked in the evenings around the environs of the castella—woods, dark and gloomy, stretched far—cloud-capt mountains reared their gigantic summits high; and, dashing amidst the jutting rocks, foaming cataracts, with sudden and impetuous course, sought the valley below.

Amid this scenery the wily Matilda usually led her victim.

One evening when the moon, rising over the gigantic outline of the mountain, silvered the far-seen cataract, Matilda and Verezzi sought the forest.

For a time neither spoke: the silence was uninterrupted, save by Matilda's sighs, which declared that violent and repressed emotions tortured the bosom within.

They silently advanced into the forest. The azure sky was spangled with stars—not a wind agitated the unruffled air—not a cloud obscured the brilliant concavity of heaven. They ascended an eminence, clothed with towering wood; the trees around formed an amphitheatre. Beneath, by a gentle ascent, an opening showed an immense extent of forest, dimly seen by the moon, which overhung the opposite mountain. The craggy heights beyond might distinctly be seen, edged by the beams of the silver moon.

Verezzi threw himself on the turf.

"What a beautiful scene, Matilda!" he exclaimed.

"Beautiful indeed," returned Matilda. "I have admired it ever, and brought you here this evening on purpose to discover whether you thought of the works of nature as I do."

"Oh! fervently do I admire this," exclaimed Verezzi, as, engrossed by the scene before him, he gazed enraptured.

"Suffer me to retire for a few minutes," said Matilda.

Without waiting for Verezzi's answer, she hastily entered a small tuft of trees. Verezzi gazed surprised; and soon sounds of such ravishing melody stole upon the evening breeze, that Verezzi thought some spirit of the solitude had made audible to mortal ears ethereal music.

He still listened—it seemed to die away—and again a louder, a more rapturous swell, succeeded.

The music was in unison with the scene—it was in unison with Verezzi's soul; and the success of Matilda's artifice, in this respect, exceeded her most sanguine expectation.

He still listened—the music ceased—and Matilda's symmetrical form emerging from the wood, roused Verezzi from his vision.

He gazed on her—her loveliness and grace struck forcibly upon his senses; her sensibility, her admiration of objects which enchanted him, flattered him; and her judicious arrangement of the music left no doubt in his mind but that, experiencing the same sensations herself, the feelings of his soul were not unknown to her.*

Thus far everything went on as Matilda desired. To touch his feelings had been her constant aim; could she find anything which interested him; anything to divert his melancholy: or could she succeed in effacing another from his mind, she had no doubt but that he would quickly and voluntarily clasp her to his bosom.

By affecting to coincide with him in everything—by feigning to possess that congeniality of sentiment and union of idea which he thought so necessary to the existence of love, she doubted not soon to accomplish her purpose.

But sympathy and congeniality of sentiment, however necessary to that love which calms every fierce emotion, fills the soul with a melting tenderness, and, without disturbing it, continually possesses the soul, was by no means consonant to the ferocious emotions, the unconquerable and ardent passion which revelled through Matilda's every vein.

When enjoying the society of him she loved, calm delight, unruffled serenity, possessed not her soul. No—but, inattentive to every object but him, even her proximity to him agitated her with almost uncontrollable emotion.

Whilst watching his look, her pulse beat with unwonted violence, her breast palpitated, and, unconscious of it herself, an ardent and voluptuous fire darted from her eyes.

Her passion too, controlled as it was in the presence of Verezzi, agitated her soul with progressively-increasing fervour. Nursed by solitude, and wound up, perhaps, beyond any pitch which another's soul might be capable of, it sometimes almost maddened her.

Still, surprised at her own forbearance, yet strongly perceiving the necessity of it, she spoke not again of her passion to Verezzi.

CHAPTER XI

At last the day arrived when Matilda expected Ferdinand's return. Punctual to his time, Ferdinand returned, and told Matilda that Zastrozzi had, for the present, taken up his abode at a cottage not far from thence, and that he there awaited her arrival.

Matilda was much surprised that Zastrozzi preferred a cottage to her castella; but, dismissing that from her mind, hastily prepared to attend him.

She soon arrived at the cottage. Zastrozzi met her—he quickened his pace towards her.

"Well, Zastrozzi," exclaimed Matilda, inquiringly.

"Oh!" said Zastrozzi, "our schemes have all, as yet, been unsuccessful. Julia yet lives, and, surrounded by wealth and power, yet defies our vengeance. I was planning her destruction, when, obedient to your commands, I came here."

"Alas!" exclaimed Matilda, "I fear it must be ever thus: but, Zastrozzi, much I need your advice—your assistance. Long have I languished in hopeless love: often have I expected, and as often have my eager expectations been blighted by disappointment."

A deep sigh of impatience burst from Matilda's bosom, as, unable to utter more, she ceased.

"'Tis but the image of that accursed Julia," replied Zastrozzi, "revelling in his breast, which prevents him from becoming instantly yours. Could you but efface that!"

"I would I could efface it," said Matilda: "the friendship which now exists between us would quickly ripen into love, and I should be for ever happy. How, Zastrozzi, can that be done? But, before we think of happiness, we must have a care to our safety: we must destroy Julia, who yet endeavours, by every means, to know the event of Verezzi's destiny. But, surrounded by wealth and power as she is, how can that be done? No bravo in Naples dare attempt her life: no rewards, however great, could tempt the most abandoned of men to brave instant destruction, in destroying her; and should *we* attempt it, the most horrible tortures of the Inquisition, a disgraceful death, and that without the completion of our desire, would be the consequence."

"Think not so, Matilda," answered Zastrozzi; "think not, because Julia possesses wealth, that she is less assailable by the dagger of one eager for revenge as I am; or that, because she lives in splendor at Naples, that a poisoned chalice, prepared by your hand, the hand of a disappointed rival, could not send her writhing and convulsed to the grave. No, no; she *can* die, nor shall we writhe on the rack."

"Oh!" interrupted Matilda, "I care not, if, writhing in the prisons of the Inquisition, I suffer the most excruciating torment; I care not if, exposed to public view, I suffer the most ignominious and disgraceful of deaths, if, before I die—if, before this spirit seeks another world, I gain my purposed design, I enjoy unutterable, and, as yet, inconceivable happiness."

The evening meanwhile came on, and, warned by the lateness of the hour to separate, Matilda and Zastrozzi parted.

Zastrozzi pursued his way to the cottage, and Matilda, deeply musing, retraced her steps to the castella.

The wind was fresh, and rather tempestuous: light fleeting clouds were driven rapidly across the dark-blue sky. The moon, in silver majesty, hung high in eastern ether, and rendered transparent as a celestial spirit the shadowy clouds, which at intervals crossed her orbit, and by degrees vanished like a vision in the obscurity of distant air. On this scene gazed Matilda—a train of confused thought took possession of her soul—her crimes, her past life, rose in array to her terror-struck imagination. Still burning love, unrepressed, unconquerable passion, revelled through every vein: her senses, rendered delirious by guilty desire, were whirled around in an inexpressible ecstasy of anticipated delight—delight, not unmixed by confused apprehensions.

She stood thus with her arms folded, as if contemplating the spangled concavity of heaven.

It was late—later than the usual hour of return, and Verezzi had gone out to meet Matilda.

"What! deep in thought, Matilda?" exclaimed Verezzi, playfully.

Matilda's cheek, as he thus spoke, was tinged with a momentary blush; it, however, quickly passed away, and she replied, "I was enjoying the serenity of the evening, the beauty of the setting sun, and then the congenial twilight induced me to wander farther than usual."

The unsuspicious Verezzi observed nothing peculiar in the manner of Matilda; but, observing that the night air was chill, conducted her back to the castella. No art was left untried, no blandishment omitted, on the part of Matilda, to secure her victim. Everything which he liked, she affected to admire: every sentiment uttered by Verezzi was always anticipated by the observing Matilda; but long was all in vain—long was every effort to obtain his love useless.

Often, when she touched the harp, and drew sounds of enchanting melody from its strings, whilst her almost celestial form bent over it, did Verezzi gaze enraptured, and, forgetful of everything else, yielding himself to a tumultuous oblivion of pleasure, listened entranced.

But all her art could not draw Julia from his memory; he was much softened towards Matilda; he felt esteem, tenderest esteem—but he yet loved not.

Thus passed the time.—Often would desperation, and an idea that Verezzi would never love her, agitate Matilda with most violent agony. The beauties of nature which surrounded the castella had no longer power to interest; borne away on swelling thought, often in the solitude of her own apartment, her spirit was wafted on the wings of anticipating fancy. Sometimes imagination portrayed the most horrible images for futurity; Verezzi's hate, perhaps his total dereliction of her, his union with Julia, pressed upon her brain, and almost drove her to distraction, for Verezzi alone filled every thought; nourished by restless reveries, the most horrible anticipations blasted the blooming Matilda.—Sometimes, however, a gleam of sense shot across her soul: deceived by visions of unreal bliss, she acquired new courage, and fresh anticipations of delight, from a beam which soon withdrew its ray; for, usually sunk in gloom, her dejected eyes were fixed on the ground; though sometimes an ardent expression, kindled by the anticipation of gratified desire, flashed from their fiery orbits.

Often, whilst thus agitated by contending emotions, her soul was shook, and, unconscious of its intentions, knew not the most preferable plan to pursue, would she seek Zastrozzi: on him, unconscious why, she relied much—his words were those of calm reflection and experience; and his sophistry, whilst it convinced her that a superior being exists not, who can control our actions, brought peace to her mind—peace to be succeeded by horrible and resistless conviction of the falsehood of her coadjutor's arguments! still, however, they calmed her; and, by addressing her reason and passions at the same time, deprived her of the power of being benefited by either.

The health of Verezzi, meanwhile, slowly mended: his mind, however, shook by so violent a trial as it had undergone, recovered not its vigour, but, mellowed by time, his grief, violent and irresistible as it had been at first, now became a fixed melancholy, which spread itself over his features, was apparent in every action, and, by resistance, inflamed Matilda's passion to tenfold fury.

The touching tenderness of Verezzi's voice, the dejected softened expression of his eye, touched her soul with tumultuous yet milder emotions. In his presence she felt calmed; and those passions which, in solitude, were almost too fierce for endurance, when with him were softened into a tender though confused delight.

It was one evening, when no previous appointment existed between Matilda and Zastrozzi, that, overcome by disappointed passion, Matilda sought the forest.

The sky was unusually obscured, the sun had sunk beneath the western mountain, and its departing ray tinged the heavy clouds with a red glare.—The rising blast sighed through the towering pines, which rose loftily above Matilda's head: the distant thunder, hoarse as the murmurs of the grove, in indistinct echoes mingled with the hollow breeze; the scintillating lightning flashed incessantly across her path, as Matilda, heeding not the storm, advanced along the trackless forest.

The crashing thunder now rattled madly above, the lightnings flashed a larger curve, and at intervals, through the surrounding gloom, showed a scathed larch, which, blasted by frequent storms, reared its bare head on a height above.

Matilda sat upon a fragment of jutting granite, and contemplated the storm which raged around her. The portentous calm, which at intervals occurred amid the reverberating thunder, portentous of a more violent tempest, resembled the serenity which spread itself over Matilda's mind—a serenity only to be succeeded by a fiercer paroxysm of passion.

CHAPTER XII

STILL sat Matilda upon the rock—she still contemplated the tempest which raged around her.

The battling elements paused: an uninterrupted silence, deep, dreadful as the silence of the tomb, succeeded. Matilda heard a noise—footsteps were distinguishable, and, looking up, a flash of vivid lightning disclosed to her view the towering form of Zastrozzi.

His gigantic figure was again involved in pitchy darkness, as the momentary lightning receded. A peal of crashing thunder again madly rattled over the zenith, and a scintillating flash announced Zastrozzi's approach, as he stood before Matilda.

Matilda, surprised at his approach, started as he addressed her, and felt an indescribable awe, when she reflected on the wonderful casualty which, in this terrific and tempestuous hour, had led them to the same spot.

"Doubtless his feelings are violent and irresistible as mine: perhaps *these* led him to meet me here."

She shuddered as she reflected; but smothering the sensations of alarm which she had suffered herself to be surprised by, she asked him what had led him to the forest.

"The same which led you here, Matilda," returned Zastrozzi: "the same influence which actuates us both, has doubtless inspired that congeniality which, in this frightful storm, led us to the same spot."

"Oh!" exclaimed Matilda, "how shall I touch the obdurate Verezzi's soul? He still despises me—he declares himself to be devoted to the memory of his Julia; and that although she be dead, he is not the less devotedly hers. What can be done?"

Matilda paused; and, much agitated, awaited Zastrozzi's reply.

Zastrozzi, meanwhile, stood collected in himself, and firm as the rocky mountain which lifts its summit to heaven.

"Matilda," said he, "to-morrow evening will pave the way for that happiness which your soul has so long panted for, if, indeed, the event which will then occur does not completely conquer

Verezzi. But the violence of the tempest increases—let us seek shelter."

"Oh! heed not the tempest," said Matilda, whose expectations were raised to the extreme of impatience by Zastrozzi's dark hints—"heed not the tempest, but proceed, if you wish not to see me expiring at your feet."

"You fear not the tumultuous elements—nor do I," replied Zastrozzi. "I assert again, that if to-morrow evening you lead Verezzi to this spot—if, in the event which will here occur, you display that presence of mind which I believe you to possess, Verezzi is yours."

"Ah! what do you say, Zastrozzi, that Verezzi will be mine?" inquired Matilda, as the anticipation of inconceivable happiness dilated her soul with sudden and excessive delight.

"I say again, Matilda," returned Zastrozzi, "that if you dare to brave the dagger's point—if you but make Verezzi owe his life to you——"

Zastrozzi paused, and Matilda acknowledged her insight of his plan, which her enraptured fancy represented as the basis of her happiness.

"Could he, after she had, at the risk of her own life, saved his, unfeelingly reject her? Would those noble sentiments, which the greatest misfortunes were unable to extinguish, suffer that?—No."

Full of these ideas, her brain confused by the ecstatic anticipation of happiness which pressed upon it, Matilda retraced her footsteps towards the castella.

The violence of the storm which so lately had raged was passed —the thunder, in low and indistinct echoes, now sounded through the chain of rocky mountains, which stretched far to the north— the azure, and almost cloudless ether, was studded with countless stars, as Matilda entered the castella, and, as the hour was late, sought her own apartment.

Sleep fled not, as usual, from her pillow; but, overcome by excessive drowsiness, she soon sank to rest.

Confused dreams floated in her imagination, in which she sometimes supposed that she had gained Verezzi; at others, that, snatched from her ardent embrace, he was carried by an invisible power over rocky mountains, or immense and untravelled heaths, and that, in vainly attempting to follow him, she had lost herself in the trackless desert.

Awakened from disturbed and unconnected dreams, she arose.

The most tumultuous emotions of rapturous exultation filled her soul as she gazed upon her victim, who was sitting at a window which overlooked the waving forest.

Matilda seated herself by him, and most enchanting, most pensive music, drawn by her fingers from a harp, thrilled his soul with an ecstasy of melancholy; tears rolled rapidly down his cheeks; deep drawn, though gentle sighs heaved his bosom: his innocent eyes were mildly fixed upon Matilda, and beamed with compassion for one whose only wish was gratification of her own inordinate desires, and destruction to his opening prospects of happiness.

She, with a ferocious pleasure, contemplated her victim; yet, curbing the passions of her soul, a meekness, a well-feigned sensibility, characterised her downcast eye.

She waited, with the smothered impatience of expectation, for the evening: then had Zastrozzi affirmed that she would lay a firm foundation for her happiness.

Unappalled, she resolved to brave the dagger's point: she resolved to bleed; and though her life-blood were to issue at the wound, to dare the event.

The evening at last arrived; the atmosphere was obscured by vapour, and the air more chill than usual; yet, yielding to the solicitations of Matilda, Verezzi accompanied her to the forest.

Matilda's bosom thrilled with inconceivable happiness, as she advanced towards the spot; her limbs, trembling with ecstasy, almost refused to support her. Unwonted sensations—sensations she had never felt before, agitated her bosom; yet, steeling her soul, and persuading herself that celestial transports would be the reward of firmness, she fearlessly advanced.

The towering pine-trees waved in the squally wind—the shades of twilight gained fast on the dusky forest—the wind died away, and a deep, a gloomy silence reigned.

They now had arrived at the spot which Zastrozzi had asserted would be the scene of an event which might lay the foundation of Matilda's happiness.

She was agitated by such violent emotions that her every limb trembled, and Verezzi tenderly asked the reason of her alarm.

"Oh, nothing, nothing!" returned Matilda; but, stung by more certain anticipation of ecstasy by his tender inquiry, her whole frame trembled with tenfold agitation, and her bosom was filled with more unconquerable transport.

On the right, the thick umbrage of the forest trees rendered undistinguishable any one who might lurk *there*; on the left, a frightful precipice yawned, at whose base a deafening cataract dashed with tumultuous violence around misshapen and enormous masses of rock; and beyond, a gigantic and blackened mountain, reared its craggy summit to the skies.

They advanced towards the precipice. Matilda stood upon the dizzy height—her senses almost failed her, and she caught the branch of an enormous pine which impended over the abyss.

"How frightful a depth!" exclaimed Matilda.

"Frightful indeed," said Verezzi, as thoughtfully he contemplated the terrific depth beneath.

They stood for some time gazing on the scene in silence.

Footsteps were heard—Matilda's bosom thrilled with mixed sensations of delight and apprehension, as, summoning all her fortitude, she turned round.—A man advanced towards them.

"What is your business?" exclaimed Verezzi.

"Revenge!" returned the villain, as, raising a dagger high, he essayed to plunge it in Verezzi's bosom, but Matilda lifted her arm, and the dagger piercing it, touched not Verezzi. Starting forward he fell to the earth, and the ruffian instantly dashed into the thick forest.

Matilda's snowy arm was tinged with purple gore: the wound was painful, but an expression of triumph flashed from her eyes, and excessive pleasure dilated her bosom: the blood streamed fast from her arm, and tinged the rock whereon they stood with a purple stain.

Verezzi started from the ground, and seeing the blood which

streamed down Matilda's garments, in accents of terror demanded where she was wounded.

"Oh! think not upon that," she exclaimed, "but tell me—ah! tell me," said she, in a voice of well-feigned alarm, "are you wounded mortally? Oh! what sensations of terror shook me, when I thought that the dagger's point, after having pierced my arm, had drunk your life-blood."

"Oh!" answered Verezzi, "I am not wounded; but let us haste to the castella."

He then tore part of his vest, and with it bound Matilda's arm. Slowly they proceeded towards the castella.

"What villain, Verezzi," said Matilda, "envious of my happiness, attempted his life, for whom I would ten thousand times sacrifice my own? Oh! Verezzi, how I thank God, who averted the fatal dagger from thy heart!"

Verezzi answered not; but his heart, his feelings, were irresistibly touched by Matilda's behaviour. Such noble contempt of danger, so ardent a passion, as to risk her life to preserve his, filled his breast with a tenderness towards her; and he felt that he could now deny her nothing, not even the sacrifice of the poor remains of his happiness, should she demand it.

Matilda's breast meanwhile swelled with sensations of unutterable delight: her soul, borne on the pinions of anticipated happiness, flashed in triumphant glances from her fiery eyes. She could scarcely forbear clasping Verezzi in her arms, and claiming him as her own; but prudence, and a fear of in what manner a premature declaration of love might be received, prevented her.

They arrived at the castella, and a surgeon from the neighbouring convent was sent for by Verezzi.

The surgeon soon arrived, examined Matilda's arm, and declared that no unpleasant consequences could ensue.—Retired to her own apartment, those transports, which before had been allayed by Verezzi's presence, now unrestrained by reason, involved Matilda's senses in an ecstasy of pleasure.

She threw herself on the bed, and, in all the exaggerated colours of imagination, portrayed the transports which Zastrozzi's artifice had opened to her view.

Visions of unreal bliss floated during the whole night in her disordered fancy; her senses were whirled around in alternate ecstasies of happiness and despair, as almost palpable dreams pressed upon her disturbed brain.

At one time she imagined that Verezzi, consenting to their union, presented her his hand: that at her touch the flesh crumbled from it, and, a shrieking spectre, he fled from her view; again, silvery clouds floated across her sight, and unconnected, disturbed visions occupied her imagination till the morning.

Verezzi's manner, as he met Matilda the following morning, was unusually soft and tender; and in a voice of solicitude, he inquired concerning her health.

The roseate flush of animation which tinged her cheek, the triumphant glance of animation which danced in her scintillating eye, seemed to render the inquiry unnecessary.

A dewy moisture filled her eyes, as she gazed with an expression of tumultuous, yet repressed rapture, upon the hapless Verezzi.

Still did she purpose, in order to make her triumph more certain, to protract the hour of victory; and, leaving her victim, wandered into the forest to seek Zastrozzi. When she arrived at the cottage, she learnt that he had walked forth.—She soon met him.

"Oh! Zastrozzi—my best Zastrozzi!" exclaimed Matilda, "what a source of delight have you opened to me! Verezzi is mine—oh! transporting thought! will be mine for ever. That distant manner which he usually affected towards me, is changed to a sweet, an ecstatic expression of tenderness. Oh! Zastrozzi, receive my best, my most fervent thanks."

"Julia need not die then," muttered Zastrozzi; "when once you possess Verezzi, her destruction is of little consequence."

The most horrible scheme of revenge at this instant glanced across Zastrozzi's mind.

"Oh! Julia must die," said Matilda, "or I shall never be safe; such an influence does her image possess over Verezzi's mind, that I am convinced, were he to know that she lived, an estrangement from me would be the consequence. Oh! quickly let me hear that she is dead. I can never enjoy uninterrupted happiness until her dissolution."

"What you have just pronounced is Julia's death-warrant," said Zastrozzi, as he disappeared among the thick trees.

Matilda returned to the castella.

Verezzi, at her return, expressed a tender apprehension, lest, thus wounded, she should have hurt herself by walking; but Matilda quieted his fears, and engaged him in interesting conversation, which seemed not to have for its object the seduction of his affection; though the ideas conveyed by her expressions were so artfully connected with it, and addressed themselves so forcibly to Verezzi's feelings, that he was convinced he ought to love Matilda, though he felt *that* within himself which, in spite of reason—in spite of reflection—told him that it was impossible.

CHAPTER XIII

> The enticing smile, the modest-seeming eye,
> Beneath whose beauteous beams, belying heaven,
> Lurk searchless cunning, cruelty, and death.
>
> THOMSON.

STILL did Matilda's blandishments—her unremitting attention—inspire Verezzi with a softened tenderness towards her. He regarded her as one who, at the risk of her own life, had saved his; who loved him with an ardent affection, and whose affection was likely to be lasting: and though he could not regard her with that enthusiastic tenderness with which he even yet adored the memory of his Julia, yet he might esteem her—faithfully esteem her—and felt not that horror at uniting himself with her as formerly. But a conversation which he had with Julia recurred to his mind: he remembered well, that when they had talked of their speedy marriage, she had expressed an idea, that a union in this life might endure to all eternity; and that the chosen of his heart on earth, might, by congeniality of sentiment, be united in heaven.

The idea was hallowed by the remembrance of his Julia; but chasing it, as an unreal vision, from his mind, again his high sentiments of gratitude prevailed.

Lost in these ideas, involved in a train of thought, and unconscious where his footsteps led him, he quitted the castella. His reverie was interrupted by low murmurs, which seemed to float on the silence of the forest: it was scarcely audible, yet Verezzi felt an undefinable wish to know what it was. He advanced towards it—it was Matilda's voice.

Verezzi approached nearer, and from within heard her voice in complaints. He eagerly listened. Her sobs rendered the words which in passionate exclamations burst from Matilda's lips, almost inaudible. He still listened—a pause in the tempest of grief which shook Matilda's soul seemed to have taken place.

"Oh! Verezzi—cruel, unfeeling Verezzi!" exclaimed Matilda, as a fierce paroxysm of passion seized her brain—"will you thus suffer one who adores you, to linger in hopeless love, and witness the excruciating agony of one who idolises you, as I do, to madness?"

As she spoke thus, a long-drawn sigh closed the sentence.

Verezzi's mind was agitated by various emotions as he stood; but rushing in at last, raised Matilda in his arms, and tenderly attempted to comfort her.

She started as he entered—she heeded not his words; but, seemingly overcome by shame, cast herself at his feet, and hid her face in his robe.

He tenderly raised her, and his expressions convinced her that the reward of all her anxiety was now about to be reaped.

The most triumphant anticipation of transports to come filled her bosom; yet, knowing it to be necessary to dissemble—knowing that a shameless claim on his affections would but disgust Verezzi, she said:

"Oh! Verezzi, forgive me: supposing myself to be alone—supposing no one overheard the avowal of the secret of my soul, with which, believe me, I never more intended to have importuned you, what shameless sentiments—shameless even in solitude—have I not given vent to. I can no longer conceal, that the passion with which I adore you is unconquerable, irresistible: but, I conjure you, think not upon what you have this moment heard to my disadvantage; nor despise a weak unhappy creature, who feels it impossible to overcome the fatal passion which consumes her.

"Never more will I give vent, even in solitude, to my love—never more shall the importunities of the hapless Matilda reach your ears. To conquer a passion fervent, tender as mine is impossible."

As she thus spoke, Matilda, seemingly overcome by shame, sank upon the turf.

A sentiment stronger than gratitude, more ardent than esteem, and more tender than admiration, softened Verezzi's heart as he raised Matilda. Her symmetrical form shone with tenfold loveliness to his heated fancy; inspired with sudden fondness, he cast himself at her feet.

A Lethean torpor crept upon his senses; and, as he lay prostrate before Matilda, a total forgetfulness of every former event of his life swam in his dizzy brain. In passionate exclamations he avowed unbounded love.

"Oh Matilda! dearest, angelic Matilda!" exclaimed Verezzi, "I am even now unconscious what blinded me—what kept me from acknowledging my adoration of thee!—adoration never to be changed by circumstances—never effaced by time."

The fire of voluptuous, of maddening love scorched his veins, as he caught the transported Matilda in his arms, and, in accents almost inarticulate with passion, swore eternal fidelity.

"And accept my oath of everlasting allegiance to thee, adored Verezzi," exclaimed Matilda; "accept my vows of eternal, indissoluble love."

Verezzi's whole frame was agitated by unwonted and ardent emotions. He called Matilda his wife—in the delirium of sudden fondness, he clasped her to his bosom—"and though love like ours," exclaimed the infatuated Verezzi, "wants not the vain ties of human laws, yet, that our love may want not any sanction which could possibly be given to it, let immediate orders be given for the celebration of our union."

Matilda exultingly consented; never had she experienced sensations of delight like these: the feelings of her soul flushed in exulting glances from her fiery eyes. Fierce, transporting triumph filled her soul as she gazed on her victim, whose mildly-beaming eyes were now characterised by a voluptuous expression. Her heart beat high with transport: and as they entered the castella, the swelling emotions of her bosom were too tumultuous for utterance.

Wild with passion, she clasped Verezzi to her beating breast; and, overcome by an ecstasy of delirious passion, her senses were whirled round in confused and inexpressible delight. A new and fierce passion raged likewise in Verezzi's breast: he returned her embrace with ardour, and clasped her in fierce transports.

But the adoration with which he now regarded Matilda, was a different sentiment from that chaste and mild emotion which had characterised his love for Julia: that passion, which he had fondly supposed would end but with his existence, was effaced by the arts of another.

Now was Matilda's purpose attained—the next day would behold her his bride—the next day would behold her fondest purpose accomplished.

With the most eager impatience, the fiercest anticipation of transport, did she wait for its arrival.

Slowly passed the day, and slowly did the clock toll each lingering hour as it rolled away.

The following morning at last arrived: Matilda arose from a sleepless couch—fierce, transporting triumph, flashed from her eyes as she embraced her victim. He returned it—he called her his dear and ever-beloved spouse; and, in all the transports of maddening love, declared his impatience for the arrival of the monk who was to unite them. Every blandishment—every thing which might dispel reflection, was this day put in practice by Matilda.

The monk at last arrived: the fatal ceremony—fatal to the peace of Verezzi—was performed.

A magnificent feast had been previously arranged; every luxurious viand, every expensive wine, which might contribute to heighten Matilda's triumph, was present in profusion.

Matilda's joy, her soul-felt triumph, was too great for utterance—too great for concealment. The exultation of her inmost soul flashed in expressive glances from her scintillating eyes, expressive of joy intense—unutterable.

Animated with excessive delight, she started from the table, and seizing Verezzi's hand, in a transport of inconceivable bliss, dragged him in wild sport and varied movements to the sound of swelling and soul-touching melody.

"Come, my Matilda," at last exclaimed Verezzi, "come, I am weary of transport—sick with excess of unutterable pleasure: let us retire, and retrace in dreams the pleasures of the day."

Little did Verezzi think that this day was the basis of his future misery; little did he think that, amid the roses of successful and licensed voluptuousness, regret, horror, and despair would arise, to blast the prospects which, Julia being forgot, appeared so fair, so ecstatic.

The morning came. Inconceivable emotions—inconceivable to

those who have never felt them—dilated Matilda's soul with an ecstasy of inexpressible bliss: every barrier to her passion was thrown down—every opposition conquered; still was her bosom the scene of fierce and contending passions.

Though in possession of every thing which her fancy had portrayed with such excessive delight, she was far from feeling that innocent and calm pleasure which soothes the soul, and, calming each violent emotion, fills it with a serene happiness. No—*her* brain was whirled around in transports; fierce, confused transports of visionary and unreal bliss: though her every pulse, her every nerve, panted with the delight of gratified and expectant desire; still was she not happy: she enjoyed not that tranquillity which is necessary to the existence of happiness.

In this temper of mind, for a short period she left Verezzi, as she had appointed a meeting with her coadjutor in wickedness.

She soon met him.

"I need not ask," exclaimed Zastrozzi, "for well do I see, in those triumphant glances, that Verezzi is thine; that the plan which we concerted when last we met, has put you in possession of that which your soul panted for."

"Oh! Zastrozzi!" said Matilda,—"kind, excellent Zastrozzi; what words can express the gratitude which I feel towards you—what words can express the bliss, exquisite, celestial, which I owe to your advice; yet still, amid the roses of successful love—amid the ecstasies of transporting voluptuousness—fear, blighting chilly fear, damps my hopes of happiness. Julia, the hated, accursed Julia's image, is the phantom which scares my otherwise certain confidence of eternal delight: could she but be hurled to destruction—could some other artifice of my friend sweep her from the number of the living——"

"'Tis enough, Matilda," interrupted Zastrozzi; "'tis enough; in six days hence meet me here; meanwhile, let not any corroding anticipations destroy your present happiness: fear not; but, on the arrival of your faithful Zastrozzi, expect the earnest of the happiness which you wish to enjoy for ever."

Thus saying, Zastrozzi departed, and Matilda retraced her steps to her castella.

Amid the delight, the ecstasy, for which her soul had so long panted—amid the embraces of him whom she had fondly supposed alone to constitute all terrestrial happiness, racking, corroding thoughts possessed Matilda's bosom.

Deeply musing on schemes of future delight—delight established by the gratification of most diabolical revenge, her eyes fixed upon the ground, heedless what path she pursued, Matilda advanced along the forest.

A voice aroused her from her reverie—it was Verezzi's—the well-known, the tenderly-adored tone, struck upon her senses forcibly: she started, and hastening towards him, soon allayed those fears which her absence had excited in the fond heart of her spouse, and on which account he had anxiously quitted the castella to search for her.

Joy, rapturous, ecstatic happiness, untainted by fear, unpolluted by reflection, reigned for six days in Matilda's bosom.

Five days passed away, the sixth arrived, and, when the evening came, Matilda, with eager and impatient steps, sought the forest.

The evening was gloomy, dense vapours overspread the air; the wind, low and hollow, sighed mournfully in the gigantic pine-trees, and whispered in low hissings among the withered shrubs which grew on the rocky prominences.

Matilda waited impatiently for the arrival of Zastrozzi. At last his towering form emerged from an interstice in the rocks.

He advanced towards her.

"Success! Victory! my Matilda," exclaimed Zastrozzi, in an accent of exultation—"Julia is——"

"You need add no more," interrupted Matilda: "kind, excellent Zastrozzi, I thank thee; but yet do say how you destroyed her—tell me by what racking, horrible torments you launched her soul into eternity. Did she perish by the dagger's point? or did the torments of poison send her, writhing in agony, to the tomb?"

"Yes," replied Zastrozzi; "she fell at my feet, overpowered by resistless convulsions. Who more ready than myself to restore the Marchesa's fleeted senses—who more ready than myself to account for her fainting, by observing, that the heat of the assembly had momentarily overpowered her? But Julia's senses were fled for ever; and it was not until the swiftest gondola in Venice had borne me far towards your castella, that il consiglio di dieci* searched for, without discovering the offender.

"Here I must remain; for, were I discovered, the fatal consequences to us both are obvious. Farewell for the present," added he; "meanwhile, happiness attend you; but go not to Venice."

"Where have you been so late, my love?" tenderly inquired Verezzi as she returned. "I fear lest the night air, particularly that of so damp an evening as this, might affect your health."

"No, no, my dearest Verezzi, it has not," hesitatingly answered Matilda.

"You seem pensive, you seem melancholy, my Matilda," said Verezzi; "lay open your heart to me. I am afraid something, of which I am ignorant, presses upon your bosom.

"Is it the solitude of this remote castella which represses the natural gaiety of your soul? Shall we go to Venice?"

"Oh! no, no!" hastily and eagerly interrupted Matilda: "not to Venice—we must not go to Venice."

Verezzi was slightly surprised, but imputing her manner to indisposition, it passed off.

Unmarked by events of importance, a month passed away. Matilda's passion, unallayed by satiety, unconquered by time, still raged with its former fierceness—still was every earthly delight centred in Verezzi; and in the air-drawn visions of her imagination, she portrayed to herself that this happiness would last for ever.

It was one evening that Verezzi and Matilda sat, happy in the society of each other, that a servant entering, presented the latter with a sealed paper.

The contents were: "Matilda Contessa di Laurentini is summoned to appear before the Holy Inquisition—to appear before its tribunal, immediately on the receipt of this summons."

Matilda's cheek, as she read it, was blanched with terror. The summons—the fatal, irresistible summons, struck her with chilly awe. She attempted to thrust it into her bosom; but, unable to conceal her terror, she assayed to rush from the apartment—but it was in vain: her trembling limbs refused to support her, and she sank fainting on the floor.

Verezzi raised her—he restored her fleeting senses; he cast himself at her feet, and in the tenderest, most pathetic accents, demanded the reason of her alarm. "And if," said he, "it is any thing of which I have unconsciously been guilty—if it is any thing in my conduct which has offended you, oh! how soon, how truly would I repent. Dearest Matilda, I adore you to madness: tell me then quickly—confide in one who loves you as I do."

"Rise, Verezzi," exclaimed Matilda, in a tone expressive of serene horror: "and since the truth can no longer be concealed, peruse that letter."

She presented him the fatal summons. He eagerly snatched it; breathless with impatience, he opened it. But what words can express the consternation of the affrighted Verezzi, as the summons, mysterious and inexplicable to him, pressed upon his straining eyeball? For an instant he stood fixed in mute and agonizing thought. At last, in the forced serenity of despair, he demanded what was to be done.

Matilda answered not: for her soul, borne on the pinions of anticipation, at that instant portrayed to itself ignominious and agonizing dissolution.

"What is to be done?" again, in a deeper tone of despair, demanded Verezzi.

"We must instantly to Venice," returned Matilda, collecting her scattered faculties; "we must to Venice; there, I believe, we may be safe. But in some remote corner of the city we must for the present fix our habitations; we must condescend to curtail our establishment; and above all, we must avoid particularity. But will my Verezzi descend from the rank of life in which his birth has placed him, and with the outcast Matilda's fortunes quit grandeur?"

"Matilda! dearest Matilda!" exclaimed Verezzi, "talk not thus; you know I am ever yours; you know I love you, and with you, could conceive a cottage elysium."

Matilda's eyes flashed with momentary triumph as Verezzi spoke thus, amid the alarming danger which impended her: under the displeasure of the Inquisition, whose motives for prosecution are inscrutable, whose decrees are without appeal, her soul, in the possession of all it held dear on earth, secure of Verezzi's affection, thrilled with pleasurable emotions, yet not unmixed with alarm.

She now prepared to depart. Taking, therefore, out of all her domestics, but the faithful Ferdinand, Matilda, accompanied by Verezzi, although the evening was far advanced, threw herself into a chariot, and leaving every one at the castella unacquainted with her intentions, took the road through the forest which led to Venice.

The convent bell, almost inaudible from distance, tolled ten as the carriage slowly ascended a steep which rose before it.

"But how do you suppose, my Matilda," said Verezzi, "that it will be possible for us to evade the scrutiny of the Inquisition?"

"Oh!" returned Matilda, "we must not appear in our true characters—we must disguise them."

"But," inquired Verezzi, "what crime do you suppose the Inquisition to allege against you?"

"Heresy, I suppose," said Matilda. "You know an enemy has nothing to do but lay an accusation of heresy against any unfortunate and innocent individual, and the victim expires in horrible tortures, or lingers the wretched remnant of his life in dark and solitary cells."

A convulsive sigh heaved Verezzi's bosom.

"And is that then to be my Matilda's destiny?" he exclaimed in horror. "No—Heaven will never permit such excellence to suffer."

Meanwhile they had arrived at the Brenta.* The Brenta's stream glided silently beneath the midnight breeze towards the Adriatic.

Towering poplars, which loftily raised their spiral forms on its bank, cast a gloomier shade upon the placid wave.

Matilda and Verezzi entered a gondola, and the grey tints of approaching morn had streaked the eastern ether, before they entered the Grand Canal at Venice; and passing the Rialto,* proceeded onwards to a small, though not inelegant mansion, in the eastern suburbs.

Everything here, though not grand, was commodious; and as

they entered it, Verezzi expressed his approbation of living here retired.

Seemingly secure from the scrutiny of the Inquisition, Matilda and Verezzi passed some days of uninterrupted happiness.

At last, one evening, Verezzi, tired even with monotony of ecstasy, proposed to Matilda to take the gondola, and go to a festival which was to be celebrated at St. Mark's Place.

CHAPTER XIV

THE evening was serene. Fleecy clouds floated on the horizon—the moon's full orb, in cloudless majesty, hung high in air, and was reflected in silver brilliancy by every wave of the Adriatic, as, gently agitated by the evening breeze, they dashed against innumerable gondolas which crowded the Laguna.

Exquisite harmony, borne on the pinions of the tranquil air, floated in varying murmurs; it sometimes died away, and then again swelling louder, in melodious undulations, softened to pleasure every listening ear.

Every eye which gazed on the fairy scene beamed with pleasure; unrepressed gaiety filled every heart but Julia's, as, with a vacant stare, unmoved by feelings of pleasure, unagitated by the gaiety which filled every other soul, she contemplated the varied scene. A magnificent gondola carried the Marchesa di Strobazzo; and the innumerable flambeaux which blazed around her rivalled the meridian sun.

It was the pensive, melancholy Julia,* who, immersed in thought, sat unconscious of every external object, whom the fierce glance of Matilda measured with a haughty expression of surprise and revenge. The dark fire which flashed from her eye, more than told the feelings of her soul, as she fixed it on her rival; and had it possessed the power of the basilisk's, Julia would have expired on the spot.

It was the ethereal form of the now forgotten Julia which first caught Verezzi's eye. For an instant he gazed with surprise upon her symmetrical figure, and was about to point her out to Matilda, when, in the downcast countenance of the enchanting female, he recognised his long-lost Julia.

To paint the feelings of Verezzi—as Julia raised her head from the attitude in which it was fixed, and disclosed to his view that countenance which he had formerly gazed on in ecstasy, the index of that soul to which he had sworn everlasting fidelity—is impossible.

The Lethean torpor, as it were, which before had benumbed him; the charm, which had united him to Matilda, was dissolved.

All the air-built visions of delight, which had but a moment before floated in gay variety in his enraptured imagination, faded away, and, in place of these, regret, horror, and despairing repentance, reared their heads amid the roses of momentary voluptuousness.

He still gazed entranced, but Julia's gondola, indistinct from distance, mocked his straining eyeball.

For a time neither spoke: the gondola rapidly passed onwards, but, immersed in thought, Matilda and Verezzi heeded not its rapidity.

They had arrived at St. Mark's Place, and the gondolier's voice, as he announced it, was the first interruption of the silence.

They started.—Verezzi now, for the first time, aroused from his reverie of horror, saw that the scene before him was real; and that the oaths of fidelity which he had so often and so fervently sworn to Julia were broken.

The extreme of horror seized his brain—a frigorific* torpidity of despair chilled every sense, and his eyes, fixedly, gazed on vacancy.

"Oh! return—instantly return!" impatiently replied Matilda to the question of the gondolier.

The gondolier, surprised, obeyed her, and they returned.

The spacious canal was crowded with gondolas; merriment and splendour reigned around, enchanting harmony stole over the scene; but, listless of the music, heeding not the splendour, Matilda sat lost in a maze of thought.

Fiercest vengeance revelled through her bosom, and, in her own mind, she resolved a horrible purpose.

Meanwhile, the hour was late, the moon had gained the zenith, and poured her beams vertically on the unruffled Adriatic, when the gondola stopped before Matilda's mansion.

A sumptuous supper had been prepared for their return. Silently Matilda entered—silently Verezzi followed.

Without speaking, Matilda seated herself at the supper-table; Verezzi, with an air of listlessness, threw himself into a chair beside her.

For a time neither spoke.

"You are not well to-night," at last stammered out Verezzi: "what has disturbed you?"

"Disturbed me!" repeated Matilda: "why do you suppose that anything had disturbed me?"

A more violent paroxysm of horror seemed now to seize Verezzi's brain. He pressed his hand to his burning forehead—the agony of his mind was too great to be concealed—Julia's form, as he had last seen her, floated in his fancy, and, overpowered by the resistlessly horrible ideas which pressed upon them, his senses failed him: he faintly uttered Julia's name—he sank forward, and his throbbing temples reclined on the table.

"Arise! awake! prostrate, perjured Verezzi, awake!" exclaimed the infuriate Matilda, in a tone of gloomy horror.

Verezzi started up, and gazed with surprise upon the countenance of Matilda, which, convulsed by passion, flashed desperation and revenge.

"'Tis plain," said Matilda, gloomily, "'tis plain, he loves me not."

A confusion of contending emotions battled in Verezzi's bosom: his marriage vow—his faith plighted to Matilda—convulsed his soul with indescribable agony.

Still did she possess a great empire over his soul—still was her frown terrible—and still did the hapless Verezzi tremble at the tones of her voice, as, in a phrensy of desperate passion, she bade him quit her for ever: "And," added she, "go, disclose the retreat of the outcast Matilda to her enemies; deliver me to the Inquisition, that a union with her you detest may fetter you no longer."

Exhausted by breathless agitation, Matilda ceased: the passions of her soul flashed from her eyes; ten thousand conflicting emotions battled in Verezzi's bosom; he knew scarce what to do; but, yielding to the impulse of the moment, he cast himself at Matilda's feet, and groaned deeply.

At last the words, "I am ever yours, I ever shall be yours," escaped his lips.

For a time Matilda stood immovable. At last she looked on Verezzi; she gazed downwards upon his majestic and youthful figure; she looked upon his soul-illumined countenance, and tenfold love assailed her softened soul. She raised him—in an oblivious delirium of sudden fondness she clasped him to her bosom, and, in wild and hurried expressions, asserted her right to his love.

Her breast palpitated with fiercest emotions; she pressed her burning lips to his; most fervent, most voluptuous sensations of ecstasy revelled through her bosom.

Verezzi caught the infection; in an instant of oblivion, every oath of fidelity which he had sworn to another, like a baseless cloud, dissolved away; a Lethean torpor crept over his senses; he forgot Julia, or remembered her only as an uncertain vision, which floated before his fancy more as an ideal being of another world, whom he might hereafter adore there, than as an enchanting and congenial female, to whom his oaths of eternal fidelity had been given.

Overcome by unutterable transports of returning bliss, she started from his embrace—she seized his hand—her face was overspread with a heightened colour as she pressed it to her lips.

"And are you then mine—mine for ever?" rapturously exclaimed Matilda.

"Oh! I am thine—thine to all eternity," returned the infatuated Verezzi: "no earthly power shall sever us; joined by congeniality of soul, united by a bond to which God himself bore witness."

He again clasped her to his bosom—again, as an earnest of fidelity, imprinted a fervent kiss on her glowing cheek; and, overcome by the violent and resistless emotions of the moment, swore, that nor heaven nor hell should cancel the union which he here solemnly and unequivocally renewed.

Verezzi filled an overflowing goblet.

"Do you love me?" inquired Matilda.

"May the lightning of heaven consume me, if I adore thee not to distraction! may I be plunged in endless torments, if my love for thee, celestial Matilda, endures not for ever!"

Matilda's eyes flashed fiercest triumph; the exultingly delightful feelings of her soul were too much for utterance—she spoke not, but gazed fixedly on Verezzi's countenance.

CHAPTER XV

> "That no compunctious visitings of nature
> Shake my fell purpose, nor keep peace between
> The effect and it. Come to my woman's breasts,
> And take my milk for gall, ye murdering ministers,
> Wherever, in your sightless substances,
> Ye wait on nature's mischief."
>
> MACBETH.

VEREZZI raised the goblet which he had just filled, and exclaimed, in an impassioned tone—

"My adored Matilda! this is to thy happiness—this is to thy every wish; and if I cherish a single thought which centres not in thee, may the most horrible tortures which ever poisoned the peace of man, drive me instantly to distraction. God of heaven! witness thou my oath, and write it in letters never to be erased! Ministering spirits, who watch over the happiness of mortals, attend! for here I swear eternal fidelity, indissoluble, unalterable affection to Matilda!"

He said—he raised his eyes towards heaven—he gazed upon Matilda. Their eyes met—hers gleamed with a triumphant expression of unbounded love.

Verezzi raised the goblet to his lips—when, lo! on a sudden, he dashed it to the ground—his whole frame was shook by horrible convulsions—his glaring eyes, starting from their sockets, rolled wildly around: seized with sudden madness, he drew a dagger from his girdle, and with fellest intent raised it high——

What phantom blasted Verezzi's eyeball! what made the impassioned lover dash a goblet to the ground, which he was about to drain as a pledge of eternal love to the choice of his soul! and why did he, infuriate, who had, but an instant before, imagined Matilda's arms an earthly paradise, attempt to rush unprepared into the presence of his Creator!—It was the mildly-beaming eyes of the lovely but forgotten Julia, which spoke reproaches to the soul of Verezzi—it was her celestial countenance, shaded by dishevelled ringlets, which spoke daggers to the false one; for, when he had raised the goblet to his lips—when, sublimed by the maddening fire of voluptuousness to the height of enthusiastic passion, he swore indissoluble fidelity to another—Julia stood before him!

Madness—fiercest madness—revelled through his brain. He raised the poniard high, but Julia rushed forwards, and, in accents of distinction, in a voice of alarmed tenderness, besought him to spare himself—to spare her—for all might yet be well.

"Oh! never, never!" exclaimed Verezzi, frantically; "no peace but in the grave for me.——I am—I am—married to Matilda."

Saying this, he fell backwards upon a sofa, in strong convulsions, yet his hand still grasped the fatal poniard.

Matilda, meanwhile, fixedly contemplated the scene. Fiercest passions raged through her breast—vengeance, disappointed love—disappointed in the instant too when she had supposed happiness to be hers for ever, rendered her bosom the scene of wildest anarchy.

Yet she spoke not—she moved not—but, collected in herself, stood waiting the issue of that event, which had so unexpectedly dissolved her visions of air-built ecstasy.

Serened to firmness from despair, Julia administered everything which could restore Verezzi with the most unremitting attention. At last he recovered.—He slowly raised himself, and starting from the sofa where he lay, his eyes rolling wildly, and his whole frame convulsed by fiercest agitation, he raised the dagger which he still retained, and, with a bitter smile of exultation, plunged it into his bosom! His soul fled without a groan, and his body fell to the floor, bathed in purple blood.

Maddened by this death-blow to all anticipation of happiness, Matilda's faculties, as she stood, whirled in wild confusion: she scarce knew where she was.

At last, a portentous, a frightful calm, spread itself over her soul. Revenge, direst revenge, swallowed up every other feeling. Her eyes scintillated with a fiend-like expression. She advanced to the lifeless corse of Verezzi—she plucked the dagger from his bosom—it was stained with his life's blood, which trickled fast from the point to the floor. She raised it on high, and impiously called upon the God of nature to doom her to endless torments, should Julia survive her vengeance.

She advanced towards her victim, who lay bereft of sense on the floor: she shook her rudely, and grasping a handful of her dishevelled hair, raised her from the earth.

"Knowest thou me?" exclaimed Matilda, in frantic passion—"knowest thou the injured Laurentini? Behold this dagger, reeking with my husband's blood—behold that pale corse, in whose now cold breast thy accursed image revelling, impelled to commit the deed which deprives me of happiness for ever."

Julia's senses, roused by Matilda's violence, returned. She cast her eyes upwards, with a timid expression of apprehension, and beheld the infuriate Matilda convulsed by fiercest passion, and a blood-stained dagger raised aloft, threatening instant death.

"Die! detested wretch," exclaimed Matilda, in a paroxysm of rage, as she violently attempted to bathe the stiletto in the life-blood of her rival; but Julia starting aside, the weapon slightly wounded her neck, and the ensanguined stream stained her alabaster bosom.

She fell on the floor, but suddenly starting up, attempted to escape her bloodthirsty persecutor.

Nerved anew by this futile attempt to escape her vengeance, the ferocious Matilda seized Julia's floating hair, and holding her back with fiend-like strength, stabbed her in a thousand places; and, with exulting pleasure, again and again buried the dagger to the hilt in her body, even after all remains of life were annihilated.

At last the passions of Matilda, exhausted by their own violence, sank into a deadly calm; she threw the dagger violently from her, and contemplated the terrific scene before her with a sullen gaze.

Before her, in the arms of death, lay him on whom her hopes of happiness seemed to have formed so firm a basis.

Before her lay her rival, pierced with innumerable wounds, whose head reclined on Verezzi's bosom, and whose angelic features, even in death, a smile of affection pervaded.

There she herself stood, an isolated guilty being. A fiercer paroxysm of passion now seized her: in an agony of horror, too great to be described, she tore her hair in handfuls—she blasphemed the power who had given her being, and imprecated eternal torments upon the mother who had borne her.

"And is it for this," added the ferocious Matilda—"is it for horror, for torments such as these, that He, whom monks call all-merciful, has created me?"

She seized the dagger which lay on the floor.

"Ah, friendly dagger," she exclaimed, in a voice of fiend-like horror, "would that thy blow produced annihilation! with what pleasure then would I clasp thee to my heart!"

She raised it high—she gazed on it—the yet warm blood of the innocent Julia trickled from its point.

The guilty Matilda shrunk at death—she let fall the upraised dagger—her soul had caught a glimpse of the misery which awaits the wicked hereafter, and, spite of her contempt of religion—spite of her, till now, too firm dependence on the doctrines of atheism, she trembled at futurity; and a voice from within, which whispers, "thou shalt never die!" spoke daggers to Matilda's soul.

Whilst thus she stood entranced in a delirium of despair, the night wore away, and the domestic who attended her, surprised at the unusual hour to which they had prolonged the banquet, came to announce the lateness of the hour; but opening the door, and perceiving Matilda's garments stained with blood, she started back with affright, without knowing the full extent of horror which the chamber contained, and alarmed the other domestics with an account that Matilda had been stabbed.

In a crowd they all came to the door, but started back in terror when they saw Verezzi and Julia stretched lifeless on the floor.

Summoning fortitude from despair, Matilda loudly called for them to return: but fear and horror overbalanced her commands, and, wild with affright, they all rushed from the chamber, except Ferdinand, who advanced to Matilda, and demanded an explanation.

Matilda gave it, in few and hurried words.

Ferdinand again quitted the apartment, and told the credulous domestics, that an unknown female had surprised Verezzi and Matilda; that she had stabbed Verezzi, and then committed suicide.

The crowd of servants, as in mute terror they listened to Ferdinand's account, entertained not a doubt of the truth. Again and again they demanded an explanation of the mysterious affair, and employed their wits in conjecturing what might be the cause of it; but the more they conjectured, the more were they puzzled; till at last, a clever fellow named Pietro, who, hating Ferdinand on account of the superior confidence with which his lady treated him, and supposing more to be concealed in this affair than met the ear, gave information to the police, and, before morning, Matilda's dwelling was surrounded by a party of officials belonging to il consiglio di dieci.

Loud shouts rent the air as the officials attempted the entrance. Matilda still was in the apartment where, during the night, so bloody a tragedy had been acted; still in speechless horror was she extended on the sofa, when a loud rap at the door aroused the horror-tranced wretch. She started from the sofa in wildest perturbation, and listened attentively. Again was the noise repeated, and the officials rushed in.

They searched every apartment; at last they entered that in which Matilda, motionless with despair, remained.

Even the stern officials, hardy, unfeeling as they were, started back with momentary horror as they beheld the fair countenance of the murdered Julia; fair even in death, and her body disfigured with numberless ghastly wounds.

"This cannot be suicide," muttered one, who by his superior manner, seemed to be their chief, as he raised the fragile form of Julia from the ground, and the blood, scarcely yet cold,* trickled from her vestments.

"Put your orders in execution," added he.

Two officials advanced towards Matilda, who, standing apart with seeming tranquillity, awaited their approach.

"What wish you with me?" exclaimed Matilda haughtily.

The officials answered not; but their chief, drawing a paper from his vest, which contained an order for the arrest of Matilda La Contessa di Laurentini, presented it to her.

She turned pale; but, without resistance, obeyed the mandate, and followed the officials in silence to the canal, where a gondola waited, and in a short time she was in the gloomy prisons of il consiglio di dieci.

A little straw was the bed of the haughty Laurentini; a pitcher of water and bread was her sustenance; gloom, horror, and despair pervaded her soul; all the pleasures which she had but yesterday tasted; all the ecstatic blisses which her enthusiastic soul had painted for futurity, like the unreal vision of a dream, faded away; and, confined in a damp and narrow cell, Matilda saw that all her hopes of future delight would end in speedy and ignominious dissolution.

Slow passed the time—slow did the clock at St. Mark's toll the revolving hours as languidly they passed away.

Night came on, and the hour of midnight struck upon Matilda's soul as her death knell.

A noise was heard in the passage which led to the prison.

Matilda raised her head from the wall against which it was reclined, and eagerly listened, as if in expectation of an event which would seal her future fate. She still gazed, when the chains of the entrance were unlocked. The door, as it opened, grated harshly on its hinges, and two officials entered.

"Follow me," was the laconic injunction which greeted her terror-struck ear.

Trembling, Matilda arose: her limbs, stiffened by confinement, almost refused to support her; but collecting fortitude from desperation, she followed the relentless officials in silence.

One of them bore a lamp, whose rays, darting in uncertain columns, showed, by strong contrasts of light and shade, the extreme massiness of the passages.

The Gothic frieze above was worked with art; and the corbels, in various and grotesque forms, jutted from the tops of clustered pilasters.

They stopped at a door. Voices were heard from within: their hollow tones filled Matilda's soul with unconquerable tremours. But she summoned all her resolution—she resolved to be collected during the trial; and even, if sentenced to death, to meet her fate with fortitude, that the populace, as they gazed, might not exclaim—"The poor Laurentini dared not to die."

These thoughts were passing in her mind during the delay which was occasioned by the officials conversing with another whom they met there.

At last they ceased—an uninterrupted silence reigned: the immense folding doors were thrown open, and disclosed to Matilda's view a vast and lofty apartment. In the centre was a table, which a lamp, suspended from the centre, overhung, and where two stern-looking men, habited in black vestments, were seated.

Scattered papers covered the table, with which the two men in black seemed busily employed.

Two officials conducted Matilda to the table where they sat, and, retiring, left her there.

CHAPTER XVI

> "Fear, for their scourge, mean villains have;
> Thou art the torturer of the brave."
>
> MARMION.

ONE of the inquisitors raised his eyes; he put back the papers which he was examining, and in a solemn tone asked her name.

"My name is Matilda; my title La Contessa di Laurentini," haughtily she answered; "nor do I know the motive for that inquiry, except it were to exult over my miseries, which you are, I suppose, no stranger to."

"Waste not your time," exclaimed the inquisitor, sternly, "in making idle conjectures upon our conduct; but do you know for what you are summoned here?"

"No," replied Matilda.

"Swear that you know not for what crime you are here imprisoned," said the inquisitor.

Matilda took the oath required. As she spoke, a dewy sweat burst from her brow, and her limbs were convulsed by the extreme of horror, yet the expression of her countenance was changed not.

"What crime have you committed which might subject you to the notice of this tribunal?" demanded he, in a determined tone of voice.

Matilda gave no answer, save a smile of exulting scorn. She fixed her regards upon the inquisitor: her dark eyes flashed fiercely but she spoke not.

"Answer me," exclaimed he, "what to confess might save both of us needless trouble."

Matilda answered not, but gazed in silence upon the inquisitor's countenance.

He stamped thrice—four officials rushed in, and stood at some distance from Matilda.

"I am unwilling," said the inquisitor, "to treat a female of high birth with indignity; but, if you confess not instantly, my duty will not permit me to withhold the question."

A deeper expression of contempt shaded Matilda's beautiful countenance: she frowned, but answered not.

"You will persist in this foolish obstinacy?" exclaimed the inquisitor. "Officials, do your duty."

Instantly the four, who till now had stood in the background, rushed forwards: they seized Matilda, and bore her into the obscurity of the apartment.

Her dishevelled ringlets floated in negligent luxuriance over her alabaster bosom: her eyes, the contemptuous glance of which had now given way to a confused expression of alarm, were almost closed; and her symmetrical form, as borne away by the four officials, looked interestingly lovely.

The other inquisitor, who, till now, busied by the papers which lay before him, had heeded not Matilda's examination, raised his eyes, and, beholding the form of a female, with a commanding tone of voice, called to the officials to stop.

Submissively they obeyed his order.—Matilda, released from the fell hands of these relentless ministers of justice, advanced to the table.

Her extreme beauty softened the inquisitor who had spoken last. He little thought that, under a form so celestial, so interesting, lurked a heart depraved, vicious as a demon's.

He therefore mildly addressed her; and telling her that, on some future day, her examination would be renewed, committed her to the care of the officials, with orders to conduct her to an apartment better suited to her rank.

The chamber to which she followed the officials was spacious and well furnished, but large iron bars secured the windows, which were high, and impossible to be forced.

Left again to solitude, again to her own gloomy thoughts—her retrospection but horror and despair—her hopes of futurity none—her fears many and horrible—Matilda's situation is better conceived than described.

Floating in wild confusion, the ideas which presented themselves to her imagination were too horrible for endurance.

Deprived, as she was, of all earthly happiness, fierce as had been her passion for Verezzi, the disappointment of which sublimed her brain to the most infuriate delirium of resistless horror, the wretched Matilda still shrunk at death—she shrunk at the punishment of those crimes, in whose perpetration no remorse had touched her soul, for which, even now, she repented not, but as they had deprived her of terrestrial enjoyments.

She thought upon the future state—she thought upon the arguments of Zastrozzi against the existence of a Deity: her inmost soul now acknowledged their falsehood, and she shuddered as she reflected that her condition was irretrievable.

Resistless horror revelled through her bosom: in an intensity of racking thought she rapidly paced the apartment; at last overpowered, she sank upon a sofa.

At last the tumultuous passions, exhausted by their own violence, subsided: the storm, which so lately had agitated Matilda's soul, ceased: a serene calm succeeded, and sleep quickly overcame her faculties.

Confused visions flitted in Matilda's imagination whilst under the influence of sleep; at last they assumed a settled shape.

Strangely brilliant and silvery clouds seemed to flit before her sight: celestial music, enchanting as the harmony of the spheres, serened Matilda's soul, and, for an instant, her situation forgotten, she lay entranced.

On a sudden the music ceased; the azure concavity of heaven seemed to open at the zenith, and a being, whose countenance beamed with unutterable beneficence, descended.

It seemed to be clothed in a transparent robe of flowing silver: its eye scintillated with super-human brilliancy, whilst her dream, imitating reality almost to exactness, caused the entranced Matilda to suppose that it addressed her in these words:—

"Poor sinning Matilda! repent, it is not yet too late.—God's mercy is unbounded. Repent! and thou mayest yet be saved."

These words yet tingled in Matilda's ears; yet were her eyes lifted to heaven, as if following the visionary phantom who had addressed her in her dream, when, much confused, she arose from the sofa.

A dream, so like reality made a strong impression upon Matilda's soul.

The ferocious passions, which so lately had battled fiercely in her bosom, were calmed: she lifted her eyes to heaven: they beamed with an expression of sincerest penitence; for sincerest penitence at this moment, agonised whilst it calmed Matilda's soul.

"God of mercy! God of heaven!" exclaimed Matilda; "my sins are many and horrible, but I repent."

Matilda knew not how to pray; but God, who from the height of heaven penetrates the inmost thoughts of terrestrial hearts, heard the outcast sinner, as in tears of true and agonising repentance, she knelt before him.

She despaired no longer—She confided in the beneficence of her Creator; and, in the hour of adversity, when the firmest heart must tremble at his power, no longer a hardened sinner, demanded mercy. And mercy, by the All-benevolent of heaven, is never refused to those who humbly, yet trusting in his goodness, ask it.

Matilda's soul was filled with a celestial tranquillity. She remained upon her knees in mute and fervent thought: she prayed; and, with trembling, asked forgiveness of her Creator.

No longer did that agony of despair torture her bosom. True, she was ill at ease: remorse for her crimes deeply affected her; and though her hopes of salvation were great, her belief in God and a future state firm, the heavy sighs which burst from her bosom, showed that the arrows of repentance had penetrated deeply.

Several days passed away, during which the conflicting passions of Matilda's soul, conquered by penitence, were mellowed into a fixed and quiet depression.

CHAPTER XVII

Si fractus illabatur orbis,
Impavidum ferient ruinæ.

HORACE.

AT last the day arrived, when, exposed to a public trial, Matilda was conducted to the tribunal of il consiglio di dieci.

The inquisitors were not, as before, at a table in the middle of the apartment; but a sort of throne was raised at one end, on which a stern-looking man, whom she had never seen before, sat: a great number of Venetians were assembled, and lined all sides of the apartment.

Many, in black vestments, were arranged behind the superior's throne; among whom Matilda recognised those who had before examined her.

Conducted by two officials, with a faltering step, a pallid cheek, and downcast eye, Matilda advanced to that part of the chamber where sat the superior.

The dishevelled ringlets of her hair floated unconfined over her shoulders: her symmetrical and elegant form was enveloped in a thin white robe.

The expression of her sparkling eyes was downcast and humble; yet, seemingly unmoved by the scene before her, she remained in silence at the tribunal.

The curiosity and pity of every one, as they gazed on the loveliness of the beautiful culprit, was strongly excited.

"Who is she? who is she?" ran in inquiring whispers round the apartment.—No one could tell.

Again deep silence reigned—not a whisper interrupted the appalling calm.

At last the superior, in a sternly solemn voice, said—

"Matilda Contessa di Laurentini, you are here arraigned on the murder of La Marchesa di Strobazzo; canst thou deny it? canst thou prove to the contrary? My ears are open to conviction. Does no one speak for the accused?"

He ceased: uninterrupted silence reigned. Again he was about —again, with a look of detestation and horror, he had fixed his penetrating eye upon the trembling Matilda, and had unclosed his mouth to utter the fatal sentence, when his attention was arrested by a man who rushed from the crowd, and exclaimed, in a hurried tone—

"La Contessa di Laurentini is innocent,"

"Who are you, who dare assert that?" exclaimed the superior, with an air of doubt.

"I am," answered he, "Ferdinand Zeilnitz, a German, the servant of La Contessa di Laurentini, and I dare assert that she is innocent."

"Your proof," exclaimed the superior, with a severe frown.

"It was late," answered Ferdinand, "when I entered the apartment, and then I beheld two bleeding bodies, and La Contessa di Laurentini, who lay bereft of sense on the sofa."

"Stop!" exclaimed the superior.

Ferdinand obeyed.

The superior whispered to one in black vestments, and soon four officials entered, bearing on their shoulders an open coffin.

The superior pointed to the ground: the officials deposited their burden, and produced, to the terror-struck eyes of the gazing multitude, Julia, the lovely Julia, covered with innumerable and ghastly gashes.

All present uttered a cry of terror—all started, shocked and amazed, from the horrible sight; yet some, recovering themselves, gazed at the celestial loveliness of the poor victim to revenge, which, unsubdued by death, still shone from her placid features.

A deep-drawn sigh heaved Matilda's bosom; tears, spite of all her firmness, rushed into her eyes; and she had nearly fainted with dizzy horror; but, overcoming it, and collecting all her fortitude, she advanced towards the corse of her rival, and, in the numerous wounds which covered it, saw the fiat of her future destiny.

She still gazed on it—a deep silence reigned—not one of the spectators, so interested were they, uttered a single word—not a whisper was heard through the spacious apartment.

"Stand off! guilt-stained, relentless woman," at last exclaimed the superior fiercely: "is it not enough that you have persecuted, through life, the wretched female who lies before you—murdered by you? Cease, therefore, to gaze on her with looks as if your vengeance was yet insatiated. But retire, wretch: officials, take her into your custody; meanwhile, bring the other prisoner."

Two officials rushed forward, and led Matilda to some distance from the tribunal: four others entered, leading a man of towering height and majestic figure. The heavy chains with which his legs were bound rattled as he advanced.

Matilda raised her eyes—Zastrozzi stood before her.

She rushed forwards—the officials stood unmoved.

"Oh Zastrozzi!" she exclaimed—"dreadful, wicked has been the tenor of our lives; base, ignominious, will be its termination: unless we repent, fierce, horrible, may be the eternal torments which will rack us, ere four-and-twenty hours are elasped. Repent then, Zastrozzi; repent! and as you have been my companion in apostasy from virtue, follow me likewise in dereliction of stubborn and determined wickedness."

This was pronounced in a low and faltering voice.

"Matilda," replied Zastrozzi, whilst a smile of contemptuous atheism played over his features—"Matilda, fear not: fate wills us to die: and I intend to meet death, to encounter annihilation, with tranquillity. Am I not convinced of the non-existence of a Deity? am I not convinced that death will but render this soul more free, more unfettered? Why need I then shudder at death? why need any one, whose mind has risen above the shackles of prejudice, the errors of a false and injurious superstition."

Here the superior interposed, and declared he could allow private conversation no longer.

Quitting Matilda, therefore, Zastrozzi, unappalled by the awful scene before him, unshaken by the near approach of agonising death, which he now fully believed he was about to suffer, advanced towards the superior's throne.

Every one gazed on the lofty stature of Zastrozzi, and admired his dignified mien and dauntless composure, even more than they had the beauty of Matilda.

Every one gazed in silence, and expected that some extraordinary charge would be brought against him.

The name of Zastrozzi, pronounced by the superior, had already broken the silence, when the culprit, gazing disdainfully on his judge, told him to be silent, for he would spare him much needless trouble.

"I am a murderer," exclaimed Zastrozzi; "I deny it not: I buried my dagger in the heart of him who injured me; but the motives which led me to be an assassin were at once excellent and meritorious: for I swore, at a loved mother's death-bed, to avenge her betrayer's falsehood.

"Think you that whilst I perpetrated the deed I feared the punishment? or whilst I revenged a parent's cause, that the futile torments which I am doomed to suffer here, had any weight in my determination? No—no. If the vile deceiver, who brought my spotless mother to a tomb of misery, fell beneath the dagger of one who swore to revenge her—if I sent him to another world, who destroyed the peace of one I loved more than myself in this, am I to be blamed?"

Zastrozzi ceased, and, with an expression of scornful triumph, folded his arms.

"Go on!" exclaimed the superior.

"Go on! go on!" echoed from every part of the immense apartment.

He looked around him. His manner awed the tumultuous multitude; and, in uninterrupted silence, the spectators gazed upon the unappalled Zastrozzi, who, towering as a demi-god, stood in the midst.

"Am I then called upon," said he, "to disclose things which bring painful remembrances to my mind? Ah, how painful! But, no matter; you shall know the name of him who fell beneath this arm: you shall know him, whose memory, even now, I detest more than I can express. I care not who knows my actions, convinced as I am, and convinced to all eternity as I shall be, of their rectitude.—Know then, that Olivia Zastrozzi was my mother; a woman in whom every virtue, every amiable and excellent quality, I firmly believe to have been centred.

"The father of him, who, by my arts committed suicide but six days ago in La Contessa di Laurentini's mansion, took advantage of a moment of weakness, and disgraced her who bore me. He swore, with the most sacred oaths, to marry her—but he was false.

"My mother soon brought me into the world—the seducer married another; and, when the destitute Olivia begged a pittance to keep her from starving, her proud betrayer spurned her from his door, and tauntingly bade her exercise her profession—'The crime I committed with thee, perjured one!' exclaimed my mother, as she left his door, 'shall be my last!'—and, by heavens! she acted nobly. A victim to falsehood, she sank early to the tomb; and, ere her thirtieth year, she died—her spotless soul fled to eternal happiness. Never shall I forget—though but fourteen when she died—never shall I forget her last commands. 'My son,' said she, 'my Pietrino, revenge my wrongs—revenge them on the perjured Verezzi—revenge them on his progeny for ever!'

"And, by heaven! I think I have revenged them. Ere I was twenty-four, the false villain, though surrounded by seemingly impenetrable grandeur; though forgetful of the offence to punish which this arm was nerved, sank beneath my dagger. But I destroyed his *body* alone," added Zastrozzi, with a terrible look of insatiated vengeance: "time has taught me better: his son's *soul* is hell-doomed to all eternity: he destroyed himself; but my machinations, though unseen, effected his destruction.

"Matilda di Laurentini! Hah! why do you shudder? When, with repeated stabs, you destroyed her who now lies lifeless before you in her coffin, did you not reflect upon what must be your fate? You have enjoyed him whom you adored—you have even been married to him—and, for the space of more than a month, have tasted unutterable joys; and yet you are unwilling to pay the price of your happiness—by heavens, I am not!" added he, bursting into a wild laugh. "Ah, poor fool, Matilda, did you think it was from friendship I instructed you to gain Verezzi? No, no—it was revenge which induced me to enter into your schemes with zeal; which induced me to lead her, whose lifeless form lies yonder, to your house, foreseeing the effect it would have upon the strong passions of your husband.

"And now," added Zastrozzi, "I have been candid with you. Judge, pass your sentence—but I know my doom; and, instead of horror, experience some degree of satisfaction at the arrival of death, since all I have to do on earth is completed."

Zastrozzi ceased; and, unappalled, fixed his expressive gaze upon the superior.

Surprised at Zastrozzi's firmness, and shocked at the crimes of which he had made so unequivocal an avowal, the superior turned away in horror.

Still Zastrozzi stood unmoved, and fearlessly awaited the fiat of his destiny.

The superior whispered to one in black vestments. Four officials rushed in, and placed Zastrozzi on the rack.

Even whilst writhing under the agony of almost insupportable torture his nerves were stretched, Zastrozzi's firmness failed him not; but, upon his soul-illumined countenance, played a smile of most disdainful scorn—and, with a wild, convulsive laugh of exulting revenge, he died.

THE END

ST. IRVYNE;

OR,

THE ROSICRUCIAN.

ST. IRVYNE;

OR,

THE ROSICRUCIAN:

A ROMANCE.

BY

A GENTLEMAN

OF THE UNIVERSITY OF OXFORD.

LONDON:

PRINTED FOR J. J. STOCKDALE,

41, PALL MALL.

1811.

ST. IRVYNE*

CHAPTER I

RED thunder-clouds, borne on the wings of the midnight whirlwind, floated, at fits, athwart the crimson-coloured orbit of the moon; the rising fierceness of the blast sighed through the stunted shrubs, which, bending before its violence, inclined towards the rocks whereon they grew: over the blackened expanse of heaven, at intervals, was spread the blue lightning's flash; it played upon the granite heights, and, with momentary brilliancy, disclosed the terrific scenery of the Alps, whose gigantic and misshapen summits, reddened by the transitory moonbeam, were crossed by black fleeting fragments of the tempest-clouds. The rain, in big drops, began to descend, and the thunder-peals, with louder and more deafening crash, to shake the zenith, till the long-protracted war, echoing from cavern to cavern, died, in indistinct murmurs, amidst the far-extended chain of mountains. In this scene, then, at this horrible and tempestuous hour, without one existent earthly being whom he might claim as friend, without one resource to which he might fly as an asylum from the horrors of neglect and poverty, stood Wolfstein;—he gazed upon the conflicting elements; his youthful figure reclined against a jutting granite rock; he cursed his wayward destiny, and implored the Almighty of Heaven to permit the thunderbolt, with crash terrific and exterminating, to descend upon his head, that a being useless to himself and to society might no longer, by his existence, mock Him who ne'er made aught in vain. "And what so horrible crimes have I committed," exclaimed Wolfstein, driven to impiety by desperation, "what crimes which merit punishment like this? What, what is death?—Ah, dissolution! thy pang is blunted by the hard hand of long-protracted suffering—suffering unspeakable, indescribable!" As thus he spoke, a more terrific paroxysm of excessive despair revelled through every vein; his brain swam around in wild confusion, and, rendered delirious by excess of misery, he started from his flinty seat, and swiftly hastened towards the precipice, which yawned widely beneath his feet. "For what then should I longer drag on the galling chain of existence?" cried Wolfstein; and his impious expression was borne onwards by the hot and sulphurous thunder-blast.

The midnight meteors danced above the gulf upon which Wolfstein wistfully gazed. Palpable, impenetrable darkness seemed to hang upon it; impenetrable even by the flaming thunderbolt. "Into this then shall I plunge myself?" soliloquized the wretched outcast, "and by one rash act endanger, perhaps, eternal happiness;—deliver myself up, perhaps, to the anticipation and experience of never-ending torments? Art thou the God then, the Creator of the universe, whom canting monks call the God of mercy and forgiveness, and sufferest thou thy creatures to become the victims of tortures such as fate has inflicted on me?*—Oh, God! take my soul; why should I longer live?" Thus having spoken, he sank on the rocky bosom of the mountains. Yet, unheeding the exclamations of the maddened Wolfstein, fiercer raged the tempest. The battling elements, in wild confusion, seemed to threaten nature's dissolution; the ferocious thunderbolt, with impetuous violence, danced upon the mountains, and, collecting more terrific strength, severed gigantic rocks from their else eternal basements; the masses, with sound more frightful than the bursting thunder-peal, dashed towards the valley below. Horror and desolation marked their track. The mountain-rills, swoln by the waters of the sky, dashed with direr impetuosity from the Alpine summits; their foaming waters were hidden in the darkness of midnight, or only became visible when the momentary scintillations of the lightning rested on their whitened waves. Fiercer still than nature's wildest uproar were the feelings of Wolfstein's bosom; his frame, at last, conquered by the conflicting passions of his soul, no longer was adequate to sustain the unequal contest, but sank to the earth. His brain swam wildly, and he lay entranced in total insensibility.

What torches are those that dispel the distant darkness of midnight, and gleam, like meteors, athwart the blackness of the tempest? They throw a wavering light over the thickness of the storm: they wind along the mountains: they pass the hollow vallies. Hark! the howling of the blast has ceased,—the thunderbolts have dispersed, but yet reigns darkness. Distant sounds of song are borne on the breeze: the sounds approach. A low bier holds the remains of one whose soul is floating in the regions of eternity: a black pall covers him. Monks support the lifeless clay: others precede, bearing torches, and chanting a requiem for the salvation of the departed one. They hasten towards the convent of the valley, there to deposit the lifeless limbs of one who has explored the frightful path of eternity before them. And now they had arrived where lay Wolfstein: "Alas!" said one of the monks, "there reclines a wretched traveller. He is dead: murdered, doubtlessly, by the fell bandits who infest these wild recesses."

They raised from the earth his form: yet his bosom throbbed with the tide of life: returning animation once more illumed his eye: he started on his feet, and wildly inquired why they had awakened him from that slumber which he had hoped to have been eternal. Unconnected were his expressions, strange and impetuous the fire darting from his restless eyeballs. At length, the monks succeeded in calming the desperate tumultuousness of his bosom, calming at least in some degree; for he accepted their proffered tenders of a lodging, and essayed to lull to sleep, for awhile, the horrible idea of dereliction which pressed upon his loaded brain.

While thus they stood, loud shouts rent the air, and, before Wolfstein and the monks could well collect their scattered faculties, they found that a troop of Alpine bandits had surrounded them. Trembling, from apprehension, the monks fled every way. None, however, could escape. "What! old grey-beards," cried one of the robbers, "do you suppose that we will permit you to evade us: you who feed upon the strength of the country, in idleness and luxury, and have compelled many of our noble fellows, who otherwise would have been ornaments to their country in peace, thunderbolts to their enemies in war, to seek precarious subsistence as Alpine bandits? If you wish for mercy, therefore, deliver unhesitatingly your joint riches." The robbers then despoiled the monks of whatever they might adventitiously have taken with them, and, turning to Wolfstein, the apparent chieftain told him to yield his money likewise. Unappalled, Wolfstein advanced towards them. The chief held a torch; its red beams disclosed the expression of stern severity and unyielding loftiness which sate upon the brow of Wolfstein. "Bandit," he answered fearlessly, "I have none,—no money—no hope—no friends; nor do I care for existence! Now judge if such a man be a fit victim for fear! No! I never trembled!"

A ray of pleasure gleamed in the countenance of the bandit as Wolfstein spoke. Grief, in inerasible traces, sate deeply implanted on the front of the outcast. At last, the chief, advancing to Wolfstein, who stood at some little distance, said, "My companions think that so noble a fellow as you appear to be, would be no unworthy member of our society; and, by Heaven, I am of their opinion. Are you willing to become one of us?"

Wolfstein's dark gaze was fixed upon the ground: his contracted eyebrow evinced deep thought: he started from his reverie, and, without hesitation, consented to their proposal.

Long was it past the hour of midnight when the banditti troop, with their newly-acquired associate, advanced along the pathless Alps. The red glare of the torches which each held, tinged the rocks and pine-trees, through woods of which they occasionally passed, and alone dissipated the darkness of night. Now had they arrived at the summit of a wild and rocky precipice, but the base indeed of another which mingled its far-seen and gigantic outline with the clouds of heaven. A door, which before had appeared part of the solid rock, flew open at the chieftain's touch, and the whole party advanced into the spacious cavern. Over the walls of the lengthened passages putrefaction had spread a bluish clamminess; damps hung around, and, at intervals, almost extinguished the torches, whose glare was scarcely sufficient to dissipate the impenetrable obscurity. After many devious windings they advanced into the body of the cavern: it was spacious and lofty. A blazing wood fire threw its dubious rays upon the misshapen and ill-carved walls. Lamps suspended from the roof, dispersed the subterranean gloom, not so completely however, but that ill-defined shades lurked in the arched distances, whose hollow recesses led to different apartments.

The gang had sate down in the midst of the cavern to supper, which a female, whose former loveliness had left scarcely any traces on her cheek, had prepared. The most exquisite and expensive wines apologised for the rusticity of the rest of the entertainment, and induced freedom of conversation, and wild, boisterous merriment, which reigned until the bandits, overcome by the fumes of the wine which they had drunk, sank to sleep. Wolfstein, left again to solitude and silence, reclining on his mat in a corner of the cavern, retraced, in mental, sorrowing review, the past events of his life: ah! that eventful existence whose fate had dragged the heir of a wealthy potentate in Germany from the lap of luxury and indulgence, to become a vile associate of viler bandits, in the wild and trackless deserts of the Alps. Around their dwellings, lofty inaccessible acclivities reared their barren summits; they echoed to no sound save the wild hoot of the night-raven, or the impatient yelling of the vulture, which hovered on the blast in quest of scanty sustenance. These were the scenes without: noisy revelry and tumultuous riot reigned within. The mirth of the bandits appeared to arise independently of themselves; their hearts were void and dreary. Wolfstein's limbs pillowed on the flinty bosom of the earth: those limbs which had been wont to recline on the softest, the most luxurious sofas. Driven from his native country by an event which imposed upon him an insuperable barrier to ever again returning thither, possessing no friends, not having one single resource from which he might obtain support, where could the wretch, the exile, seek for an asylum but with those whose fortunes, expectations, and characters were desperate, and marked as darkly, by fate, as his own?

Time fled, and each succeeding day inured Wolfstein more and more to the idea of depriving his fellow-creatures of their possessions. In a short space of time the high-souled and noble Wolfstein, though still high-souled and noble, became an experienced bandit. His magnanimity and courage, even whilst surrounded by the most threatening dangers, and the unappalled expression of countenance with which he defied the dart of death, endeared him to the robbers; whilst with him they all asserted that they felt, as it were, instinctively impelled to deeds of horror and danger, which, otherwise, must have remained unattempted even by the boldest. His was every daring expedition, his the scheme which demanded depth of judgment and promptness of execution. Often, whilst at midnight the band lurked perhaps beneath the overhanging rocks, which were gloomily impended above them, in the midst, perhaps, of one of those horrible tempests whereby the air, in those Alpine regions, is so frequently convulsed, would the countenance of the bandits betray some slight shade of alarm and awe; but that of Wolfstein was fixed, unchanged, by any variation of scenery of action. One day it was when the chief communicated to the banditti, notice which he had received by means of spies, that an Italian Count of immense wealth was journeying from Paris to his native country, and, at a late hour the following evening, would pass the Alps near this place; "They have but few attendants," added he, "and those few will not come this way; the postilion is in our interest, and the horses are to be overcome with fatigue when they approach the destined spot: you understand."

The evening came. "I," said Wolfstein, "will roam into the country, but will return before the arrival of our wealthy victim." Thus saying, he left the cavern, and wandered out amidst the mountains.

It was autumn. The mountain-tops, the scattered oaks which occasionally waved their lightning-blasted heads on the summits of the far-seen piles of rock, were gilded by the setting glory of the sun; the trees, yellowed by the waning year, reflected a glowing teint from their thick foliage; and the dark pine-groves which were stretched half way up the mountain sides, added a more deepened gloom to the shades of evening, which already began to gather rapidly above the scenery.

It was at this dark and silent hour, that Wolfstein, unheeding the surrounding objects,—objects which might have touched with awe, or heightened to devotion, any other breast,—wandered alone—pensively he wandered—dark images for futurity possessed his soul: he shuddered when he reflected upon what had passed; nor was his present situation calculated to satisfy a mind eagerly panting for liberty and independence. Conscience too, awakened conscience, upbraided him for the life which he had selected, and, with silent whisperings, stung his soul to madness. Oppressed by thoughts such as these, Wolfstein yet proceeded, forgetful that he was to return before the arrival of their destined victim—forgetful indeed was he of every external existence; and, absorbed in himself, with arms folded, and eyes fixed upon the earth, he yet advanced. At last he sank on a mossy bank, and, guided by the impulse of the moment, inscribed on a tablet the following lines; for the inaccuracy of which, the perturbation of him who wrote them, may account; he thought of past times while he marked the paper with—

'Twas dead of the night, when I sat in my dwelling;
  One glimmering lamp was expiring and low;
Around, the dark tide of the tempest was swelling,
Along the wild mountains night-ravens were yelling,—
  They bodingly presaged destruction and woe.

'Twas then that I started!—the wild storm was howling,
  Nought was seen, save the lightning, which danc'd in the sky;
Above me, the crash of the thunder was rolling,
  And low, chilling murmurs, the blast wafted by.

My heart sank within me—unheeded the war
  Of the battling clouds, on the mountain-tops, broke—
Unheeded the thunder-peal crash'd in mine ear—
This heart, hard as iron, is stranger to fear;
  But conscience in low, noiseless whispering spoke.

'Twas then that her form on the whirlwind upholding,
  The ghost of the murder'd Victoria strode;
In her right hand, a shadowy shroud she was holding,
  She swiftly advanced to my lonesome abode.
I wildly then call'd on the tempest to bear me—— *

Overcome by the wild retrospection of ideal horror, which these swiftly-written lines excited in his soul, Wolfstein tore the paper, on which he had written them, to pieces, and scattered them about him. He arose from his recumbent posture, and again advanced through the forest. Not far had he proceeded, ere a mingled murmur broke upon the silence of night—it was the sound of human voices. An event so unusual in these solitudes, excited Wolfstein's momentary surprise; he started, and looking around him, essayed to discover whence those sounds proceeded.—What was the astonishment of Wolfstein, when he found that a detached party, who had been sent in pursuit of the Count, had actually overtaken him, and, at this instant, were dragging from the carriage the almost lifeless form of a female, whose light symmetrical figure, as it leant on the muscular frame of the robber who supported it, afforded a most striking contrast.—They had, before his arrival, plundered the Count of all his riches, and, enraged at the spirited defence which he had made, had inhumanly murdered him, and cast his lifeless body adown the yawning precipice. Transfixed by a jutting point of granite rock, it remained there to be devoured by the ravens. Wolfstein joined the banditti; and, although he could not recall the deed, lamented the wanton cruelty which had been practised upon the Count. As for the female, whose grace and loveliness made so strong an impression upon him, he demanded that every soothing attention should be paid to her, and his desire was enforced by the commands of the chief, whose dark eye wandered wildly over the beauties of the lovely Megalena de Metastasio, as if he had secretly destined them for himself.

At last they arrived at the cavern; every resource which the cavern of a gang of lawless and desperate villains might afford, was brought forward to restore the fainted Megalena to life: she soon recovered—she slowly opened her eyes, and started with surprise to behold herself surrounded by a rough set of desperadoes, and the gloomy walls of the cavern, upon which darkness hung, awfully visible. Near her sate a female, whose darkened expression of countenance seemed perfectly to correspond with the horror prevalent throughout the cavern; her face, though bearing the marks of an undeniable expression of familiarity with wretchedness, had some slight remains of beauty.

It was long past midnight when each of the robbers withdrew to repose. But his mind was too much occupied by the events of the evening to allow the unhappy Wolfstein to find quiet;—at an early hour he rose from his sleepless couch, to inhale the morning breeze. The sun had but just risen; the scene was beautiful; everything was still, and seemed to favour that reflection, which even propinquity to his abandoned associates imposed no indefinably insuperable bar to. In spite of his attempts to think upon other subjects, the image of the fair Megalena floated in his mind.

Her loveliness had made too deep an impression on it to be easily removed; and the hapless Wolfstein, ever the victim of impulsive feeling, found himself bound to her by ties, more lasting than he had now conceived the transitory tyranny of woe could have imposed. For never had Wolfstein beheld so singularly beautiful a form;—her figure cast in the mould of most exact symmetry; her blue and love-beaming eyes, from which occasionally emanated a wild expression, seemingly almost superhuman; and the auburn hair which hung in unconfined tresses down her damask cheek—formed a resistless *tout ensemble*.

Heedless of every external object, Wolfstein long wandered.—The protracted sound of the bandits' horn struck at last upon his ear, and aroused him from his reverie. On his return to the cavern, the robbers were assembled at their meal; the chief regarded him with marked and jealous surprise as he entered, but made no remark. They then discussed their uninteresting and monotonous topics, and the meal being ended, each villain departed on his different business.

Megalena, finding herself alone with Agnes (the only woman, save herself, who was in the cavern, and who served as an attendant on the robbers), essayed, by the most humble entreaties and supplications, to excite pity in her breast: she conjured her to explain the cause for which she was thus imprisoned, and wildly inquired for her father. The guilt-bronzed brow of Agnes was contracted by a sullen and malicious frown: it was the only reply which the inhuman female deigned to return. After a pause, however, she said, "Thou thinkest thyself my superior, proud girl; but time may render us equals.—Submit to that, and you may live on the same terms as I do."

There appeared to lurk a meaning in these words, which Megalena found herself incompetent to develop; she answered not, therefore, and suffered Agnes to depart unquestioned. The wretched Megalena, a prey to despair and terror, endeavoured to revolve in her mind the events which had brought her to this spot, but an unconnected stream of ideas pressed upon her brain. The sole light in her cell was that of a dismal lamp which, by its uncertain flickering, only dissipated the almost palpable obscurity, in a sufficient degree more assuredly to point out the circumambient horrors. She gazed wistfully around, to see if there were any outlet; none there was, save the door whereby Agnes had entered, which was strongly barred on the outside. In despair she threw herself on the wretched pallet.—"For what cause, then, am I thus entombed alive?" soliloquized the hapless Megalena; "would it not be preferable at once to annihilate the spark of life which burns but faintly within my bosom?—O my father! where art thou? Thy tombless corse, perhaps, is torn into a thousand pieces by the fury of the mountain cataract.—Little didst thou presage misfortunes such as these!—little didst thou suppose that our last journey would have caused thy immature dissolution—my infamy and misery, not to end but with my hapless existence!—Here there is none to comfort me, none to participate my miseries!" Thus speaking, overcome by a paroxysm of emotion, she sank on the bed, and bedewed her fair face with tears.

Whilst, oppressed by painful retrospection, the outcast orphan was yet kneeling, Agnes entered, and, not even noticing her distress, bade her prepare to come to the banquet where the troop of bandits was assembled. In silence, along the vaulted and gloomy passages, she followed her conductress, from whose stern and forbidding gaze her nature shrunk back enhorrored, till they reached that apartment of the cavern where the revelry waited but for her arrival to commence. On her entering, Cavigni, the chief, led her to a seat on his right hand, and paid her every attention which his froward nature could stoop to exercise towards a female; she received his civilities with apparent complacency; but her eye was frequently fascinated, as it were, towards the youthful Wolfstein, who had caught her attention the evening before. His countenance, spite of the shade of woe with which the hard hand of suffering had marked it, was engaging and beautiful; not that beauty which may be freely acknowledged, but inwardly confessed by every beholder with sensations penetrating and resistless; his figure majestic and lofty, and the fire which flashed from his expressive eye, indefinably to herself, penetrated the inmost soul of the isolated Megalena. Wolfstein regarded Cavigni with indignation and envy; and, though almost ignorant himself of the dreadful purpose of his soul, resolved in his own mind an horrible deed. Cavigni was enraptured with the beauty of Megalena, and secretly vowed that no pains should be spared to gain to himself the possession of an object so lovely. The anticipated delight of gratified voluptuousness revelled in every vein as he gazed upon her; his eye flashed with a triumphant expression of lawless love, yet he determined to defer the hour of his happiness till he might enjoy more free, unrestrained delight, with his adored fair one. She gazed on the chief, however, with an ill-concealed aversion; his dark expression of countenance, the haughty severity, and contemptuous frown, which habitually sate on his brow, invited not, but rather repelled a reciprocality of affection, which the haughty chief, after his own attachment, entertained not the most distant doubt of. He was, notwithstanding, conscious of her coldness, but attributing it to virgin modesty, or to the novel situation into which she had suddenly been thrown, paid her every attention; nor did he omit to promise her every little comfort which might induce her to regard him with esteem. Still, though veiled beneath the most artful dissimulation, did the fair Megalena pant ardently for liberty—for, oh! liberty is sweet, sweeter even than all the other pleasures of life, to full satiety, without it.

Cavigni essayed, by every art, to gain her over to his desires; but Megalena, regarding him with aversion, answered with an haughtiness which she was unable to conceal, and which his proud spirit might ill brook. Cavigni could not disguise the vexation which he felt, when, increased by resistance, Megalena's dislike towards him remained no longer a secret: "Megalena," said he, at last, "fair girl, thou shalt be mine—we will be wedded to-morrow, if you think the bands of love not sufficiently forcible to unite us."

"No bands shall ever unite me to you!" exclaimed Megalena. "Even though the grave were to yawn beneath my feet, I would willingly precipitate myself into its gulf, if the alternative of that, or an union with you, were proposed to me."

Rage swelled Cavigni's bosom almost to bursting—the conflicting passions of his soul were too tumultuous for utterance;—in an hurried tone, he commanded Agnes to show Megalena to her cell: she obeyed, and they both quitted the apartment.

Wolfstein's soul, sublimed by the most infuriate paroxysms of contending emotions, battled wildly. His countenance retained, however, but one expression,—it was of dark and deliberate revenge. His stern eye was fixed upon Cavigni;—he decided at this instant to perpetrate the deed he had resolved on. Leaving his seat, he intimated his intention of quitting the cavern for an instant.

Cavigni had just filled his goblet. Wolfstein, as he passed, dexterously threw a little white powder into the wine of the chief.

When Wolfstein returned, Cavigni had not yet quaffed the deadly draught: rising, therefore, he exclaimed aloud, "Fill your goblets, all." Every one obeyed, and sat in expectation of the toast which he was about to propose.

"Let us drink," he exclaimed, "to the health of the chieftain's bride—let us drink to their mutual happiness." A smile of pleasure irradiated the countenance of the chief:—that he whom he had supposed to be a dangerous rival, should thus publicly forego any claim to the affections of Megalena, was indeed pleasure.

"Health and mutual happiness to the chieftain and his bride!" re-echoed from every part of the table.

Cavigni raised the goblet to his lips: he was about to quaff the tide of death, when Ginotti, one of the robbers, who sat next to him, upreared his arm, and dashed the cup of destruction to the earth. A silence, as if in expectation of some terrible event, reigned throughout the cavern.

Wolfstein turned his eyes towards the chief;—the dark and mysterious gaze of Ginotti arrested his wandering eyeball; its expression was too marked to be misunderstood:—he trembled in his inmost soul, but his countenance yet retained its unchangeable expression. Ginotti spoke not, nor willed he to assign any reason for his extraordinary conduct; the circumstance was shortly forgotten, and the revelry went on undisturbed by any other event.

Ginotti was one of the boldest of the robbers; he was the distinguished favourite of the chief, and, although mysterious and reserved, his society was courted with more eagerness, than such qualities might, abstractedly considered, appear to deserve. None knew his history—*that* he concealed within the deepest recesses of his bosom; nor could the most suppliant entreaties, or threats of the most horrible punishments, have wrested from him one particular concerning it. Never had he once thrown off the mysterious mask, beneath which his character was veiled, since he had become an associate of the band. In vain the chief required him to assign some reason for his late extravagant conduct; he said it was mere accident, but with an air, which more than convinced every one, that something lurked behind which yet remained unknown. Such, however, was their respect for Ginotti, that the occurrence passed almost without a comment.

Long now had the hour of midnight gone by, and the bandits had retired to repose. Wolfstein retired too to his couch, but sleep closed not his eyelids; his bosom was a scene of the wildest anarchy; the conflicting passions revelled dreadfully in his burning brain:—love, maddening, excessive, unaccountable idolatry, as it were, which possessed him for Megalena, urged him on to the commission of deeds which conscience represented as beyond measure wicked, and which Ginotti's glance convinced him were by no means unsuspected. Still so unbounded was his love for Megalena (madness rather than love), that it overbalanced every other consideration, and his unappalled soul resolved to persevere in its determination even to destruction!

Cavigni's commands respecting Megalena had been obeyed:—the door of her cell was fastened, and the ferocious chief resolved to let her lie there till the suffering and confinement might subdue her to his will. Megalena endeavoured, by every means, to soften the obdurate heart of her attendant; at length, her mildness of manner induced Agnes to regard her with pity; and before she quitted her cell, they were so far reconciled to each other that they entered into a comparison of their mutual situations; and Agnes was about to relate to Megalena the circumstances which had brought her to the cavern, when the fierce Cavigni entered, and, commanding Agnes to withdraw, said, "Well, proud girl, are you now in a better humour to return the favour with which your superior regards you?"

"No!" heroically answered Megalena.

"Then," rejoined the chief, "if within four-and-twenty hours you hold yourself not in readiness to return my love, force shall wrest the jewel from its casket." Thus having said, he abruptly quitted the cell.

So far had Wolfstein's proposed toast, at the banquet, gained on the unsuspecting ferociousness of Cavigni, that he accepted the former's artful tender of service, in the way of persuasion with Megalena, supposing, by Wolfstein's manner, that they had been cursorily acquainted before. Wolfstein, therefore, entered the apartment of Megalena.

At the sight of him Megalena arose from her recumbent posture, and hastened joyfully to meet him; for she remembered that Wolfstein had rescued her from the insults of the banditti, on the eventful evening which had subjected her to their control.

"Lovely, adored girl," he exclaimed, "short is my time: pardon, therefore, the abruptness of my address. The chief has sent me to persuade you to become united to him; but I love you, I adore you to madness. I am not what I seem. Answer me!—time is short."

An indefinable sensation, unfelt before, swelled through the passion-quivering frame of Megalena. "Yes, yes," she cried, "I will—I love you——" At this instant the voice of Cavigni was heard in the passage. Wolfstein started from his knees, and pressing the fair hand presented to his lips with exulting ardour, departed hastily to give an account of his mission to the anxious Cavigni, who restrained himself in the passage without, and, slightly mistrusting Wolfstein, was about to advance to the door of the cell to listen to their conversation, when Wolfstein quitted Megalena.

Megalena, again in solitude, began to reflect upon the scenes which had been lately acted. She thought upon the words of Wolfstein, unconscious wherefore they were a balm to her mind: she reclined upon her wretched pallet. It was now night: her thoughts took a different turn; the melancholy wind sighing along the crevices of the cavern, and the dismal sound of rain, which pattered fast, inspired mournful reflection. She thought of her father,—her beloved father;—a solitary wanderer on the face of the earth; or, most probably, thought she, his soul rests in death. Horrible idea! If the latter, she envied his fate; if the former, she even supposed it preferable to her present abode. She again thought of Wolfstein; she pondered on his last words:—an escape from the cavern: oh, delightful idea! Again her thoughts recurred to her father: tears bedewed her cheeks; she took a pencil, and, actuated by the feelings of the moment, inscribed on the wall of her prison these lines:—

Ghosts of the dead! have I not heard your yelling
  Rise on the night-rolling breath of the blast,*
When o'er the dark ether the tempest is swelling,
  And on eddying whirlwind the thunder-peal past?

For oft have I stood on the dark height of Jura,
  Which frowns on the valley that opens beneath;
Oft have I braved the chill night-tempest's fury,
  Whilst around me, I thought, echo'd murmurs of death.

And now, whilst the winds of the mountain are howling,
  O father! thy voice seems to strike on mine ear;
In air whilst the tide of the night-storm is rolling,
  It breaks on the pause of the elements' jar.

On the wing of the whirlwind which roars o'er the mountain
  Perhaps rides the ghost of my sire who is dead;
On the mist of the tempest which hangs o'er the fountain,
  Whilst a wreath of dark vapour encircles his head.

Here she paused, and, ashamed of the exuberance of her imagination, obliterated from the wall the characters which she had traced: the wind still howled dreadfully: in fearful anticipation of the morrow, she threw herself on the bed, and, in sleep, forgot the misfortunes which impended over her.

Meantime, the soul of Wolfstein was disturbed by ten thousand conflicting passions; revenge and disappointed love agonized his soul to madness; and he resolved to quench the rude feelings of his bosom in the blood of his rival. But, again he thought of Ginotti; he thought of the mysterious intervention which his dark glances proved not to be accidental. To him it was an inexplicable mystery; which the more he reflected upon, the less able was he to unravel. He had mixed the poison, unseen, as he thought, by any one; certainly unseen by Ginotti, whose back was unconcernedly turned at the time. He planned, therefore, a second attempt, unawed by what had happened before, for the destruction of Cavigni, which he resolved to put into execution this night.

Before he had become an associate with the band of robbers, the conscience of Wolfstein was clear; clear, at least, from the commission of any wilful and deliberate crime; for, alas! an event almost too dreadful for narration, had compelled him to quit his native country, in indigence and disgrace. His courage was equal to his wickedness; his mind was unalienable from its purpose; and whatever his will might determine, his boldness would fearlessly execute, even though hell and destruction were to yawn beneath his feet, and essay to turn his unappalled soul from the accomplishment of his design. Such was the guilty Wolfstein; a disgraceful fugitive from his country, a vile associate of a band of robbers, and a murderer, at least in intent, if not in deed. He shrunk not at the commission of crimes; he was now the hardened villain; eternal damnation, tortures inconceivable on earth, awaited him. "Foolish, degrading idea!" he exclaimed, as it momentarily glanced through his mind; "am I worthy of the celestial Megalena, if I shrink at the price which it is necessary I should pay for her possession?" This idea banished every other feeling from his heart; and, smothering the stings of conscience, a decided resolve of murder took possession of him—the determining, within himself, to destroy the very man who had given him an asylum, when driven to madness by the horrors of neglect and poverty. He stood in the night-storm on the mountains; he cursed the intervention of Ginotti, and secretly swore that nor heaven nor hell again should dash the goblet of destruction from the mouth of the detested Cavigni. The soul of Wolfstein too, insatiable in its desires, and panting for liberty, ill could brook the confinement of idea, which the cavern of the bandits must necessarily induce. He longed again to try his fortune; he longed to re-enter that world which he had never tried but once, and that indeed for a short time; sufficiently long, however, to blast his blooming hopes, and to graft on the stock, which otherwise might have produced virtue, the fatal seeds of vice.

CHAPTER II

> The fiends of fate are heard to rave,
> And the death-angel flaps his broad wing o'er the wave.

It was midnight; and all the robbers were assembled in the banquet-hall, amongst whom, bearing in his bosom a weight of premeditated crime, was Wolfstein; he sat by the chief. They discoursed on indifferent subjects; the sparkling goblet went round; loud laughter succeeded. The ruffians were rejoicing over some plunder which they had taken from a traveller, whom they had robbed of immense wealth; they had left his body a prey to the vultures of the mountains. The table groaned with the pressure of the feast. Hilarity reigned around: reiterated were the shouts of merriment and joy; if such could exist in a cavern of robbers.

It was long past midnight: another hour, and Megalena must be Cavigni's. This idea rendered Wolfstein callous to every sting of conscience; and he eagerly awaited an opportunity when he might, unperceived, infuse poison into the goblet of one who confided in him. Ginotti sat opposite to Wolfstein: his arms were folded, and his gaze rested fixedly upon the fearless countenance of the murderer. Wolfstein shuddered when he beheld the brow of the mysterious Ginotti contracted, his marked features wrapped in inexplicable mystery.

All were now heated by wine, save the wily villain who destined murder; and the awe-inspiring Ginotti, whose reservedness and mystery, not even the hilarity of the present hour could dispel.

Conversation appearing to flag, Cavigni exclaimed, "Steindolph, you know some old German stories; cannot you tell one, to deceive the lagging hours?"

Steindolph was famed for his knowledge of metrical spectre tales, and the gang were frequently wont to hang delighted on the ghostly wonders which he related.

"Excuse, then, the mode of my telling it," said Steindolph, "and I will with pleasure. I learnt it whilst in Germany; my old grandmother taught it me, and I can repeat it as a ballad."—"Do, do," re-echoed from every part of the cavern.—Steindolph thus began:

BALLAD

I

The death-bell beats!—
The mountain repeats
The echoing sound of the knell;
And the dark monk now
Wraps the cowl round his brow,
As he sits in his lonely cell.

II

And the cold hand of death
Chills his shuddering breath,
As he lists to the fearful lay
Which the ghosts of the sky,
As they sweep wildly by,
Sing to departed day.
And they sing of the hour
When the stern fates had power
To resolve Rosa's form to its clay.

III

But that hour is past;
And that hour was the last
Of peace to the dark monk's brain.
Bitter tears, from his eyes, gush'd silent and fast;
And he strove to suppress them in vain.

IV

Then his fair cross of gold he dash'd on the floor
When the death-knell struck on his ear,
Delight is in store
For her evermore;
But for me is fate, horror, and fear.

V

Then his eyes wildly roll'd,
When the death-bell toll'd,
And he raged in terrific woe.
And he stamp'd on the ground,—
But when ceased the sound
Tears again began to flow.

VI

And the ice of despair
Chill'd the wild throb of care,
And he sat in mute agony still;
Till the night-stars shone through the cloudless air
And the pale moonbeam slept on the hill.

VII

Then he knelt in his cell:—
And the horrors of hell
Were delights to his agonized pain.
And he pray'd to God to dissolve the spell,
Which else must for ever remain.

VIII

And in fervent prayer he knelt on the ground,
Till the abbey bell struck One:
His feverish blood ran chill at the sound:
A voice hollow and horrible murmur'd around,—
"The term of thy penance is done!"

IX

Grew dark the night;
The moonbeam bright
Wax'd faint on the mountain high;
And, from the black hill,
Went a voice cold and still,—
"Monk! thou art free to die."

X

Then he rose on his feet,
And his heart loud did beat,
And his limbs they were palsied with dread;
Whilst the grave's clammy dew
O'er his pale forehead grew;
And he shudder'd to sleep with the dead.

XI

And the wild midnight storm
Raved around his tall form,
As he sought the chapel's gloom:
And the sunk grass did sigh
To the wind, bleak and high,
As he searched for the new-made tomb.

XII

And forms, dark and high,
Seem'd around him to fly,
And mingle their yells with the blast:
And on the dark wall
Half-seen shadows did fall,
As enhorror'd he onward pass'd.

XIII

And the storm-fiend's wild rave
O'er the new-made grave,
And dread shadows, linger around.
The Monk call'd on God his soul to save,
And, in horror, sank on the ground.

XIV

Then despair nerved his arm
To dispel the charm,
And he burst Rosa's coffin asunder.
And the fierce storm did swell
More terrific and fell,
And louder peal'd the thunder.

XV

And laugh'd, in joy, the fiendish throng,
Mix'd with ghosts of the mouldering dead:
And their grisly wings, as they floated along,
Whistled in murmurs dread.

XVI

And her skeleton form the dead Nun rear'd,
Which dripp'd with the chill dew of hell.
In her half-eaten eyeballs two pale flames appear'd,
And triumphant their gleam on the dark Monk glared,
As he stood within the cell.

XVII

And her lank hand lay on his shuddering brain;
But each power was nerved by fear.—
"I never, henceforth, may breathe again;
Death now ends mine anguish'd pain.—
The grave yawns,—we meet there."

XVIII

And her skeleton lungs did utter the sound,
So deadly, so lone, and so fell,
That in long vibrations shudder'd the ground;
And as the stern notes floated around,
A deep groan was answer'd from hell.

As Steindolph concluded, an universal shout of applause echoed through the cavern. Every one had been so attentive to the recitation of the robber, that no opportunity of perpetrating his resolve had appeared to Wolfstein. Now all again was revelry and riot, and the wily designer eagerly watched for the instant when universal confusion might favour his attempt to drop, unobserved, the powder into the goblet of the chief. With a gaze of insidious and malignant revenge was the eye of Wolfstein fixed upon the chieftain's countenance. Cavigni perceived it not; for he was heated with wine, or the unusual expression of his associate's face must have awakened suspicion, or excited remark. Yet was Ginotti's gaze fixed upon Wolfstein, who, like a sanguinary and remorseless ruffian, sat expectantly waiting the instant of death. The goblet passed round:—at the moment when Wolfstein mingled the poison with Cavigni's wine, the eyes of Ginotti, which before had regarded him with the most dazzling scrutiny, were intentionally turned away. He then arose from the table, and, complaining of sudden indisposition, retired. Cavigni raised the goblet to his lips—

"Now, my brave fellows," he exclaimed, "the hour is late; but before we retire, I here drink success and health to every one of you."

Wolfstein involuntarily shuddered.—Cavigni quaffed the liquor to the dregs!—the cup fell from his trembling hand. The chill dew of death sat upon his forehead: in terrific convulsions he fell headlong; and, inarticulately uttering, "I am poisoned," sank seemingly lifeless on the earth. Sixty robbers at once rushed forward to raise him; and, reclining in their arms, with an horrible and harrowing shriek, the spark of life fled from his body for ever. A robber, skilled in surgery, opened a vein; but no blood followed the touch of the lancet.—Wolfstein advanced to the body, unappalled by the crime which he had committed, and tore aside the vest from its bosom; that bosom was discoloured by large spots of livid purple, which, by their premature appearance, declared the poison which had been used to destroy him, to be excessively powerful.

Every one regretted the death of the brave Cavigni; every one was surprised at the mode of his death; and, by his abruptly quitting the apartment, the suspicion fell upon Ginotti, who was consequently sent for by Ardolph, a robber whom they had chosen chieftain, Wolfstein having declined the proffered distinction.

Ginotti arrived. His stern countenance was changed not by the execrations showered on him by every one. He yet remained unmoved, and apparently careless what sentiments others might entertain of him; he deigned not even to deny the charge. This coolness seemed to have convinced every one, the new chief in particular, of his innocence.

"Let every one," said Ardolph, "be searched; and if his pockets contain poison which could have effected this, let him die." This method was universally applauded. As soon as the acclamations were stilled, Wolfstein advanced forwards and spoke thus:

"Any longer to conceal that it was I who perpetrated the deed, were useless. Megalena's loveliness inflamed me:—I envied one who was about to possess it.—I have murdered him!"

Here he was interrupted by the shouts of the bandits; and he was about to be delivered to death, when Ginotti advanced. His superior and towering figure inspired awe even in the hearts of the bandits. They were silent.

"Suffer Wolfstein," he exclaimed, "to depart unhurt. *I* will answer for his never publishing our retreat: *I* will promise that never more shall you behold him."

Every one submitted to Ginotti: for who could resist the superior Ginotti? From the gaze of Ginotti Wolfstein's soul shrank, enhorrored, in confessed inferiority: he who had shrunk not at death, had shrunk not to avow himself guilty of murder, and had prepared to meet its reward, started from Ginotti's eye-beam as from the emanation of some superior and preter-human being.

"Quit the cavern!" said Ginotti.—"May I not remain here until the morrow?" inquired Wolfstein.—"If to-morrow's rising sun finds you in this cavern," returned Ginotti, "I must deliver you up to the vengeance of those whom you have injured."

Wolfstein retired to his solitary cell, to retrace, in his mind, the occurrences of this eventful night. What was he now?—an isolated wicked wanderer; not a being on earth whom he could call a friend, and carrying with him that never-dying tormenter—conscience. In half-waking dreams passed the night: the ghost of him whom he had so inhumanly destroyed, seemed to cry for justice at the throne of God; bleeding, pale, and ghastly, it pressed on his agonized brain; and confused, inexplicable visions flitted in his imagination, until the freshness of the morning breeze warned him to depart. He collected together all those valuables which had fallen to his share as plunder, during his stay in the cavern: they amounted to a large sum. He rushed from the cavern; he hesitated;—he knew not whither to fly. He walked fast, and essayed, by exercise, to smother the feelings of his soul; but the attempt was fruitless. Not far had he proceeded, ere, stretched on the earth apparently lifeless, he beheld a female form. He advanced towards it—it was Megalena!

A tumult of exulting and inconceivable transport rushed through his veins as he beheld her—her for whom he had plunged into the abyss of crime. She slept, and, apparently overcome by the fatigues which she had sustained, her slumber was profound. Her head reclined upon the jutting root of a tree; the tint of health and loveliness sat upon her cheek.

When the fair Megalena awakened, and found herself in the arms of Wolfstein, she started: yet, turning her eyes, she beheld it was no enemy, and the expression of terror gave way to pleasure. In the general confusion had Megalena escaped from the abode of the bandits. The destinies of Wolfstein and Megalena were assimilated by similarity of situations; and, before they quitted the spot, so far had this reciprocal feeling prevailed, that they swore mutual affection. Megalena then related her escape from the cavern, and showed Wolfstein jewels, to an immense amount, which she had secreted.

"At all events, then," said Wolfstein, "we may defy poverty; for I have about me jewels to the value of ten thousand zechins."

"We will go to Genoa," said Megalena. "We will, my fair one. There, entirely devoted to each other, we will defy the darts of misery."

Megalena returned no answer, save a look of else inexpressible love.

It was now the middle of the day; neither Wolfstein nor Megalena had tasted food since the preceding night; and faint, from fatigue, Megalena scarce could move onwards. "Courage, my love," said Wolfstein; "yet a little way, and we shall arrive at a cottage, a sort of inn, where we may wait until the morrow, and hire mules to carry us to Placenza,* whence we can easily proceed to the goal of our destination."

Megalena collected her strength: in a short time they arrived at the cottage, and passed the remainder of the day in plans respecting the future. Wearied with unusual exertions, Megalena early retired to an inconvenient bed, which, however, was the best the cottage could afford; and Wolfstein, lying along the bench by the fireplace, resigned himself to meditation; for his mind was too much disturbed to let him sleep.

Although Wolfstein had every reason to rejoice at the success which had crowned his schemes; although the very event had occurred which his soul had so much and so eagerly panted for; yet, even now, in possession of all he held valuable on earth, was he ill at ease. Remorse for his crimes tortured him: yet, steeling his conscience, he essayed to smother the fire which burned in his bosom; to change the tenour of his thoughts—in vain! he could not. Restless passed the night, and the middle of the day beheld Wolfstein and Megalena far from the habitation of the bandits.

They intended, if possible, to reach Breno that night, and thence, on the following day, to journey towards Genoa. They had descended the southern acclivity of the Alps. It was now hastening towards spring, and the whole country began to gleam with the renewed loveliness of nature. Odoriferous orange-groves scented the air. Myrtles bloomed on the sides of the gentle eminences which they occasionally ascended. The face of nature was smiling and gay; so was Megalena's heart: with exulting and speechless transport it bounded within her bosom. She gazed on him who possessed her soul; although she felt no inclination in her bosom to retrace the events, by means of which an obscure bandit, undefinable to herself, had gained the eternal love of the former haughty Megalena de Metastasio.

They soon arrived at Breno.* Wolfstein dismissed the muleteer, and conducted Megalena into the interior of the inn, ordering at the same time a supper. Again were repeated protestations of eternal affection, avowals of indissoluble love; but it is sufficient to conceive what cannot be so well described.

It was near midnight; Wolfstein and Megalena sat at supper, and conversed with that unrestrainedness and gaiety which mutual confidence inspired, when the door was opened, and the innkeeper announced the arrival of a man who wished to speak with Wolfstein.

"Tell him," exclaimed Wolfstein, rather surprised, and wishing to guard against the possibility of danger, "that I will not see him."

The landlord left the room, and in a short time returned. A man accompanied him: he was of gigantic stature, and masked. "He would take no denial, Signor," said the landlord, in exculpation, as he left the room.

The stranger advanced to the table at which Wolfstein and Megalena sat: he threw aside his mask, and disclosed the features of—Ginotti! Wolfstein's frame became convulsed with involuntary horror: he started. Megalena was surprised.

Ginotti, at length, broke the terrible silence.

"Wolfstein," he said, "I saved you from, otherwise, inevitable death; by *my* means alone have you gained Megalena:—what do I then deserve in return?" Wolfstein looked on the countenance: it was stern and severe, yet divested of the terrible expression which had before caused his frame to shudder with excess of alarm.

"My eternal gratitude," returned Wolfstein, hesitatingly.

"Will you promise, that when, destitute and a wanderer, I demand your protection, when I beseech you to listen to the tale which I shall relate, you *will* listen to me; that, when I am dead, you will bury me, and suffer my soul to rest in the endless slumber of annihilation? Then will you repay me for the benefits which I have conferred upon you."

"I will," replied Wolfstein; "I will perform all that you require."

"Swear it!" exclaimed Ginotti.

"I swear."

Ginotti then abruptly quitted the apartment; the sound of his footsteps was heard descending the stairs; and, when they were no longer audible, a weight seemed to have been taken from the breast of Wolfstein.

"How did that man save your life?" inquired Megalena.

"He was one of our band," replied Wolfstein, evasively; "and, on a plundering excursion, his pistol-ball entered the heart of the man, whose sabre, lifted aloft, would else have severed my head from my body."

"Dear Wolfstein, who are you?—whence came you?—for you were not always an Alpine bandit?"

"That is true, my adored one; but fate presents an insuperable barrier to my ever relating the events which occurred previously to my connexion with the banditti. Dearest Megalena, if you love me, never question me concerning my *past* life, but rest satisfied with the conviction, that my future existence shall be devoted to you, and to you alone." Megalena felt surprise; but, although eagerly desiring to unravel the mystery in which Wolfstein shrouded himself, desisted from inquiry.

Ginotti's mysterious visit had made too serious an impression on the mind of Wolfstein to be lightly erased. In vain he essayed to appear easy and unembarrassed, while he conversed with Megalena. He attempted to drown thought in wine—but in vain:—Ginotti's strange injunction pressed, like a load of ice, upon his breast. At last, the hour being late, they both retired to their respective rooms.

Early on the following morning, Wolfstein arose, to arrange the necessary preparations for their journey to Genoa; whither he had sent a servant whom he hired at Breno, to prepare accommodations for their arrival.—Needless were it minutely to describe each trivial event which occurred during their journey to Genoa.

On the morning of the fourth day, they found themselves within a short distance of the city. They determined on the plan they should adopt, and, in a short space of time, arriving at Genoa, took up their residence in a mansion on the outermost extremity of the city.

CHAPTER III

> Whence, and what art thou, execrable shape,
> That darest, though grim and terrible, advance
> Thy miscreated front athwart my way?
>
> PARADISE LOST.*

TIME passed; and, settled in their new habitation, Megalena and Wolfstein appeared to defy the arrows of vengeful destiny.

Wolfstein resolved to allow some time to elapse before he spoke of the subject nearest to his heart, of herself, to Megalena. One evening, however, overcome by the passion which, by mutual indulgence, had become resistless, he cast himself at her feet, and, avowing most unbounded love, demanded the promised return. A slight spark of virtue yet burned in the bosom of the wretched girl; she essayed to fly from temptation; but Wolfstein, seizing her hand, said, "And is my adored Megalena a victim then to prejudice? Does she believe, that the Being who created us gave us passions which never were to be satiated? Does she suppose that Nature created us to become the tormentors of each other?"

"Ah! Wolfstein," Megalena said tenderly, "rise!—You know too well the chain which unites me to you is indissoluble; you know that I must be thine; where, therefore, is there an appeal?"

"To thine own heart, Megalena; for, if my image implanted there is not sufficiently eloquent to confirm your hesitating soul, I would wish not for a casket that contains a jewel unworthy of my possession."

Megalena involuntarily started at the strength of his expression; she felt how completely she was his, and turned her eyes upon his countenance, to read in it the meaning of his words.—His eyes gleamed with excessive and confiding love.

"Yes," exclaimed Megalena, "yes, prejudice avaunt! once more reason takes her seat, and convinces me, that to be Wolfstein's is not criminal. O Wolfstein! if for a moment Megalena has yielded to the imbecility of nature, believe that she yet knows how to recover herself, to reappear in her proper character. Ere I knew you, a void in my heart, and a tasteless carelessness of those objects which now interest me, confessed your unseen empire; my heart longed for something which now it has attained. I scruple not, Wolfstein, to aver that it is you:—Be mine, then, and let our affection end not but with our existence!"

"Never, never shall it end!" enthusiastically exclaimed Wolfstein. "Never!—What can break the bond joined by congeniality of sentiment, cemented by an union of soul which must endure till the intellectual particles which compose it become annihilated? Oh! never shall it end; for when, convulsed by nature's latest ruin, sinks the fabric of this perishable globe; when the earth is dissolved away, and the face of heaven is rolled from before our eyes like a scroll; then will we seek each other, and, in eternal, indivisible, although immaterial union, shall we exist to all eternity."

Yet the love with which Wolfstein regarded Megalena, notwithstanding the strength of his expressions, though fervent and excessive, at first, was not of that nature which was likely to remain throughout existence; it was like the blaze of the meteor at midnight, which glares amid the darkness for awhile, and then expires; yet did he love her now; at least if heated admiration of her person and accomplishments, independently of mind, be love.

* * * * * *

Blessed in mutual affection, if so it may be called, the time passed swift to Wolfstein and Megalena. No incident worthy of narration occurred to disturb the uninterrupted tenour of their existence. Tired, at last, even with delight, which had become monotonous from long continuance, they began to frequent the public places. It was one evening, nearly a month subsequent to their first residence at Genoa, that they went to a party at the Duca di Thice. It was there that he beheld the gaze of one of the crowd fixed upon him. Indefinable to himself were the emotions which shook him; in vain he turned to every part of the saloon to avoid the scrutiny of the stranger's gaze; he was not able to give formation, in his own mind, to the ideas which struck him; they were acknowledged, however, in his heart, by sensations awful, and not to be described. He knew that he had before seen the features of the stranger; but he had forgotten Ginotti; for it was Ginotti—from whose scrutinizing glance Wolfstein turned appalled;—it was

Ginotti, of whose strangely and fearfully gleaming eyeball Wolfstein endeavoured to evade the fascination in vain. His eyes, resistlessly attracted to the sphere of chill horror that played around Ginotti's glance, in vain were fixed on vacuity; in vain attempted to notice other objects. Complaining to Megalena of sudden and violent indisposition, Wolfstein with her retired, and they quickly reached the steps of their mansion. Arrived there, Megalena tenderly inquired the cause of Wolfstein's illness, but his vague answers, and unconnected exclamations, soon led her to suppose it was not corporeal. She entreated him to acquaint her with the reason of his indisposition; Wolfstein, however, wishing to conceal from Megalena the true cause of his emotions, evasively told her that he had felt excessively faint from the heat of the assembly; she well knew, by his manner, that he had not told her truth, but affected to be satisfied, resolving, at some future period, to develope the mystery with which he evidently was environed. Retired to rest, Wolfstein's mind, torn by contending paroxysms of passion, admitted not of sleep; he ruminated on the mysterious reappearance of Ginotti; and the more he reflected, the more did the result of his reflections lead him astray. The strange gaze of Ginotti, and the consciousness that he was completely in the power of so indefinable a being; the consciousness that, wheresoever he might go, Ginotti would still follow him, pressed upon Wolfstein's heart. Ignorant of what connexion they could have with this mysterious observer of his actions, his crimes recurred in hideous and disgustful array to the bewildered mind of Wolfstein; he reflected, that, although now exulting in youthful health and vigour, the time would come, the dreadful day of retribution, when endless damnation would yawn beneath his feet, and he would shrink from eternal punishment before the tribunal of that God whom he had insulted. To evade death, unconscious why, became an idea on which he dwelt with earnestness; he thought on it for a time, and being mournfully convinced of its impossibility, strove to change the tenour of his reflections.

While these thoughts dwelt in his mind, sleep crept imperceptibly over his senses; yet, in his visions, was Ginotti present. He dreamed that he stood on the brink of a frightful precipice, at whose base, with deafening and terrific roar, the waves of the ocean dashed; that, above his head, the blue glare of the lightning dispelled the obscurity of midnight, and the loud crashing of the thunder was rolled franticly from rock to rock; that, along the cliff on which he stood, a figure, more frightful than the imagination of man is capable of portraying, advanced towards him, and was about to precipitate him headlong from the summit of the rock whereon he stood, when Ginotti advanced, and rescued him from the grasp of the monster; that no sooner had he done this, than the figure dashed Ginotti from the precipice—his last groans were borne on the blast which swept the bosom of the ocean. Confused visions then obliterated the impressions of the former, and he rose in the morning restless and unrefreshed.

A weight which his utmost efforts could not remove, pressed upon the bosom of Wolfstein; his mind, superior and towering as it was, found all its energies inefficient to conquer it. As a last resource, therefore, this wretched victim of vice and folly sought the gaming-table; a scene which alone could raise the spirits of one who required something important, even in his pastimes, to interest him. He staked large sums; and, although he concealed his haunts from Megalena, she soon discovered them. For a time, fortune smiled; till one evening he entered his mansion, desperate from ill luck, and, accusing his own hapless destiny, could no longer conceal the truth from Megalena. She reproved him mildly, and her tenderness had such an effect on Wolfstein that he burst into tears, and promised her that never again would he yield to the vicious influence of folly.

The rapid days rolled on, and each one brought the conviction to Wolfstein more strongly, that Megalena was not the celestial model of perfection which his warm imagination had portrayed; he began to find in her, not the exhaustless mine of interesting converse which he had once supposed. Possession, which, when unassisted by real, intellectual love, clogs man, increases the ardent, uncontrollable passions of woman even to madness. Megalena yet adored Wolfstein with most fervent love:—although yet greatly attached to Megalena, although he would have been uneasy were she another's, Wolfstein no longer regarded her with that idolatrous affection which had filled his bosom towards her. Feelings of this nature naturally drove Wolfstein occasionally from home to seek for employment—and what employment, save gaming, could Genoa afford to Wolfstein?—In what other occupation was it possible that he could engage? It was done: he broke his promise to Megalena, and became even a more devoted votary to gambling than before.

How powerful are the attractions of delusive vice! Wolfstein soon staked large sums—larger even than ever. With what anxiety did he watch the dice!—How were his eyeballs strained with mingled anticipation of wealth and poverty! Now fortune smiled; yet he concealed even his good luck from Megalena. At length the tide changed again: he lost immense sums; and desperate from a series of ill success, cursed his hapless destiny, and with wildest emotions rushed into the street. Again he solemnly swore to Megalena, that never more would he risk their mutual happiness by his folly.

Still, hurried away by the impulse of a burning desire of interesting his deadened feelings, did Wolfstein, false to his promise, seek the gaming-table; he had staked an enormous amount; and the fatal throw was at this instant about to decide the fate of the unhappy Wolfstein.

A pause, as if some dreadful event were about to occur, ensued; each gazed upon the countenance of Wolfstein, which, desperate from danger, retained, however, an expressive firmness.

A stranger stood before Wolfstein on the opposite side of the table. He appeared to have no interest in what was going forward, but, with unmoved gaze, fixed his eyes upon his countenance.

Wolfstein felt an instinctive shuddering thrill through his frame, when, oh horrible confirmation of his wildest apprehensions! it was —Ginotti!—the terrible, the mysterious Ginotti, whose dire scrutiny, resting upon Wolfstein, chilled his soul with excessive affright.

A sensation of extreme and conflicting emotions shook the inmost recesses of Wolfstein's heart; for an instant his brain swam around in wildest commotion, yet he steeled his resolution, even to the horrors of hell and destruction; he gazed on the mysterious scrutineer who stood before him, and, regardless of the sum he had staked, and which before had engaged his whole attention, and excited his liveliest interest, dashed the box convulsively upon the table, and followed Ginotti, who was about to quit the apartment, resolving to clear up a fatality which hung around him, and appeared to blast his prospects; for of the misfortunes which had succeeded his association with the bandits, he had not the slightest doubt in his own mind, that Ginotti was the cause.

With reflections a scene of the wildest anarchy, Wolfstein resolved to unravel the mystery in which he saw Ginotti was shrouded; and resolved, therefore, to devote that night towards finding out his abode. With feelings such as these, he rushed into the street, and followed the gigantic form of Ginotti, who stalked onwards majestically, as if conscious of safety, and wholly ignorant of the eager scrutiny with which Wolfstein watched his every movement.

It was midnight—yet they continued to advance; a feeling of desperation urged Wolfstein onwards; he resolved to follow Ginotti, even to the extremity of the universe. They passed through many bye and narrow streets; the darkness was complete; but the rays of the lamps, as they fell upon the lofty form of Ginotti, guided the footsteps of Wolfstein.

They had reached the end of the Strada Nuova; the lengthened sound of Ginotti's footsteps was all that struck upon Wolfstein's ear. On a sudden, Ginotti's figure disappeared from Wolfstein's gaze; in vain he looked around him, in vain he searched every recess, wherein he might have secreted himself—Ginotti was gone!

To describe the surprise mingled with awe, which possessed Wolfstein's bosom, is impossible. In vain he searched every part. He proceeded to the bridge; a party of fishermen were waiting there; he inquired of them, had they seen a man of superior stature pass? they appeared surprised at his question and unanimously answered in the negative. While varying emotions tumultuously contended within his bosom, Wolfstein, ever the victim of extraordinary events, paused awhile, revolving the mystery both of Ginotti's appearance and disappearance. That business of an important nature led him to Genoa, he doubted not; his indifference at the gaming-table, his particular regard of Wolfstein, left, in the mind of the latter, no doubt, but that he took a terrible and mysterious interest in whatever related to him.

All now was silent. The inhabitants of Genoa lay wrapped in sleep, and, save the occasional conversation of the fishermen who had just returned, no sound broke on the uninterrupted stillness, and thick clouds obscured the star-beams of heaven.

Again Wolfstein searched that part of the city which lay near Strada Nuova; but no one had seen Ginotti; although all wondered at the wild expressions and disordered mien of Wolfstein. The bell tolled the hour of three ere Wolfstein relinquished his pursuit; finding, however, further inquiry fruitless, he engaged a chair to take him to his habitation, where he doubted not that Megalena anxiously awaited his return.

Proceeding along the streets, the obscurity of the night was not so great but that he observed the figure of one of the chairmen to be above that of common men, and that he had drawn his hat forwards to conceal his countenance. His appearance, however, excited no remark; for Wolfstein was too much absorbed in the idea which related individually to himself, to notice what, perhaps, at another time, might have excited wonder. The wind sighed moaningly along the stilly colonnades, and the grey light of morning began to appear above the eastern eminences.

They entered the street which soon led to the abode of Wolfstein, who fixed his eyes upon the chairman. His gigantic proportions struck him with involuntary awe: such is the unaccountable connexion of idea in the mind of man. He shuddered. Such a man, thought he, is Ginotti: such a man is he who watches my every action, whose power I feel within myself is resistless, and not to be evaded. He sighed deeply when he reflected on the terrible connexion, dreadful although mysterious, which subsisted between himself and Ginotti. His soul sank within him at the idea of his own littleness, when a fellow-mortal might be able to gain so strong, though sightless, an empire over him. He felt that he was no longer independent. Whilst these thoughts agitated his mind, the chair had stopped at his habitation. He turned round to discharge the chairman's fare, when, casting his eyes on his countenance, which hitherto had remained concealed, oh horrible and chilling conviction! he recognized in his dark features those of the terrific Ginotti. As if hell had yawned at the feet of the hapless Wolfstein, as if some spectre of the night had blasted his straining eyeball, so did he stand transfixed. His soul shrank with mingled awe and abhorrence from a being who, even to himself, was confessedly superior to the proud and haughty Wolfstein. Ere well he could calm his faculties, agitated by so unexpected an interview, Ginotti said,

"Wolfstein! long have I known you; long have I marked you as the only man who now exists, worthy, and appreciating the value of what I have in store for you. Inscrutable are my intentions; seek not, therefore, to develope them: time will do it in a far more complete manner. You shall not now know the motive for my, to you, unaccountable actions: strive not, therefore, to unravel them. You may frequently see me: never attempt to speak or follow; for, if you do——" Here the eyes of Ginotti flashed with coruscations of inexpressible fire, and his every feature became animated by the tortures which he was about to describe; but he suddenly checked himself, and only added; "Attend to these my directions, but try, if possible, to forget me. I am not what I seem. The time may come, *will* most probably arrive, when I shall appear in my real character to you. You, Wolfstein, have I singled out from the whole world to make the depositary——" He ceased, and abruptly quitted the spot.

CHAPTER IV

—Nature shrinks back
Enhorror'd from the lurid gaze of vengeance,
E'en in the deepest caverns, and the voice
Of all her works lies hush'd.

OLYMPIA.

ON Wolfstein's return to his habitation, he found Megalena in anxious expectation of his arrival. She feared that some misfortune had befallen him. Wolfstein related to her the events of the preceding night; they appeared to her mysterious and inexplicable; nor could she offer any consolation to the wretched Wolfstein.

The occurrences of the preceding evening left a load upon his breast, which all the gaieties of Genoa were insufficient to dispel: eagerly he longed for the visit of Ginotti. Slow dragged the hours: each day did he expect it, and each succeeding day brought but disappointment to his expectations.

Megalena too, the beautiful, the adored Megalena, was no longer what formerly she was, the innocent girl hanging on his support, and depending wholly upon him for defence and protection; no longer, with mild and love-beaming eyes, she regarded the haughty Wolfstein as a superior being, whose look or slightest word was sufficient to decide her on any disputed point. No; dissipated pleasures had changed the former mild and innocent Megalena. Far, far different was she than when she threw herself into his arms on their escape from the cavern, and, with a blush, smiled upon the first declaration of Wolfstein's affection.

Now, immersed in a succession of gay pleasures, Megalena was no longer the gentle interesting she, whose soul of sensibility* would tremble if a worm beneath her feet expired; whose heart would sink within her at the tale of other's woe. She had become a fashionable belle, and forgot, in her new character, the fascinations of her old one. Still, however, was she ardently, solely, and resistlessly attached to Wolfstein: his image was implanted in her soul, never to be effaced by casualty, never erased by time. No coolness apparently took place between them; but, although unperceived and unacknowledged by each, an indifference evidently did exist between them. Among the various families whom their residence in Genoa had rendered familiar to Wolfstein and Megalena, none were more so than that of il Conte della Anzasca; it consisted of himself, la Contessa, and a daughter of exquisite loveliness, named Olympia.

This girl, mistress of every fascinating accomplishment, uniting in herself to great brilliancy and playfulness of wit, a person alluring beyond description, was in her eighteenth year. From habitual indulgence, her passions, naturally violent and excessive, had become irresistible; and when once she had fixed a determination in her mind, that determination must either be effected, or she must cease to exist. Such, then, was the beautiful Olympia, and as such she conceived a violent and unconquerable passion for Wolfstein. His towering and majestic form, his expressive and regular features, beaming with somewhat of softness; yet pregnant with a look as if woe had beat to the earth a mind whose native and unconfined energies aspired to heaven—all, all told her, that, without him, she must either cease to be, or drag on a life of endless and irremediable woe. Nourished by restless imagination, her passion soon attained a most unbridled height: instead of conquering a feeling which honour, generosity, virtue, all forbade ever to be gratified, she gloried within herself at having found one on whom she might with justice fix her burning attachment; for although the object of them had never before been present to her mind, the desires for that object, although unseen, had taken root long, long ago. A false system of education, and a wrong expansion of ideas, as they became formed, had been put in practice with respect to her youthful mind; and indulgence strengthened the passions which it behoved restraint to keep within proper bounds, and which might have unfolded themselves as coadjutors of virtue, and not as promoters of vicious and illicit love. Fiercer, nevertheless, in proportion as greater obstacles appeared in the prosecution of her resolve, flamed the passion of the devoted Olympia. Her brain was whirled round in the fiercest convulsions of expectant happiness; the anticipation of gratified voluptuousness swelled her bosom even to bursting, yet did she rein in the boiling emotions of her soul, and resolved to be sufficiently cool, more certainly to accomplish her purpose.

It was one night when Wolfstein's mansion was the scene of gaiety, that this idea first suggested itself to the mind of Olympia, and unfolded itself to her, as it really was love for Wolfstein. In vain the suggestions of generosity, the voice of conscience, which told her how doubly wicked would be the attempt of alienating from her the lover of her friend Megalena, in audible, though noiseless, accents spoke; in vain the native modesty of her sex represented in its real and hideous colours what she was about to do: still Olympia was resolved.

That night, in the solitude of her own chamber, in the palazzo of her father, she retraced in her mind the various events which had led to her present uncontrollable passion, which had employed her whole thoughts, and rendered her, as it were, dead to every other outward existence. The wild transports of maddening desire raved terrific within her breast: she endeavoured to smother the ideas which presented themselves; but the more she strove to erase them from her mind, the more vividly were they represented in her heated and enthusiastic imagination. "And will he not return my love?" she exclaimed: "will he not?—ah! a bravo's dagger shall pierce his heart, and thus will I reward him for his contempt of Olympia della Anzasca. But no! it is impossible. I will cast myself at his feet; I will avow to him the passion which consumes me,—will swear to be ever, ever his! Can he then cast me from him? Can he despise a woman whose only fault is love, nay, idolatry, adoration for him?"

She paused.—The tumultuous passions of her soul were now too fierce for utterance—too fierce for concealment or restraint. The hour was late; the moon poured its mildly-lustrous beams upon the lengthened colonnades of Genoa, when Olympia, overcome by emotions such as these, quitted her father's palazzo, and hastened, with rapid and unequal footsteps, towards the mansion of Wolfstein. The streets were by no means crowded; but those who yet lingered in them gazed with slight surprise on the figure of Olympia, which, light and symmetrical as a celestial sylphid, passed swiftly onwards.

She soon arrived at the habitation of Wolfstein, and sent the domestic to announce that one wished to speak with him, whose business was pressing and secret. She was conducted into an apartment, and there awaited the arrival of Wolfstein. A confused expression of awe played upon his features as he entered; but it suddenly gave place to that of surprise. He started upon perceiving Olympia, and said,

"To what, Lady Olympia, do I owe the unforeseen pleasure of your visit? What so mysterious business have you with me?" continued he playfully. "But come, we had just sat down to supper; Megalena is within."——"Oh! if you wish to see me expire in horrible torments at your feet, inhuman Wolfstein, call for Megalena! and then will your purpose be accomplished."—"Dearest Lady Olympia, compose yourself, I beseech you," said Wolfstein; "what, what agitates you?"—"Oh! pardon, pardon me," she exclaimed, with maniac wildness: "pardon a wretched female who knows not what she does! Oh! resistlessly am I impelled to this avowal: resistlessly am I impelled to declare to you, that I love you! adore you to distraction!—Will you return my affection? But ah! I rave! Megalena, the beloved Megalena, claims you as her own; and the wretched Olympia must moan the blighted prospects which were about to open fair before her eyes."

"For Heaven's sake, dear lady, compose yourself; recollect who you are; recollect the loftiness of birth and loveliness of form which are so eminently yours. This, this is far beneath Olympia."

"Oh!" she exclaimed, franticly casting herself at his feet, and bursting into a passion of tears, "what are birth, fame, fortune, and all the advantages which are casually given to me! I swear to thee, Wolfstein, that I would sacrifice not only these, but even all my hopes of future salvation, even the forgiveness of my Creator, were it required from me. O Wolfstein, kind, pitying Wolfstein, look down with an eye of indulgence on a female whose only crime is resistless, unquenchable adoration of you."*

She panted for breath, her pulses beat with violence, her eyes swam, and, overcome by the conflicting passions of her soul, the frame of Olympia fell, sickening with faintness, on the ground. Wolfstein raised her, and tenderly essayed to recall the senses of the hapless girl. Recovering, and perceiving her situation, Olympia started, seemingly horrified, from the arms of Wolfstein. The energies of her high mind instantly resumed their functions, and she exclaimed, "Then, base and ungrateful Wolfstein, you refuse to unite your fate with mine? My love is ardent and excessive, but the revenge which may follow the despiser of it is far more impetuous; reflect well then ere you drive Olympia della Anzasca to despair."—"No reflection, in the present instance, is needed, lady," replied Wolfstein, coolly, yet determinedly. "What man of honour needs a moment's rumination to discover what nature has so inerasibly implanted in his bosom—the sense of right and wrong? I am connected with a female whom I love, who confides in me; in what manner should I merit her confidence, if I join myself to another? nor can the loveliness, the exquisite, the unequalled loveliness of the beautiful Olympia della Anzasca compensate me for breaking an oath sworn to another."

He paused.—Olympia spake not, but appeared to be awaiting the dreadful fiat of her destiny.

"Olympia," Wolfstein continued, "pardon me! Were I not irrevocably Megalena's, I must be thine: I esteem you, I admire you, but my love is another's."

The passion which before had choked Olympia's utterance, appeared to give way to the impetuousness of her emotions.

"Then," she said, as a solemnity of despair toned her voice to firmness, "then you are irrevocably another's?"

"I am compelled to be explicit; I am compelled to say, I am another's for ever!" fervently returned Wolfstein.

Again fainting from the excess of painful feeling which vibrated through her frame, Olympia fell at Wolfstein's feet: again he raised her, and, in anxious solicitude, watched her varying countenance. At the critical instant when Olympia had just recovered from the faintness which had oppressed her, the door burst open, and disclosed to the view of the passion-grieving Olympia, the detested form of Megalena. A silence, resembling that when a solemn pause in the midnight-tempest announces that the elements only hesitate to collect more terrific force for the ensuing explosion, took place, while Megalena surveyed Olympia and

Wolfstein. Still she spoke not; yet the silence, even more terrible than the commotion which followed, continued to prevail. Olympia dashed by Megalena, and faintly articulating "Vengeance!" rushed into the street, and bent her rapid flight to the Palazzo di Anzasca.

"Wolfstein," said Megalena, her voice quivering with excessive emotion, "Wolfstein, how have I deserved this? How have I deserved a dereliction so barbarous and unprovoked? But no!" she added in a firmer tone, "no, I will leave you! I will show that I can bear the tortures of disappointed love, better than you can evade the scrutiny of one who did adore thee."

In vain Wolfstein put in practice every soothing art to tranquillize the agitation of Megalena. Her frame trembled with violent shuddering; yet her soul, as it were, superior to the form which enshrined it, loftily towered, and retained its firmness amidst the frightful chaos which battled within.

"Now," said she to Wolfstein, "I will leave you."

"O God! Megalena, dearest, adored Megalena!" exclaimed Wolfstein, passionately, "stop—I love you, must ever love you: deign, at least, to hear me."—"What good would accrue from that?" gloomily inquired Megalena.

Wolfstein rushed towards her; he threw himself at her feet and exclaimed, "If ever, for one instant, my soul was alienated from thee—if ever it swerved from the affection which I have sworn to thee—may the red right hand of God instantaneously dash me beneath the lowest abyss of hell! O Megalena! is it as a victim of groundless jealousy that I have immolated myself at the altar of thy perfections? Have I only raised myself to this summit of happiness to feel more deeply the fall of which thou art the cause? O Megalena! if yet one spark of thy former love lingers in thy breast, oh! believe one who swears that he must be thine even till the particles which compose the soul devoted to thee, become annihilated."—He paused.

Megalena heard his wildly enthusiastic expressions in sullen silence. She looked upon him with a stern and severe gaze:—he yet lay at her feet, and, hiding his face upon the earth, groaned deeply. "What proof," exclaimed Megalena, impatiently, "what proof will Wolfstein, the deceiver, bring to satisfy me that his love is still mine?"

"Seek for proof in my heart," returned Wolfstein, "that heart which yet is bleeding from the thorns which thou, cruel girl, hast implanted in it: seek it in my every action, and then will the convinced Megalena know that Wolfstein is hers irrevocably—body and soul, for ever!"

"Yet, I believe thee not!" said Megalena: "for the haughty Olympia della Anzasca would scarcely recline in the arms of a man who was not entirely devoted to her."

Yet were the charms of Megalena unfaded; yet their empire over Wolfstein excessive and complete.

"Still I believe thee not," continued she, as a smile of expectant malice sat upon her cheek. "I require some proof which will assuredly convince me that I am yet beloved: give me proof, and Megalena will again be Wolfstein's."—"Oh!" said Wolfstein, mournfully, "what farther proof can I give, but my oath, that never in soul or body have I broken the allegiance that I formerly swore to thee?"

"The death of Olympia!" gloomily returned Megalena.

"What mean you?" said Wolfstein, starting.

"I mean," continued Megalena, collectedly, as if what she was about to utter had been the result of serious cogitation: "I mean that, if ever you wish again to possess my affections, ere to-morrow morning, Olympia must expire!"

"Murder the innocent Olympia?"

"Yes!"

A pause ensued, during which the mind of Wolfstein, torn by ten thousand warring emotions, knew not on what to resolve. He gazed upon Megalena: her symmetrical form shone with tenfold loveliness to his enraptured imagination: again he resolved to behold those eyes beam with affection for him, which were now gloomily fixed upon the ground. "Will nothing else convince Megalena that Wolfstein is eternally hers?"

"Nothing."

"'Tis done, then," exclaimed Wolfstein, "'tis done. Yet," he muttered, "I may suffer for this premeditated act tortures now inconceivable; I may writhe, convulsed, in immaterial agony, for ever and for ever—ah! I cannot. No!" he continued, "Megalena, I am again yours; I will immolate the victim which thou requirest as a sacrifice to our love. Give me a dagger, which may sweep off from the face of the earth, one who is hateful to thee! Adored creature, give me the dagger, and I will restore it to thee dripping with Olympia's hated blood; it shall have first been buried in her heart."

"Then, then again art thou mine own! again art thou the idolized Wolfstein, whom I was wont to love!" said Megalena, enfolding him in her embrace. Perceiving her returning softness, Wolfstein essayed to induce her to spare him the frightful proof of the ardour of his attachment; but she started from his arms as he spoke, and exclaimed:

"Ah! base deceiver, do you hesitate?"

"Oh, no! I do not hesitate, dearest Megalena;—give me a dagger, and I go."

"Here, follow me then," returned Megalena. He followed her to the supper-room.

"It is useless to go yet, it has but yet struck one; the inhabitants of il Palazzo della Anzasca will, about two, be nearly all retired to rest; till then, let us converse on what we were about to do." So far did Megalena's seductive blandishment, her artful selection of converse, win upon Wolfstein, that, when the destined hour approached, his sanguinary soul thirsted for the blood of the comparatively innocent Olympia.

"Well!" he cried, swallowing down an overflowing goblet of wine, "now the time is come; now suffer me to go, and tear the soul of Olympia from her hated body." His fury amounted almost to delirium, as masked, and having a dagger, which Megalena had given him, concealed beneath his garments, he proceeded rapidly along the streets towards the Palazzo della Anzasca. So eager was he to shed the life-blood of Olympia, that he flew, rather than ran, along the silent streets of Genoa. The colonnades of the lofty Palazzo della Anzasca resounded to his rapid footsteps; he stopped at its lofty portal:—it was open; unperceived he entered, and, hiding himself behind a column, according to the directions of Megalena, waited there. Soon advancing through the hall, he saw the sylph-like figure of the lovely Olympia; with silent tread he followed it, experiencing not the slightest sentiment of remorse within his bosom for the deed which he was about to perpetrate. He followed her to her apartment, and secreting himself until Olympia might have sunk into sleep, with sanguinary and remorseless patience, when her loud breathing convinced him that her slumber was profound, he arose from his place of concealment, and advanced to the bed, wherein Olympia lay. Her light tresses, disengaged from the band which had confined them, floated around a countenance, superhumanly beautiful, and whose expression, even in slumber, appeared to be tinted by Wolfstein's refusal; convulsive sighs heaved her fair bosom, and tears, starting from under her eyelids, fell profusely down her damask cheek. Wolfstein gazed upon her in silence. "Cruel, inhuman Megalena!" he mentally soliloquized, "could nothing but immolation of this innocence appease thee?" Again he stifled the stings of rebelling conscience; again the unquenchable ardour of his love for Megalena stimulated him to the wildest pitch of fury: he raised high the dagger, and, drawing aside the covering which veiled her alabaster bosom, paused an instant, to decide in what place it were most instantaneously destructive to strike. Again a mournful smile irradiated her lovely features; it played with a sweet softness on her countenance: it seemed as though she smiled in defiance of the arrows of destiny, but that her soul, nevertheless, lingered witht* he wretch who sought her life. Maddened by the sight of so much beauteous innocence, even the desperate Wolfstein, forgetful of the danger which he must thereby incur, hurled the dagger from him. The sound awakened Olympia: she started up in surprise; but her alarm was changed into ecstasy, when she beheld the idolized possessor of her soul standing before her.

"I was dreaming of you," said Olympia, scarcely knowing whether this were not a dream; but, impulsively following the first emotions of her soul. "I dreamed that you were about to murder me. It is not so, Wolfstein, no! you would not murder one who adores you?"

"Murder Olympia! O God! no!—I take Heaven to witness, that I never *now* could do it!"

"Nor could you ever, I hope, dear Wolfstein; but drive away thoughts like these, and remember that Olympia lives but for thee; and the moment which takes from her your affections seals the death-like fiat of her destiny." These asseverations, strengthened by the most solemn and deadly vows that he would return to Megalena the destroyer of Olympia, flashed across Wolfstein's mind. Perpetrate the deed, now, he could not; his soul became a scene of most terrific agony. "Wilt thou be mine?" exclaimed the enraptured Olympia, as a ray of hope arose in her mind. "Never! never can I," groaned the agitated Wolfstein; "I am irrevocably, indissolubly another's." Maddened by this death-blow to all expectations of happiness, which the deluded Olympia had so fondly anticipated, she leaped wildly from the bed. A light and flowing night-dress alone veiled her form, her alabaster bosom was shaded by the light ringlets of her hair which rested unconfined upon it. She threw herself at the feet of Wolfstein. On a sudden, as if struck by some thought, she started convulsively from the earth: for an instant she paused.

The rays of a lamp, which stood in a recess of the apartment, fell full upon the dagger of Wolfstein. Eagerly Olympia sprung towards it; and, ere Wolfstein was aware of her dreadful intent, plunged it into her bosom. Weltering in purple gore, she fell; no groan, no sigh escaped her lips. A smile, which the pangs of dissolution could not dispel, played on her convulsed countenance; it irradiated her features with celestially awful, although terrific expression. "Ineffectually have I endeavoured to conquer the ardent feelings of my soul; now I overcome them," were her last words. She uttered them in a tone of firmness, and, falling back, expired in torments, which her fine, her expressive features declared that she gloried in.

All was silent in the chamber of death: the stillness was frightful. The agonies which Wolfstein endured were past description: for a time he neither moved nor spoke. The pale glare of the lamp fell upon the features of Olympia, from which the tinge of life had fled for ever. Suddenly, and in despite of himself, were the affections of Wolfstein turned from Megalena: he could not but now regard her as a fiend, who had been the cause of Olympia's destruction; who had urged him to a deed from which his nature now shrunk as from annihilation. A wild paroxysm of awful alarm seized upon him: he knelt by the side of Olympia's corpse; he kissed it, bathed it with his tears, and imprecated a thousand curses on himself. Her features, although convulsed by the agonies of violent dissolution, retained an unchanging image of loveliness, which never might fade away. Her beautiful bosom, in which her hand yet held the fatal dagger, was discoloured with blood, and those affection-beaming orbs were now closed in the never-ending slumber of the grave. Unable longer to endure a sight of so much horror, Wolfstein started up, and, forgetful of everything save the frightful deed which he had witnessed, rushed from the Palazzo della Anzasca, and mechanically retraced his way towards his own habitation.

Not once that night had Megalena closed her eyes. Her infuriate passions had wound her soul up to a deadly calmness of expectation. She had not, during the whole of the night, retired to rest, but sat, with sanguinary patience, cursing the lagging hours that they passed so slowly, and waiting to hear tidings of death. Morning had begun to streak the eastern sky with gray, when Wolfstein hurried into the supper-room, where Megalena still sat, wildly exclaiming, "The deed is done!" Megalena entreated him to be calm, and, more collectedly, to communicate the events which had occurred during the night.

"In the first place," he said in an accent of feigned horror, "the officers of justice are alarmed!"

Deadly affright chilled the soul of Megalena: she turned pale, and, gasping for breath, inquired eagerly respecting the success of his attempt.

"O God!" exclaimed Wolfstein, "that has succeeded but too well! the hapless Olympia welters in her life-blood!"

"Joy! joy!" franticly exclaimed Megalena, her eagerness for revenge overcoming, for the moment, every other feeling.

"But, Megalena," continued Wolfstein, "she fell not by my hand: no, she smiled on me in her sleep, and when she awoke, finding me deaf to her solicitations, snatched my dagger, and buried it in her bosom."

"Did you *wish* to prevent the deed?" inquired Megalena.

"Oh, good God of Heaven! thou knowest my heart: I would sacrifice every remaining earthly good were Olympia again alive!"

Megalena spoke not, but a smile of exquisitely gratified malice illumined her features with terrific flame.

"We must instantly quit Genoa," said Wolfstein: "the name on the mask which I left in the Palazzo della Anzasca, will remove all doubt that I was the murderer of Olympia. Yet indeed I care not much for death; if you will it so, Megalena, we will even, as it is, remain in Genoa."

"Oh! no, no!" eagerly cried Megalena: "Wolfstein, I love you beyond expression, and Genoa is destruction: let us seek, therefore, some retired spot, where we may for awhile at least secrete ourselves. But, Wolfstein, are you persuaded that I love you? need there more proof be required than that I wished the death of another for thee? it was on *that* account alone that I desired the destruction of Olympia, that thou mightest be more completely and irresistibly mine."

Wolfstein answered not: the feelings of his soul were far different; the expression of his countenance plainly evinced them: and Megalena regretted that her effervescent passions should have led her to so rash an avowal of her contempt of virtue. They then separated to arrange their affairs, prior to their departure, which, on account of the pressing necessity of the case, must take place immediately. They took with them but two domestics, and, collecting all their stock of money, they were soon far from pursuit and Genoa.

CHAPTER VII *

Yes! 'tis the influence of that sightless fiend,
Who guides my every footstep, that I feel:
An iron grasp arrests each fluttering sense,
And a fell voice howls in mine anguish'd ear,
"Wretch, thou mayest rest no more."

OLYMPIA.

How sweet are the scenes endeared to us by ideas which we have cherished in the society of one we have loved! How melancholy to wander amongst them again after an absence, perhaps of years; years, which have changed the tenour of our existence,—have changed even the friend, the dear friend, for whose sake alone the landscape lives in the memory, for whose sake tears flow at the each varying feature of the scenery, which catches the eye of one who has never seen them since he saw them with the being who was dear to him!

Dark, autumnal, and gloomy was the hour; the winds whistled hollow, and over the expanse of heaven was spread an unvarying sombreness of vapour: nothing was heard save the melancholy shriekings of the night-bird, which, soaring on the evening blast, broke the stillness of the scene, interrupting the meditations of frenzied enthusiasm; mingled with the sighing of the wind, which swept in languid and varying cadence amidst the leafless boughs.

Ah! of whom shall the poor outcast wanderer demand protection? Far, far, has she wandered. The vice and unkindness of the world hath torn her tender heart. In whose bosom shall she repose the secret of her sufferings? Who will listen with pity to the narrative of her woe, and heal the wounds which the selfish unkindness of man hath made, and then sent her with them, unbound, on the wide and pitiless world? Lives there one whose confidence the sufferer might seek?

Cold and dreary was the night: November's blast had chilled the air. Is the blast so pitiless as ingratitude and selfishness? Ah, no! thought the wanderer; it is unkind indeed, but not *so* unkind as that. Poor Eloise de St. Irvyne! many, many are in thy situation; but few have a heart so full of sensibility and excellence for the demoniac malice of man to deform, and then glut itself with hellish pleasure in the conviction of having ravaged the most lovely of the works of their Creator. She gazed upon the sky: the moon had just risen; its full orb was occasionally shaded by a passing cloud: it rose from behind the turrets of le Château de St. Irvyne. The poor girl raised her eyes towards it, streaming with tears: she scarce could recognize the once-loved building. She thanked God for permitting her again to behold it; and hastened on with steps tottering from fatigue, yet nerved with the sanguineness of anticipation.

Yes, St. Irvyne was the same as when she had left it five years ago. The same ivy mantled the western tower; the same jasmine, which bloomed so luxuriantly when she left it, was still there, though leafless from the season.* Thus was it with poor Eloise: she had left St. Irvyne, blooming, and caressed by every one; she returned to it, pale, downcast, and friendless. The jasmine encircled the twisted pillars which supported the portal. Alas! whose assistance had prevented Eloise from sinking to the earth?—no one's. She knocked at the door—it was opened, and an instant's space beheld her in the arms of a beloved sister. Needless were it to describe the mutual pleasure, needless to describe the delight, of recognition; suffice it to say, that Eloise once more enjoyed the society of her dearest friend; and, in the happiness of her society, forgot the horrors which had preceded her return to St. Irvyne.

Now were it well to leave Eloise at St. Irvyne, and retrace the events which, since five years, had so darkly tinged the fate of the unsuspecting female, who trusted to the promises of man. It was a beautiful morning in May, and the loveliness of the season had spread a deeper shade of gloom over the features of Eloise, for she knew that not long would her mother live. They journeyed on towards Geneva, whither the physicians had ordered Madame de St. Irvyne to repair, as the last resort of a hope that she might, thereby, escape a rapid decline. On account of the illness of her mother, they proceeded slowly; and ere long they had entered the region of the Alps, the shades of evening, which rapidly began to increase, announced approaching night. They had expected, before this time, to have reached a town; but, either owing to a miscalculation of their route, or the remissness of the postillion, they had not yet done so. The majestic moon which hung above their heads, tinged with silver the fleecy clouds which skirted the far-seen horizon; and, borne on the soft wing of the evening zephyr, shadowy lines of vapour, at intervals, crossed her orbit; then vanishing into the dark blue expansiveness of ether, their fantastic forms, like the phantoms of midnight, became invisible. Now might we almost suppose, that the sightless spirits of the departed good, enthroned on the genial breeze of night, watched over those whom they had loved on earth, and poured into the bosom, to the dictates of which, in this world, they had listened with idolatrous attention, that tranquillity and confidence in the goodness of the Creator, which is necessary for us to experience ere we go to the next. Such tranquillity felt Madame de St. Irvyne: she tried to stifle the ideas which arose within her mind; but the more she strove to repress them, in the more vivid characters were they imprinted on the imagination.

Now had they gained the summit of the mountain, when, suddenly, a crash announced that the carriage had given way.

"What is to be done?" inquired Eloise The postillion appeared to take no notice of her question. "What is to be done?" again she inquired.

"Why, I scarcely know," answered the postillion; "but 'tis impossible to proceed."

"Is there no house nearer than——"

"Oh yes," replied he; "here is a house quite near, but a little out of the way; and, perhaps, Ma'am'selle will not——"

"Oh, lead on, lead on to it," quickly rejoined Eloise.

They followed the postillion, and soon arrived at the house. It was large and plain; and although there were lights in some of the windows, it bore an indefinable appearance of desolation.

In a large hall sat three or four men, whose marked countenances almost announced their profession to be bandits. *One* of superior and commanding figure, whispering to the rest, and himself advancing with the utmost and most unexpected politeness, accosted the travellers. For the ideas with which the countenance of this man inspired Eloise she in vain endeavoured to account. It appeared to her that she had seen him before; that the deep tone of his voice was known to her; and that eye, scintillating with a coruscation of mingled sternness and surprise, found some counterpart in herself. Of gigantic stature, yet formed in the mould of exactest symmetry, was the figure of the stranger who sate before Eloise. His countenance of excessive beauty even, but dark, emanated with an expression of superhuman loveliness; not that grace which may freely be admired, but acknowledged in the inmost soul by sensations mysterious, and before unexperienced. He tenderly inquired, whether the night air had injured the ladies, and pressed them to partake of a repast which the other three men had prepared; he appeared to unbend a severity, which evidently was habitual, and by extreme brilliancy and playfulness of wit, joined to talents for conversation possessed by few, made Madame de St. Irvyne forget that she was dying; and her daughter, as in rapturous attention she listened to each accent of the stranger, remembered no more that she was about to lose her mother.

In the stranger's society, they almost forgot the lapse of time: a pause in the conversation at last occurred.

"Can Ma'am'selle sing?" inquired the stranger.

"I can," replied Eloise; "and with pleasure."

Song

How swiftly through heaven's wide expanse
  Bright day's resplendent colours fade!
How sweetly does the moonbeam's glance
  With silver tint St. Irvyne's glade!

No cloud along the spangled air,
  Is borne upon the evening breeze;
How solemn is the scene! how fair
  The moonbeams rest upon the trees!

Yon dark gray turret glimmers white,
  Upon it sits the mournful owl;
Along the stillness of the night,
  Her melancholy shriekings roll.

But not alone on Irvyne's tower,
  The silver moonbeam pours her ray;
It gleams upon the ivied bower,
  It dances in the cascade's spray.

"Ah! why do darkening shades conceal
 The hour, when man must cease to be?*
Why may not human minds unveil
 The dim mists of futurity?

"The keenness of the world hath torn
 The heart which opens to its blast;
Despised, neglected, and forlorn,
 Sinks the wretch in death at last."

She ceased;—the thrilling accents of her interestingly sweet voice died away in the vacancy of stillness;—yet listened the charmed auditors; their imaginations prolonged the tender strain; the uncouth attendants of the stranger were chained in silence, and the enthusiastic gaze of their host was fixed upon the timid countenance of Eloise with wild and mysterious expression. It seemed to say to Eloise, "We meet again;"—and, as the idea struck her imagination, convulsed by a feeling of indescribable and excessive awe, she started.

At last, the hour being late, they all retired. Eloise sought the couch prepared for her; her mind, perturbed by emotions, the cause of which she in vain essayed to develope, could bring its intellectual energies to act on no one particular point; her imagination was fertile, and, under its fantastic guidance, she felt her judgment and reason irresistibly fettered. The image of the fascinating, yet awful stranger, dwelt on her mind. She sank on her knees to return thanks to her Creator for His mercies; yet even then, faithless to the task on which it was employed, her mind returned to the stranger. She felt no particular affection or esteem for him;—no, she rather feared him; and, when she endeavoured to connect the chain of ideas which pressed upon her mind, tears started into her eyes, and she looked around the apartment with the timid terror of a person who converses at midnight on a subject at once awful and interesting: but poor Eloise was no philosopher; and to explain sensations like these, were even beyond the power of the wisest of them. She felt alarmed, herself, at the violence of the feelings which shook her bosom, and attempted to compose herself to sleep. Yet even in her dream was the stranger present. She thought that she met him on a flowery plain; that the feelings of her bosom, whether she would or not, impelled her towards him; that, before she had been enfolded in his arms, a torrent of scintillating flame, accompanied by a terrific crash of thunder, made the earth yawn beneath her feet;—the gay vision vanished from her fancy, and, in place of the flowery plain, a rugged and desolate heath extended far before her; its monotonous solitude unbroken, save by the low and barren rocks which rose occasionally from its surface. From dreams such as these, dreams which left on her mind painful presentiments of her future life, Eloise arose, restless and unrefreshed from slumber.

Why gleams that dark eyeball upon the countenance of Eloise, as she tenderly inquired for the health of her mother? Why did a hidden expression of exulting joy light up that demoniac gaze, when Madame de St. Irvyne said to her daughter, "I feel rather faint to-day, my child;—would we were at Geneva!"—It beams with hell and destruction!—Let me look again: that, when I see another eye which gleams so fiendishly, I may know that it is a villain's.—Thus might have thought the sightless minister of the beneficence of God, as it hovered round the spotless Eloise. But, hush! what was that scream which was heard by the ear of listening enthusiasm? It was the shriek of the fair Eloise's better genius; it screamed to see the foe of the innocent girl so near—it is fled fast to Geneva. "There, Eloise, will we meet again," methought it whispered; whilst a low hollow tone, hoarse from the dank vapours of the grave, seemed lowly to howl in the ear of rapt Fancy, "We meet again likewise."

Their courteous host conducted Madame de St. Irvyne and Eloise to their chaise, which was now repaired, and ready for the journey; the stranger bowed respectfully as they went away. The expression of his dark eye, as he beheld them for the last time, was even stronger than ever; it seemed not to affect her mother; but the mystic feelings which it excited in the bosom of Eloise were beyond description powerful. The paleness of Madame de St. Irvyne's cheek, on which the only teint was an occasional and hectic flush, announced that the illness which consumed her, rapidly increased, and would soon lead her gently to the gates of death. She talked calmly of her approaching dissolution, and only regretted, that to no one protector could she entrust the care of her orphaned daughters. Marianne, her eldest daughter, had, by her mother's particular desire, remained at the château; and though much wishing to accompany her mother, she urged it no longer, when she knew Madame de St. Irvyne to be resolved against it. Now had the illness which had attacked her assumed so serious and so decided an appearance, that she could no longer doubt the event;—could no longer doubt that she was quickly about to enter a better world.

"My daughter," said she, "there is a banker at Geneva, a worthy man, to whom I shall bequeath the guardianship of my child; on that head are all my doubts quieted. But, Eloise, my child, you are yet young; you know not the world; but bear in mind these words of your dying mother, so long as you remember herself:—When you see a man enveloped in deceit and mystery; when you see him dark, reserved, and suspicious, carefully avoid him. Should such a man seek your friendship or affection, should he seek, by any means, to confer an obligation upon you, or make you confer one on him, spurn him from you as you would a serpent; as one who aimed to lure your unsuspecting innocence to the paths of destruction."

The affecting solemnity of her voice, as thus she spoke, touched Eloise deeply; she wept. "I must remember my mother for ever," was her almost inarticulate reply; deep sobs burst from her agitated bosom; and the varying crowds of imagery which followed each other in her mind, were too complicated to be defined. Still, though deeply grieved at the approaching death of her mother, was the mysterious stranger uppermost in her thoughts; his image excited ideas painful and unpleasant. She wished to turn the tide of them; but the more she attempted it, with the more painful recurrence of almost *mechanical* force, did his recollection press upon her disturbed intellect.

Eloise de St. Irvyne was a girl, whose temper and disposition was most excellent; she was, indeed, too, possessed of uncommon sensibility; yet was her mind moulded in an inferior degree of perfection. She was susceptible of prejudice, to a great degree; and resigned herself, careless of the consequences which might follow, to the feelings of the moment. Every accomplishment, it is true, she enjoyed in the highest excellence; and the very convent at which she was educated, which afforded the adventitious advantages so highly esteemed by the world, prevented her mind from obtaining that degree of expansiveness and excellence which, otherwise, might have rendered Eloise nearer approaching to perfection; the very routine of a convent education gave a false and pernicious bias to the ideas, as, luxuriant in youth, they unfolded themselves; and those sentiments which, had they been allowed to take the turn which nature intended, would have become coadjutors of virtue, and strengtheners of that mind, which now they had rendered *comparatively* imbecile. Such was Eloise, and as such she required unexampled care to prevent those feelings which agitate every mind of sensibility, to get the better of the judgment which had, by an erroneous system of education, become relaxed. Her mother was about to die—who now would care for Eloise?

They entered Geneva at the close of a fine, yet sultry day. The illness of Madame de St. Irvyne had increased so as now to threaten instant danger: she was conveyed to bed. A deadly paleness sat on her cheek: it was flushed, however, as she spoke, with momentary hectics; and, as she conversed with her daughter, a fire, which almost partook of ethereality, shone in her sunken eye. It was evening; the yellow beams of the sun, as his orb shed the parting glory on the verge of the horizon, penetrated the bed-curtains; and by their effulgence contrasted the deadliness of her countenance. The poor Eloise sat, watching, with eyes dimmed by tears, each variation in the countenance of her mother. Silent, from an ecstasy of grief, she gazed fixedly upon her, and felt every earthly hope die within her, when the conviction of a fast-approaching dissolution pressed upon her disturbed brain. Madame de St. Irvyne, at length exhausted, fell into a quiet slumber; Eloise feared to disturb her, but, motionless with grief, sate behind the curtain. Now had sunk the orb of day, and the shades of twilight began to scatter duskiness through the chamber of death. All was silent; and, save by the catchings of breath in her mother's slumber, the stillness was uninterrupted. Yet even in this awful, this terrific crisis of her existence, the mind of Eloise seemed compelled to exert its intellectual energies but on one subject;—in vain she essayed to pray;—in vain she attempted to avert the horror of her meditations, by contemplating the pallid features of her dying mother: her thoughts were not within her own control, and she trembled as she reflected on the appalling and mysterious influence which the image of a man, whom she had seen but once, and whom she neither loved nor cared for, had gained over her mind. With the indefinable terror of one who dreads to behold some phantom, Eloise fearfully cast her eyes around the gloomy apartment; occasionally she shrank from the ideal form which an unconnected imagination had conjured up, and could scarcely but suppose that the *stranger's* gaze, as last he had looked upon her, met her own with an horrible and mixed scintillation of mysterious cunning and interest. She felt no prepossession in his favour; she rather detested him, and gladly would never have again beheld him. Yet, were the circumstances which introduced him to their notice alluded to, she would turn pale, and blush, by turns; and Jeanette, their maid, was fully persuaded in her own mind, and prided herself on her penetration in the discovery, that Ma'am'selle was violently in love with the hospitable Alpine hunter.

Madame de St. Irvyne had now awakened; she beckoned her daughter to approach. Eloise obeyed; and, kneeling, kissed the chill hand of her mother, in a transport of sorrow, and bathed it with her tears.

"Eloise," said her mother, her voice trembling from excessive weakness, "Eloise, my child, farewell—farewell for ever. I feel I am about to die; but, before I die, willingly would I say much to my dearest daughter. You are now left on the hard-hearted, pitiless world; and perhaps, oh! perhaps, about to become an immolated victim of its treachery. Oh!——" Here, overcome by extreme pain, she fell backwards; a transient gleam of animation lighted up her expressive countenance; she smiled, and—expired. All was still; and over the gloomy chamber reigned silence and horror. The yellow moonbeam, with sepulchral effulgence, gleamed on the countenance of her who had expired, and lighted her features, sweet even in death, with a dire and horrible contrast to the dimness which prevailed around!—Ah! such was the contrast of the peace enjoyed by the spirit of the departed one, with the misery which awaited the wretched Eloise. Poor Eloise! she had now lost almost her only friend!

In excessive and silent grief, knelt the mourning girl; she spoke not, she wept not; her sorrow was too violent for tears, but, oh! her heart was torn by pangs of unspeakable acuteness. But even amid the alarm which so melancholy an event must have excited, the idea of the *stranger in the Alps* sublimed the soul of Eloise to the highest degree of horror, and despair the most infuriate. For the ideas which crowded into her mind at this crisis, so eventful, so terrific, she endeavoured to account; but, alas! her attempt was fruitless! Still knelt she; still did she press to her burning lips the lifeless hand of departed excellence, when the morning's ray announced to her that longer continuing there might excite suspicion of intellectual derangement. She arose, therefore, and, quitting the apartment, announced the melancholy event which had taken place. She gave orders for the funeral; it was to be solemnized as soon as decency would permit, as the poor friendless Eloise wished speedily to quit Geneva. She wrote to announce the fatal event to her sister. Slowly dragged the time. Eloise followed to its latest bed the corpse of her mother, and was returning from the convent, when a stranger put into her hand a note, and quickly disappeared:—

"Will Eloise de St. Irvyne meet her friend at —— Abbey, to-morrow night, at ten o'clock?"

CHAPTER VIII

——Why then unbidden gush'd the tear?
* * * * *
Then would cold shudderings seize his brain,
  As gasping he labour'd for breath;
The strange gaze of his meteor eye,
Which, frenzied, and rolling dreadfully,
  Glar'd with hideous gleam,
Would chill like the spectre gaze of Death,
  As, conjured by feverish dream,
He seems o'er the sick man's couch to stand,
And shakes the fell lance in his skeleton hand.*

WANDERING JEW.

YES;—they fled from Genoa; they had eluded pursuit and justice, but could not escape the torments of an outraged and avenging conscience, which, with stings the most acute, pursued them whithersoever they might go. Fortune even seemed to favour them: for fortune will, sometimes, in this world, appear to side with the wicked. Wolfstein had received notice that an uncle, possessed of immense wealth, had died in Bohemia, and bequeathed to him the whole of his estate. Thither, then, with Megalena, went Wolfstein. Their journey produced no event of consequence; suffice it to say, that they arrived at the spot where Wolfstein's possessions were situated.

Dark and desolate were the scenes which surrounded the no less desolate castle. Gloomy heaths, in unvarying sadness of immensity, stretched far and wide. A scathed pine or oak, blasted by the thunderbolts of heaven, alone broke the monotonous sameness of the imagery. Needless were it to describe the castle, built like all those of the Bohemian barons, in mingled Gothic and barbarian architecture. Over the dark expanse the dim moon beaming, and faintly, with its sepulchral radiance, dispersing the thickness of the vapours which lowered around (for her waning horn, which hung low above the horizon, added but tenfold horror to the terrific desolation of the scene); the night-raven pouring on the dull ear of evening her frightful screams, and breaking on the otherwise uninterrupted stillness,—were the melancholy greetings to their new habitation.

They alighted at the antique entrance, and, passing through a vast and comfortless hall, were conducted into a saloon not much less so. The coolness of the evening, for it was late in the autumn, made the wood fire, which had been lighted, disperse a degree of comfort; and Wolfstein, having arranged his domestic concerns, continued talking with Megalena until midnight.

"But you have never yet correctly explained to me," said Megalena, "the mystery which encircled that strange man whom we met at the inn at Breno. I think I have seen him once since, or I should not now have thought of the circumstance."

"Indeed, Megalena, I know of no mystery. I suppose the man was mad, or wished to make us think so; for my part, I have never thought of him since; nor intend to think of him."

"Do you not?" exclaimed a voice, which enchained motionless to his seat the horror-struck Wolfstein—when turning round, and starting in agonized frenzy from his chair, Ginotti himself—*Ginotti*—from whose terrific gaze never had he turned unappalled, stood in cool and fearless contempt before him!

"Do you not?" continued the mysterious stranger. "Never again intendest thou to think of me?—me! who have watched each expanding idea, conscious to what I was about to apply them, conscious of the great purpose for which each was formed. Ah! Wolfstein, by my agency shalt thou——" He paused, assuming a smile expressive of exultation and superiority.

"Oh! do with me what thou wilt, strange, inexplicable being!—Do with me what thou wilt!" exclaimed Wolfstein, as an ecstasy of frenzied terror overpowered his astonished senses. Megalena still sat unmoved: she was surprised, it is true; but most was she surprised, that an event like this should have power so to shake Wolfstein; for even then he stood gazing in enhorrored silence on the majestic figure of Ginotti.

"Fool, then, that thou art, to deny me!" continued Ginotti, in a tone less solemn, but more severe. "Wilt thou promise me that, when I come to demand what thou covenantedst with me at Breno, I meet no fears, no scruples, but that, then, thou wilt perform what there thou didst swear, and that *this* oath shall be inviolable?"

"It shall," replied Wolfstein.

"Swear it."

"As I keep my vows with you, may God reward me hereafter!"

"'Tis done, then," returned Ginotti. "Ere long shall I claim the performance of this covenant—now farewell." Speaking thus, Ginotti dashed away; and, mounting a horse which stood at the gate, sped swiftly across the heath. His form lessened in the clear moonlight; and when it was no longer visible to the straining eyeballs of Wolfstein, he felt, as it were, a spell which had enthralled him, to be dissolved.

Reckless of Megalena's earnest entreaties, he threw himself into a chair, in deep and gloomy melancholy; he answered them not, but, immersed in a train of corroding ideas, remained silent. Even when retired to repose, and he could, occasionally, sink into a transitory slumber, would he again start from it, as he thought that Ginotti's majestic form leaned over him, and that the glance which, last, his fearful eye had thrown, chilled his breast with indescribable agony. Slowly lagged the time to Wolfstein: Ginotti, though now gone, and far away perhaps, dwelt in his disturbed mind; his image was there imprinted in characters terrific and indelible. Oft would he wander along the desolate heath; on every blast of wind which sighed over the scattered remnants of what was once a forest, Ginotti's, the terrific Ginotti's voice seemed to float; and in every dusky recess, favoured by the descending shades of gloomy night, his form appeared to lurk, and, with frightful glare, his eye to penetrate the conscience-stricken Wolfstein as he walked. A falling leaf, or a hare starting from her heathy seat, caused him to shrink with affright; yet, though dreading loneliness, he was irresistibly compelled to seek for solitude. Megalena's charms had now no longer power to speak comfort to his soul: ephemeral are the friendships of the wicked, and involuntary disgust follows the attachment founded on the visionary fabric of passion or interest. It sinks in the merited abyss of ennui, or is followed by apathy and carelessness, which amply its origin deserved.

The once ardent and excessive passion of Wolfstein for Megalena, was now changed into disgust and almost detestation; he sought to conceal it from her, but it was evident, in spite of his resolution. He regarded her as a woman capable of the most shocking enormities; since, without any adequate temptation to vice, she had become sufficiently depraved to consider an inconsequent crime the wilful and premeditated destruction of a fellow-creature; still, whether it were from the indolence which he had contracted, or an indefinably sympathetic connexion of soul, which forbade them to part during their mortal existence, was Wolfstein irremediably linked to his mistress, who was as depraved as himself, though originally of a better disposition. He likewise had, at first, resisted the allurements of vice; but, overpowered by its incitements, had resigned himself, indeed reluctantly, to its influence. But Megalena had courted its advances, and endeavoured to conquer neither the suggestions of crime, nor the dictates of a nature prone to the attacks of *appetite*—let me not call it passion.

Fast advanced winter; cheerless and solitary were the days. Wolfstein, occasionally, followed the chase; but even *that* was wearisome: and the bleeding image of the murdered Olympia, or the still more dreaded idea of the terrific Ginotti, haunted him in the midst of its tumultous pleasures, and embittered every moment of his existence. The pale corpse too of Cavigni, blackened by poison, reigned in his chaotic imagination and stung his soul with tenfold remorse, when he reflected that he had murdered one who never had injured him, for the sake of a being whose depraved society every succeeding day rendered more monotonous and insipid.

It was one evening when, according to his custom, Wolfstein wandered late: it was in the beginning of December, and the weather was peculiarly mild for the season and latitude. Over the cerulean expanse of ether the dim moon, shrouded in the fleeting fragments of vapour, which, borne on the pinions of the northern blast, crossed her pale orb; at intervals, the dismal hooting of the owl, which, searching for prey, flitted her white wings over the dusky heath; the silver beams which slept on the outline of the far-seen forests, and the melancholy stillness, uninterrupted save by these concomitants of gloom, conduced to sombre reflection. Wolfstein reclined upon the heath; he retraced, in mental review, the past events of his life, and shuddered at the darkness of his future destiny. He strove to repent of his crimes; but, though conscious of the connexion which existed between the ideas, as often as repentance presented itself to his mind, Ginotti rushed upon his troubled imagination, and a dark veil seemed to separate him for ever from contrition, notwithstanding he was constantly subjected to the tortures inflicted by it. At last, wearied with the corroding recollections, the acme of which progressively increased, he bent his steps again towards his habitation.

As he was entering the portal, a grasp of iron arrested his arm, and, turning round, he recognized the tall figure of Ginotti, which, enveloped in a mantle, had leaned against a jutting buttress. Amazement, for a time, chained the faculties of Wolfstein in motionless surprise: at last he recollected himself, and, in a voice trembling from agitation, inquired, did he now demand the performance of the promise?

"I come," he said, "I come to demand it, Wolfstein! Art thou willing to perform what thou hast promised?—but come——"

A degree of solemnity, mixed with concealed fierceness, toned his voice as he spoke; yet was he fixed in the attitude in which first he had addressed Wolfstein. The pale ray of the moon fell upon his dark features, and his coruscating eye fixed on his trembling victim's countenance, flashed with almost intolerable brilliancy. A chill horror darted through Wolfstein's sickening frame; his brain swam around wildly, and most appalling presentiments of what was about to happen, pressed upon his agonized intellect. "Yes, yes, I have promised, and I will perform the covenant I have entered into," said Wolfstein; "I swear to you that I will!" and as he spoke, a kind of mechanical and inspired feeling steeled his soul to fortitude; it seemed to arise independently of himself; nor could he, though he eagerly desired to do so, control in the least his *own* resolves. Such an impulse as this had first induced him to promise at all. Ah! how often in Ginotti's absence had he resisted it! but when the mysterious disposer of the events of his existence was before him, a consciousness of the inutility of his refusal compelled him to submit to the mandates of a being, whom his heart sickening to acknowledge, it unwillingly confessed as a superior.

"Come," continued Ginotti; "the hour is late, I must dispatch."

Unresisting, yet speaking not, Wolfstein conducted Ginotti to an apartment.

"Bring wine, and light a fire," said he to his servant, who quickly obeyed him. Wolfstein swallowed an overflowing goblet, hoping thereby to acquire courage; for he found that, with every moment of Ginotti's stay, the visionary and awful terrors of his mind augmented.

"Do you not drink?"

"No," replied Ginotti, sullenly.

A pause ensued; during which the eyes of Ginotti, glaring with demoniacal scintillations, spoke tenfold terrors to the soul of Wolfstein. He knitted his brows, and bit his lips, in vain attempting to appear unembarrassed. "Wolfstein!" at last said Ginotti, breaking the fearful silence; "Wolfstein!"

The colour fled from the cheek of his victim, as thus Ginotti spoke: he moved his posture, and awaited, in anxious and horrible solicitude, the declaration which was, as he supposed, to ensue. "My name, my family, and the circumstances which have attended my career through existence, it neither boots you to know, nor me to declare."

"Does it not?" said Wolfstein, scarcely knowing what to say; yet convinced, from the pause, that something was expected.

"No! nor canst thou, nor any other existent being, even attempt to dive into the mysteries which envelope me. Let it be sufficient for you to know, that every event in your life has not only been known to me, but has occurred under my particular machinations."

Wolfstein started. The terror which had blanched his cheek now gave way to an expression of fierceness and surprise; he was about to speak, but Ginotti, noticing not his motion, thus continued:

"Every opening idea which has marked, in so decided and so eccentric an outline, the fiat of your future destiny, has not been unknown to or unnoticed by me. I rejoiced to see in you, whilst young, the progress of that genius which in mature time would entitle you to the reward which I destine for you, and for you alone. Even when far, far away, when the ocean perhaps has roared between us, have I known your thoughts, Wolfstein; yet have I known them neither by conjecture nor inspiration. Never would your mind have attained that degree of expansion or excellence, had not I watched over its every movement, and taught the sentiment, as it unfolded itself, to despise contented vulgarity. For this, and for an event far more important than any your existence yet has been subjected to, have I watched over you: say, Wolfstein, have I watched in vain?"

Each feeling of resentment vanished from Wolfstein's bosom, as the mysterious intruder spoke: his voice at last died, in a clear and melancholy cadence, away; and his expressive eye, divested of its fierceness and mystery, rested on Wolfstein's countenance with a mild benignity.

"No, no; thou hast not watched in vain, mysterious disposer of my existence. Speak! I burn with curiosity and solicitude to learn for what thou hast thus superintended me:" and, as thus he spoke, a feeling of resistless anxiety to know what would be the conclusion of the night's adventure, took place of horror. Inquiringly he gazed on the countenance of Ginotti, the features of whom were brightened with unwonted animation. "Wolfstein," said Ginotti, "often hast thou sworn that I should rest in the grave in peace:—now listen."

CHAPTER IX

> If Satan had never fallen,
> Hell had been made for thee.*
>
> The Revenge.

Ah! poor, unsuspecting innocence! and is that fair flower about to perish in the blasts of dereliction and unkindness? Demon indeed must be he who could gaze on those mildly-beaming eyes, on that perfect form, the emblem of sensibility, and yet plunge the spotless mind of which it was an index, into a sea of repentance and unavailing sorrow. I should scarce suppose even a demon would act so, were there not many with hearts more depraved even than those of fiends, who first have torn some unsophisticated soul from the pinnacle of excellence, on which it sat smiling, and then triumphed in their hellish victory when it writhed in agonized remorse, and strove to hide its unavailing regret in the dust from which the fabric of her virtues had arisen. "*Ah! I fear me, the unsuspecting girl will go;*" she knows not the malice and the wiles of perjured man—and she is gone!

It was late in the evening, and Eloise had returned from her mother's funeral, sad and melancholy; yet, even amidst the oppression of grief, surprise, and astonishment, pleasure and thankfulness, that any one should notice her, possessed her mind as she read over and over the characters traced on the note which she still held in her hand. The hour was late, the moon was down, yet countless stars bedecked the almost boundless hemisphere. The mild beams of Hesper slept on the glassy surface of the lake, as, scarcely agitated by the zephyr of evening, its waves rolled in slow succession; the solemn umbrage of the pine-trees, mingled with the poplar, threw their undefined shadows on the water; and the nightingale, sitting solitary in the hawthorn, poured on the listening stillness of evening, her grateful lay of melancholy. Hark! her full strains swell on the silence of night, and now they die away, with lengthened and solemn cadence, insensibly into the breeze, which lingers, with protracted sweep, along the valley.

Ah! with what enthusiastic ecstasy of melancholy does he whose friend, whose dear friend, is far, far away, listen to such strains as these! perhaps he has heard them with that friend,—with one he loves: never again may they meet his ear. Alas! 'tis melancholy; I even now see him sitting on the rock which looks over the lake, in frenzied listlessness; and counting in mournful review, the days which are past since they fled so quickly with one who was dear to him.

It was to the ruined abbey which stood on the southern side of the lake that, so swiftly, Eloise is hastening. A presentiment of awe filled her mind; she gazed, in inquiring terror, around her, and scarce could persuade herself that shapeless forms lurked not in the gloomy recesses of the scenery.

She gained the abbey; in melancholy fallen grandeur its vast ruins reared their pointed casements to the sky. Masses of disjointed stone were scattered around; and, save by the whirrings of the bats, the stillness which reigned, was uninterrupted. Here then was Eloise to meet the strange one who professed himself to be her friend. Alas! poor Eloise believed him. It yet wanted an hour to the time of appointment; the expiration of that hour Eloise awaited. The abbey brought to her recollection a similar ruin which stood near St. Irvyne; it brought with it the remembrance of a song which Marianne had composed soon after her brother's death. She sang, though in a low voice:

Song

How stern are the woes of the desolate mourner,
  As he bends in still grief o'er the hallowed bier,
As enanguish'd he turns from the laugh of the scorner,
  And drops, to perfection's remembrance, a tear;
When floods of despair down his pale cheek are streaming,
When no blissful hope on his bosom is beaming,
Or, if lull'd for awhile, soon he starts from his dreaming,
  And finds torn the soft ties to affection so dear.

Ah! when shall day dawn on the night of the grave,
  Or summer succeed to the winter of death;
Rest awhile, hapless victim, and Heaven will save
  The spirit, that faded away with the breath.
Eternity points in its amaranth bower,
Where no clouds of fate o'er the sweet prospect lower,
Unspeakable pleasure, of goodness the dower,
  When woe fades away like the mist of the heath.

She ceased: the melancholy cadence of her angelic voice died in faint reverberations of echo away, and once again reigned stillness.

Now fast approached the hour; and, ere ten had struck, a stranger of towering and gigantic proportions walked along the ruined refectory; without stopping to notice other objects, he advanced swiftly to Eloise, who sat on a misshapen piece of ruin, and throwing aside the mantle which enveloped his figure, discovered to her astonished sight the stranger of the Alps, who of late had been incessantly present to her mind. Amazement, for a time, chained each faculty in stupefaction; she would have started from her seat, but the stranger, with gentle violence grasping her hand, compelled her to remain where she was.

"Eloise," said the stranger, in a voice of the most fascinating tenderness—"Eloise!"

The softness of his accents changed, in an instant, what was passing in the bosom of Eloise. She felt no surprise that he knew her name; she experienced no dread at this mysterious meeting with a person, at the bare mention of whose name she was wont to tremble: no, the ideas which filled her mind were indefinable. She gazed upon his countenance for a moment, then, hiding her face in her hands, sobbed loudly.

"What afflicts you, Eloise?" said the stranger: "how cruel, that such a breast as thine should be tortured by pain!"

"Ah!" cried Eloise, forgetting that she spoke to a stranger; "how can one avoid sorrow, when there, perhaps, is scarce a being in the world whom I can call my friend; when there is no one on whom I lay claim for protection?"

"Say not, Eloise," cried the stranger, reproachfully, yet benignly; "say not that you can claim none as a friend—you may claim me. Ah! that I had ten thousand existences, that each might be devoted to the service of one whom I love more than myself! Make me then the repository of your every sorrow and secret. I love you, indeed I do, Eloise, and why will you doubt me?"

"I do not doubt you, stranger," replied the unsuspecting girl; "why should I doubt you? for you could have no interest in saying so, if you did not.—I thank you for loving one who is quite, quite friendless; and, if you will allow me to be your friend, I will love you too. I never loved any one, before, but my poor mother and Marianne. Will you then, if you are a friend to me, come and live with me and Marianne, at St. Irvyne's?"

"St. Irvyne's!" exclaimed the stranger, almost convulsively, as he interrupted her; then, as fearing to betray his emotions, he paused, yet quitted not the grasp of Eloise's hand, which trembled within his with feelings which her mind distrusted not.

"Yes, sweet Eloise, I love you indeed," at last he said, affectionately. "And I thank you much for believing me; but I cannot live with you at St. Irvyne's. Farewell, for to-night, however; for my poor Eloise has need of sleep." He then was quitting the abbey, when Eloise stopped him to inquire his name.

"Frederic de Nempere."

"Ah! then I shall recollect Frederic de Nempere, as the name of a friend, even if I never again behold him."

"Indeed I am not faithless; soon shall I see you again. Farewell, beloved Eloise." Thus saying, with rapid step he quitted the ruin.

Though he was now gone, the sound of his tender farewell yet seemed to linger on the ear of Eloise; but with each moment of his absence, became lessened the conviction of his friendship, and heightened the suspicions which, though unaccountable to herself, possessed her bosom. She could not conceive what motive could have led her to own her love for one whom she feared, and felt a secret terror, from the conviction of the resistless empire which he possessed within her: yet though she shrank from the bare idea of ever becoming his, did she ardently, though scarcely would she own it to herself, desire again to see him.

Eloise now returned to Geneva: she resigned herself to sleep, but even in her dreams was the image of Nempere present to her imagination. Ah! poor deluded Eloise, didst thou think a *man* would merit thy love through disinterestedness? didst thou think that one who supposed himself superior, yet inferior in reality, to you, in the scale of existent beings, would desire thy society from *love?* yet superior as the fool here supposes himself to be to the creature whom he injures, superior as he boasts himself, he may howl with the fiends of darkness, in never-ending misery, whilst thou shalt receive, at the throne of the God whom thou hast loved, the rewards of that unsuspecting excellence, which he who boasts his superiority, shall *suffer* for trampling upon. Reflect on *this*, ye libertines, and, in the full career of the lasciviousness which has unfitted your souls for enjoying the *slightest* real happiness here or hereafter, tremble! Tremble! I say; for the day of retribution will arrive. But the poor Eloise need not tremble; the victims of your detested cunning need not fear that day: no!—then will the cause of the broken-hearted be avenged by Him to whom their wrongs cry for redress.

Within a few miles of Geneva, Nempere possessed a country-house: thither did he persuade Eloise to go with him; "For," said he, "though I cannot come to St. Irvyne's, yet my friend will live with me."

"Yes indeed I will," replied Eloise; for, whatever she might feel when he was absent, in his presence she felt insensibly softened, and a sentiment nearly approaching to love would, at intervals, take possession of her soul. Yet was it by no means an easy task to lure Eloise from the paths of virtue; it is true she knew but little, nor was the expansion of her mind such as might justify the exultations of a fiend at a triumph over her virtue; yet was it that very timid, simple innocence which prevented Eloise from understanding to what the deep-laid sophistry of her false friend tended; and, not understanding it, she could not be influenced by its arguments. Besides, the principles and morals of Eloise were such as could not *easily* be shaken by the allurements which temptation might throw out to her unsophisticated innocence.

"Why," said Nempere, "are we taught to believe that the union of two who love each other is wicked, unless authorized by certain rites and ceremonials, which certainly cannot change the tenour of sentiments which it is destined that these two people should entertain of each other?"

"It is, I suppose," answered Eloise, calmly, "because God has willed it so; besides," continued she, blushing at she knew not what, "it would——"

"And is then the superior and towering soul of Eloise subjected to sentiments and prejudices so stale and vulgar as these?" interrupted Nempere indignantly. "Say, Eloise, do not you think it an insult to two souls, united to each other in the irrefragable covenants of love and congeniality, to promise, in the sight of a Being whom they know not, that fidelity which is certain otherwise?"

"But I do know that Being!" cried Eloise, with warmth; "and when I cease to know him, may I die! I pray to him every morning, and, when I kneel at night, I thank him for the mercy which he has shown to a poor friendless girl like me! He is the protector of the friendless, and I love and adore him!"

"Unkind Eloise! how canst thou call thyself friendless? Surely, the adoration of two beings unfettered by restraint, must be most acceptable!—But, come, Eloise, this conversation is nothing to the purpose: I see we both think alike, although the *terms* in which we express our sentiments are different. Will you sing to me, dear Eloise?" Willingly did Eloise fetch her harp; she wished not to scrutinize what was passing in her mind, but, after a short prelude, thus began:—

Song

I

Ah! faint are her limbs, and her footstep is weary,
  Yet far must the desolate wanderer roam;
Though the tempest is stern, and the mountain is dreary,
  She must quit at deep midnight her pitiless home.
I see her swift foot dash the dew from the whortle,
As she rapidly hastes to the green grove of myrtle;
And I hear, as she wraps round her figure the kirtle,
  "Stay thy boat on the lake,—dearest Henry, I come."

II

High swell'd in her bosom the throb of affection
  As lightly her form bounded over the lea,
And arose in her mind every dear recollection;
  "I come, dearest Henry, and wait but for thee."
How sad, when dear hope every sorrow is soothing,
When sympathy's swell the soft bosom is moving,
And the mind the mild joys of affection is proving,
  Is the stern voice of fate that bids happiness flee!

III

Oh! dark lower'd the clouds on that horrible eve,
  And the moon dimly gleam'd through the tempested air;
Oh! how could fond visions such softness deceive?
  Oh! how could false hope rend a bosom so fair?
Thy love's pallid corse the wild surges are laving,
O'er his form the fierce swell of the tempest is raving;
But, fear not, parting spirit; thy goodness is saving,
  In eternity's bowers, a seat for thee there.

"How soft is that strain!" cried Nempere, as she concluded.

"Ah!" said Eloise, sighing deeply: "'tis a melancholy song; my poor brother wrote it, I remember, about ten days before he died. 'Tis a gloomy tale concerning him; he ill deserved the fate he met. Some future time I will tell it you; but now, 'tis very late.—Good-night."

Time passed, and Nempere, finding that he must proceed more warily, attempted no more to impose upon the understanding of Eloise by such palpably baseless arguments; yet, so great and so unaccountable an influence had he gained on her unsuspecting soul, that ere long, on the altar of vice, pride, and malice, was immolated the innocence of the spotless Eloise. Ah, ye proud! in the severe consciousness of unblemished reputation, in the fallacious opinion of the world, why turned ye away, as if fearful of contamination, when yon poor frail one drew near? See the tears which steal adown her cheek!—*She* has repented, *ye* have not!

And thinkest thou, libertine, from a principle of depravity—thinkest thou that thou hast raised thyself to the level of Eloise, by trying to sink her to thine own?—No!—Hopest thou that thy curse has passed away unheeded or unseen? The God whom thou hast insulted has marked thee!—In the everlasting tablets of heaven is thine offence written!—but poor Eloise's crime is obliterated by the mercy of Him, who knows the innocence of her heart.

* * * * * *

Yes—thy sophistry hath prevailed, Nempere!—'tis but blackening the memoir of thine offences! Hark! what shriek broke upon the enthusiastic silence of twilight? 'Twas the fancied scream of one who loved Eloise long ago, but now is—dead. It warns thee—alas! 'tis unavailing!!—'Tis fled, but not for ever.

It is evening; the moon, which rode in cloudless and unsullied majesty, in the leaden-coloured east, hath hidden her pale beams in a dusky cloud, as if blushing to contemplate a scene of so much wickedness.

'Tis done; and amidst the vows of a transitory delirium of pleasure, regret, horror, and misery, arise! they shake their Gorgon locks at Eloise! appalled she shudders with affright, and shrinks from the contemplation of the consequences of her imprudence. Beware, Eloise!—a precipice, a frightful precipice yawns at thy feet! advance yet a step further, and thou perishest! No, give not up thy religion—it is that alone which can support thee under the miseries, with which imprudence has so darkly marked the progress of thine existence!

CHAPTER X

> The elements respect their Maker's seal!
>   Still like the scathed pine-tree's height,
>   Braving the tempests of the night,
> Have I 'scaped the bickering flame.
> Like the scathed pine, which a monument stands
> Of faded grandeur, which the brands
>   Of the tempest-shaken air
> Have riven on the desolate heath;
> Yet it stands majestic even in death,
>   And rears its wild form there.
>
> WANDERING JEW.

YET, in an attitude of attention, Wolfstein was fixed, and, gazing upon Ginotti's countenance, awaited his narrative.

"Wolfstein," said Ginotti, "the circumstances which I am about to communicate to you are, many of them, you may think, trivial; but I must be minute, and, however the recital may excite your astonishment, suffer me to proceed without interruption."

Wolfstein bowed affirmatively—Ginotti thus proceeded:—

"From my earliest youth, before it was quenched by complete satiation, *curiosity*, and a desire of unveiling the latent mysteries of nature, was the passion by which all the other emotions of my mind were intellectually organized. This desire first led me to cultivate, and with success, the various branches of learning which led to the gates of wisdom. I then applied myself to the cultivation of philosophy, and the éclât with which I pursued it, exceeded my most sanguine expectations. *Love* I cared not for; and wondered why men perversely sought to ally themselves with weakness. Natural philosophy at last became the peculiar science to which I directed my eager inquiries; thence was I led into a train of labyrinthic meditations. I thought of *death*—I shuddered when I reflected, and shrank in horror from the idea, *selfish and self-interested* as I was, of entering a new existence to which I was a stranger. I must either dive into the recesses of futurity, or I must not, I cannot die.—'Will not this nature—will not the *matter* of which it is composed—exist to all eternity? Ah! I know it will; and, by the exertions of the energies with which nature has gifted me, well I know it shall.' This was my opinion at that time: I then believed that there existed no God. Ah! at what an exorbitant price have I bought the conviction that there is one!!! Believing that priestcraft and superstition were all the religion which *man* ever practised, it could not be supposed that I thought there existed supernatural beings of any kind. I believed *nature* to be self-sufficient and excelling; I supposed not, therefore, that there could be anything beyond nature.

"I was now about seventeen: I had dived into the depths of metaphysical calculations. With sophistical arguments had I convinced myself of the non-existence of a First Cause, and, by every combined modification of the essences of matter, had I apparently proved that no existences could possibly be, unseen by human vision. I had lived, hitherto, completely for myself; I cared not for others; and, had the hand of fate swept from the list of the living every one of my youthful associates, I should have remained immoved and fearless. I had not a friend in the world;—I cared for nothing but *self*. Being fond of calculating the effects of poison, I essayed one, which I had composed, upon a youth who had offended me; he lingered a month, and then expired in agonies the most terrific. It was returning from his funeral, which all the students of the college where I received my education (Salamanca)* had attended, that a train of the strangest thought pressed upon my mind. I feared, more than ever, now, to die; and, although I had no right to form hopes or expectations for longer life than is allotted to the rest of mortals, yet did I think it were possible to protract existence. And why, reasoned I with myself, relapsing into melancholy, why am I to suppose that these muscles or fibres are made of stuff more durable than those of other men? I have no right to suppose otherwise than that, at the end of the time allotted by nature, for the existence of the atoms which compose my being, I must, like all other men, perish, perhaps everlastingly.—Here, in the bitterness of my heart, I cursed that nature and chance which I believed in; and, in a paroxysmal frenzy of contending passions, cast myself, in desperation, at the foot of a lofty ash-tree, which reared its fantastic form over a torrent which dashed below.

"It was midnight; far had I wandered from Salamanca; the passions which agitated my brain, almost to delirium, had added strength to my nerves, and swiftness to my feet; but, after many hours' incessant walking, I began to feel fatigued. No moon was up, nor did one star illume the hemisphere. The sky was veiled by a thick covering of clouds; and, to my heated imagination, the winds, which in stern cadence swept along the night-scene, whistled tidings of death and annihilation. I gazed on the torrent, foaming beneath my feet; it could scarcely be distinguished through the thickness of the gloom, save at intervals, when the white-crested waves dashed at the base of the bank on which I stood. 'Twas then that I contemplated self-destruction; I had almost plunged into the tide of death, had rushed upon the unknown regions of eternity, when the soft sound of a bell from a neighbouring convent, was wafted in the stillness of the night. It struck a chord in unison with my soul; it vibrated on the secret springs of rapture. I thought no more of suicide, but, reseating myself at the root of the ash-tree, burst into a flood of tears;—never had I wept before; the sensation was new to me; it was inexplicably pleasing. I reflected by what rules of science I could account for it: *there* philosophy failed me. I acknowledged its inefficacy; and, almost at *that* instant, allowed the existence of a superior and beneficent *Spirit*, in whose image is made the soul of man; but quickly chasing these ideas, and, overcome by excessive and unwonted fatigue of mind and body, I laid my head upon a jutting projection of the tree, and, forgetful of every thing around me, sank into a profound and quiet slumber. Quiet, did I say? No—It was not quiet. I dreamed that I stood on the brink of a most terrific precipice, far, far above the clouds, amid whose dark forms which lowered beneath, was seen the dashing of a stupendous cataract: its roarings were borne to mine ear by the blast of night. Above me rose, fearfully embattled and rugged, fragments of enormous rocks, tinged by the dimly gleaming moon; their loftiness, the grandeur of their misshapen proportions, and their bulk, staggering the imagination; and scarcely could the mind itself scale the vast loftiness of their aërial summits. I saw the dark clouds pass by, borne by the impetuosity of the blast, yet felt no wind myself. Methought darkly gleaming forms rode on their almost palpable prominences.

"Whilst thus I stood, gazing on the expansive gulf which yawned before me, methought a silver sound stole on the quietude of night. The moon became as bright as polished silver, and each star sparkled with scintillations of inexpressible whiteness. Pleasing images stole imperceptibly upon my senses, when a ravishingly sweet strain of dulcet melody seemed to float around. Now it was wafted nearer, and now it died away in tones to melancholy dear. Whilst I thus stood enraptured, louder swelled the strain of seraphic harmony; it vibrated on my inmost soul, and a mysterious softness lulled each impetuous passion to repose. I gazed in eager anticipation of curiosity on the scene before me; for a mist of silver radiance rendered every object but myself imperceptible; yet was it brilliant as the noon-day sun. Suddenly, whilst yet the full strain swelled along the empyrean sky, the mist in one place seemed to dispart, and through it, to roll clouds of deepest crimson. Above them, and seemingly reclining on the viewless air, was a form of most exact and superior symmetry. Rays of brilliancy, surpassing expression, fell from his burning eye, and the emanations from his countenance tinted the transparent clouds below with silver light. The phantasm advanced towards me; it seemed then, to my imagination, that his figure was borne on the sweet strain of music which filled the circumambient air. In a voice which was fascination itself, the being addressed me, saying, 'Wilt thou come with me? wilt thou be mine?' I felt a decided wish never to be his. 'No, no,' I unhesitatingly cried, with a feeling which no language can either explain or describe. No sooner had I uttered these words, than methought a sensation of deadly horror chilled my sickening frame; an earthquake rocked the precipice beneath my feet; the beautiful being vanished; clouds, as of chaos, rolled around, and from their dark masses flashed incessant meteors. I heard a deafening noise on every side; it appeared like the dissolution of nature; the blood-red moon, whirled from her sphere, sank beneath the horizon. My neck was grasped firmly, and, turning round in an agony of horror, I beheld a form more hideous than the imagination of man is capable of portraying, whose proportions, gigantic and deformed, were seemingly blackened by the inerasible traces of the thunderbolts of God; yet in its hideous and detestable countenance, though seemingly far different, I thought I could recognize that of the lovely vision: 'Wretch!' it exclaimed, in a voice of exulting thunder; 'saidst thou that thou wouldst not be mine? Ah! thou art mine beyond redemption; and I triumph in the conviction, that no power can ever make thee otherwise. Say, art thou willing to be mine?' Saying this, he dragged me to the brink of the precipice: the contemplation of approaching death frenzied my brain to the highest pitch of horror. 'Yes, yes, I am thine,' I exclaimed. No sooner had I pronounced these words than the visionary scene vanished, and I awoke. But even when awake, the contemplation of what I had suffered, whilst under the influence of sleep, pressed upon my disordered fancy; my intellect, wild with unconquerable emotions, could fix on no one particular point to exert its energies; they were strained beyond their power of exerting.

"Ever, from that day, did a deep-corroding melancholy usurp the throne of my soul. At last, during the course of my philosophical inquiries, I ascertained the method by which *man* might exist for ever, and it was connected with my dream. It would unfold a tale of too much horror to trace, in review, the circumstances as then they occurred; suffice it to say, that I became acquainted that a *superior* being really exists: and ah! how dear a price have I paid for the knowledge! To one man alone, Wolfstein, may I communicate this secret of immortal life: then must I forego *my* claim to it,—and oh! with what pleasure shall I forego it! To you I bequeath the secret; but first you must swear that if . . . . you wish God may . . . ."

"I swear," cried Wolfstein, in a transport of delight; burning ecstasy revelled through his veins; pleasurable coruscations were emitted from his eyes. "I swear," continued he; "and if ever . . . . may God . . . ."

"Needless were it for me," continued Ginotti, "to expatiate further upon the *means* which I have used to become master over your every action; that will be sufficiently explained when you have followed my directions. Take," continued Ginotti, "—— and —— and ——; mix them according to the directions which this book will communicate to you. Seek, at midnight, the ruined abbey near the castle of St. Irvyne, in France; and there—I need say no more—there you will meet with me."

CHAPTER XI

THE varying occurrences of time and change, which bring anticipation of better days, brought none to the hapless Eloise. Nempere now having gained the point which his villainy had projected, felt little or no attachment left for the unhappy victim of his baseness; he treated her indeed most cruelly, and his unkindness added greatly to the severity of her afflictions. One day, when, weighed down by the extreme asperity of her woes, Eloise sat leaning her head on her hand, and mentally retracing, in sickening and mournful review, the concatenated occurrences which had led her to become what she was, she sought to change the bent of her ideas, but in vain. The feelings of her soul were but exacerbated by the attempt to quell them. Her dear brother's death, that brother so tenderly beloved, added a sting to her sensations. Was there any one on earth to whom she was now attracted by a wish of pouring in the friend's bosom ideas and feelings indefinable to any one else? Ah, no! that friend existed not; never, never more would she know such a friend. Never did she really love any one; and now had she sacrificed her conviction of right and wrong to a man who neither knew how to appreciate her excellence, nor was adequate to excite other sensation than of terror and dread.

Thus were her thoughts engaged, when Nempere entered the apartment, accompanied by a gentleman, whom he unceremoniously announced as the Chevalier Mountfort, an Englishman of rank, and his friend. He was a man of handsome countenance and engaging manners. He conversed with Eloise with an ill-disguised conviction of his own superiority, and seemed indeed to assert, as it were, a right of conversing with her; nor did Nempere appear to dispute his apparent assumption. The conversation turned upon music; Mountfort asked Eloise her opinion; "Oh!" said Eloise, enthusiastically, "I think it sublimes the soul to heaven; I think it is, of all earthly pleasures, the most excessive. Who, when listening to harmoniously-arranged sounds of music, exists there, but must forget his woes, and lose the memory of every earthly existence in the ecstatic emotions which it excites? Do you not think so, Chevalier?" said she; for the liveliness of his manner enchanted Eloise, whose temper, naturally elastic and sprightly, had been damped as yet by misery and seclusion. Mountfort smiled at the energetic avowal of her feelings; for, whilst she yet spoke, her expressive countenance became irradiated by the emanation of sentiment.

"Yes," said Mountfort, "it is indeed powerfully efficient to excite the interests of the soul; but does it not, by the very act of resuscitating the feelings, by working upon the, perhaps, long dead chords of secret and enthusiastic rapture, awaken the powers of grief as well as pleasure?"

"Ah! it may do both," said Eloise, sighing.

He approached her at that instant. Nempere arose, as if intentionally, and left the room. Mountfort pressed her hand to his heart with earnestness: he kissed it, and then resigning it, said, "No, no, spotless untainted Eloise; untained even by surrounding depravity: not for worlds would I injure you. Oh! I can conceal it no longer—will conceal it no longer—Nempere is a villain."

"Is he?" said Eloise, apparently resigned, *now*, to the severest shocks of fortune: "then, then indeed I know not with whom to seek an asylum. Methinks all are villains."

"Listen, then, injured innocence, and reflect in whom thou hast confided. Ten days ago, in the gaming-house at Geneva, Nempere was present. He engaged in play with me, and I won of him considerable sums. He told me that he could not pay me now, but that he had a beautiful girl, whom he would give to me, if I would release him from the obligation. 'Est-elle une fille de joie?' I inquired. 'Oui, et de vertu praticable.' This quieted my conscience. In a moment of licentiousness, I acceded to his proposal; and, as money is almost valueless to me, I tore the bond for three thousand zechins: but did I think that an angel was to be sacrificed to the degraded avarice of the being to whom her fate was committed? By heavens, I will this moment seek him—upbraid him with his inhuman depravity,—and——"

"Oh! stop, stop," cried Eloise, "do not seek him; all, all is well—

I will leave him. Oh! how I thank you, stranger, for this unmerited pity to a wretch who is, alas! too conscious that she deserves it not."—"Ah! you deserve every thing," interrupted the impassioned Mountfort; "you deserve paradise. But leave this perjured villain; and do not say, unkind fair-one, that you have no friend: indeed, you have a most warm, disinterested friend in me."—"Ah! but," said Eloise, hesitatingly, "what will the——"

"World say," she was about to have added; but the conviction of having so lately and so flagrantly violated every regard to its opinion—she only sighed. "Well," continued Mountfort, as if not perceiving her hesitation; "you will accompany me to a cottage ornée, which I possess at some little distance hence? Believe that your situation shall be treated with the deference which it requires; and, however I may have yielded to habitual licentiousness, I have too much honour to disturb the sorrows of one who is a victim to that of another." Licentious and free as had been the career of Mountfort's life, it was by no means the result of a nature naturally prone to vice; it had been owing to the unchecked sallies of an imagination not sufficiently refined. At the desolate situation of Eloise, however, every good propensity in his nature urged him to take compassion on her. His heart, originally susceptible of the finest feelings, was touched, and he really and sincerely—yes, a libertine, but not one from principle, sincerely meant what he said.

"Thanks, generous stranger," said Eloise, with energy; "indeed I *do* thank you." For not yet had acquaintance with the world sufficiently bidden Eloise distrust the motives of its disciples. "I accept your offer, and only hope that my compliance may not induce you to regard me otherwise than I am."

"Never, never can I regard you as other than a suffering angel," replied the impassioned Mountfort. Eloise blushed at what the energetic force of Mountfort's manner assured her was not intended as a compliment.

"But may I ask my generous benefactor, *how*, *where*, and *when* am I to be released?"

"Leave that to me," returned Mountfort: "be ready to-morrow night at ten o'clock. A chaise will wait beneath."

Nempere soon entered; their conversation was uninterrupted, and the evening passed away uninteresting and slow.

Swiftly fled the intervening hours, and fast advanced the moment when Eloise was about to try, again, the compassion of the world. Night came, and Eloise entered the chaise; Mountfort leaped in after her. For awhile her agitation was excessive. Mountfort at last succeeded in calming her; "Why, my dearest Ma'am'selle," said he, "why will you thus needlessly agitate yourself? I *swear* to hold your honour far dearer than my own life; and my companion ——"

"What companion?" Eloise interrupted him, inquiringly.

"Why," replied he, "a friend of mine, who lives at my cottage; he is an Irishman, and so *very* moral, and so averse to every species of *gaieté de cœur*, that you need be under no apprehensions. In short, he is a love-sick swain, without ever having found what he calls a *congenial* female. He wanders about, writes poetry, and, in short, is much *too sentimental* to occasion you any alarm on that account. And, I assure you," added he, assuming a more serious tone, "although I may not be quite so far gone in romance, yet I have feelings of honour and humanity which teach me to respect your sorrows as my own."

"Indeed, indeed I believe you, generous stranger; nor do I think that you *could* have a friend whose principles are dishonourable."

Whilst yet she spoke, the chaise stopped, and Mountfort, springing from it, handed Eloise into his habitation. It was neatly fitted up in the English taste.

"Fitzeustace," said Mountfort to his friend, "allow me to introduce you to Madame Eloise de ——." Eloise blushed, as did Fitzeustace.

"Come," said Fitzeustace, to conquer *mauvaise honte*, "supper is ready, and the lady doubtlessly fatigued."

Fitzeustace was finely formed, yet there was a languor which pervaded even his whole figure: his eyes were dark and expressive, and as, occasionally, they met those of Eloise, gleamed with excessive brilliancy, awakened doubtlessly by curiosity and interest. He said but little during supper, and left to his more vivacious friend the whole of Eloise's conversation, who, animated at having escaped a persecutor, and one she hated, displayed extreme command of social powers. Yes, once again was Eloise vivacious: the sweet spirit of social intercourse was not dead within,—that spirit which illumes even slavery, which makes its horrors less terrific, and is not annihilated in the dungeon itself.

At last arrived the hour of retiring.—Morning came.

The cottage was situated in a beautiful valley. The odorous perfume of roses and jasmine wafted on the zephyr's wing, the flowery steep which rose before it, and the umbrageous loveliness of the surrounding country, rendered it a spot the most fitted for joyous seclusion. Eloise wandered out with Mountfort and his friend to view it; and so accommodating was her spirit, that, ere long, Fitzeustace became known to her as familiarly as if they had been acquainted all their lives.

Time fled on, and each day seemed only to succeed the other purposely to vary the pleasures of this delightful retreat. Eloise sung in the summer evenings, and Fitzeustace, whose taste for music was most exquisite, accompanied her on his oboe.

By degrees the society of Fitzeustace, to which before she had preferred Mountfort's, began to be more interesting. He insensibly acquired a power over the heart of Eloise, which she herself was not aware of. She involuntarily almost sought his society; and when, which frequently happened, Mountfort was absent at Geneva, her sensations were indescribably ecstatic in the society of his friend. She sat in mute, in silent rapture, listening to the notes of his oboe, as they floated on the stillness of evening: she feared not for the future, but, as it were, in a dream of rapturous delight, supposed that she must ever be as now—happy; not reflecting that, were he who caused that happiness absent, it would exist no longer.

Fitzeustace madly, passionately doted on Eloise; in all the energy of incontaminated nature, he sought but the happiness of the object of his whole affections. He sought not to investigate the causes of his woe; sufficient was it for him to have found one who could *understand*, could *sympathize in*, the feelings and sensations which every child of nature whom the world's refinements and luxury have not vitiated, must feel,—that affection, that contempt of selfish gratification, which every one, whose soul towers at all above the multitude, must acknowledge. He destined Eloise, in his secret soul, for his own. He resolved to die—he wished to live with her; and would have purchased one instant's happiness for her with ages of hopeless torments to be inflicted on himself. He loved her with passionate and excessive tenderness: were he absent from her but a moment, he would sigh with love's impatience for her return; yet he feared to avow his flame, lest this, perhaps, baseless dream of rapturous and enthusiastic happiness might fade;—then, indeed, Fitzeustace felt that he must die.

Yet was Fitzeustace mistaken; Eloise loved him with all the tenderness of innocence; she confided in him unreservedly; and, though unconscious of the nature of the love she felt for him, returned each enthusiastically energetic prepossession of his towering mind with ardour excessive and unrestrained. Yet did Fitzeustace suppose that she loved him not. Ah! why did he think so?

Late one evening, Mountfort had gone to Geneva, and Fitzeustace wandered with Eloise towards that spot which Eloise selected as their constant evening ramble on account of its superior beauty. The tall ash and oak, in mingled umbrage, sighed far above their heads; beneath them were walks, artificially cut, yet imitating nature. They wandered on, till they came to a pavilion which Mountfort had caused to be erected. It was situated on a piece of land entirely surrounded by water, yet peninsulated by a rustic bridge which joined it to the walk.

Hither, urged mechanically, for their thoughts were otherwise employed, wandered Eloise and Fitzeustace. Before them hung the moon in cloudless majesty; her orb was reflected by every movement of the crystalline water, which, agitated by the gentle zephyr, rolled tranquilly. Heedless yet of the beauties of nature, the loveliness of the scene, they entered the pavilion.

Eloise convulsively pressed her hand on her forehead.

"What is the matter, my dearest Eloise?" inquired Fitzeustace, whom awakened tenderness had thrown off his guard.

"Oh! nothing, nothing; but a momentary faintness. It will soon go off; let us sit down."

They entered the pavilion.

"'Tis nothing but drowsiness," said Eloise, affecting gaiety; "'twill soon go off. I sate up late last night; that I believe was the occasion."

"Recline on this sofa, then," said Fitzeustace, reaching another pillow to make the couch easier; "and I will play some of those Irish tunes which you admire so much."

Eloise reclined on the sofa, and Fitzeustace, seated on the floor, began to play; the melancholy plaintiveness of his music touched Eloise; she sighed, and concealed her tears in her handkerchief. At length she sunk into a profound sleep: still Fitzeustace continued playing, noticing not that she slumbered. He now perceived that she spoke, but in so low a tone, that he knew she slept.

He approached. She lay wrapped in sleep; a sweet and celestial smile played upon her countenance, and irradiated her features with a tenfold expression of etheriality. Suddenly the visions of her slumbers appeared to have changed; the smile yet remained, but its expression was melancholy; tears stole gently from under her eyelids:—she sighed.

Ah! with what eagerness of ecstasy did Fitzeustace lean over her form! He dared not speak, he dared not move; but pressing a ringlet of hair which had escaped its band, to his lips, waited silently.

"Yes, yes; I think—it may——" at last she muttered; but so confusedly, as scarcely to be distinguishable.

Fitzeustace remained rooted in rapturous attention, listening.

"I thought, I thought he looked as if he could love me," scarcely articulated the sleeping Eloise. "Perhaps, though he may not love me, he may allow me to love him.—Fitzeustace!"

On a sudden, again were changed the visions of her slumbers; terrified she started from sleep, and cried, "Fitzeustace!"

CHAPTER XII

For love is heaven, and heaven is love.
LAY OF THE LAST MINSTREL.

NEEDLESS were it to expatiate on their transports; they loved each other, and that is enough for those who have felt like Eloise and Fitzeustace.

One night, rather later indeed than it was Mountfort's custom to return from Geneva, Eloise and Fitzeustace sat awaiting his arrival. At last it was too late any longer even to expect him; and Eloise was about to bid Fitzeustace good-night, when a knock at the door aroused them. Instantly, with a hurried and disordered step, his clothes stained with blood, his countenance convulsed and pallid as death, in rushed Mountfort.

An involuntary exclamation of surprise burst from the terrified Eloise.

"What—what is the matter?"

"Oh, nothing, nothing!" answered Mountfort, in a tone of hurried, yet desperate agony. The wildness of his looks contradicted his assertions. Fitzeustace, who had been inquiring whether he was wounded, on finding that he was not, flew to Eloise.

"Oh! go, go!" she exclaimed. "Something, I am convinced, is wrong. Tell me, dear Mountfort, what it is—in pity tell me."

"Nempere is dead!" replied Mountfort, in a voice of deliberate desperation; then, pausing for an instant, he added in an undertone: "And the officers of justice are in pursuit of me. Adieu, Eloise!—Adieu, Fitzeustace! You know I must part with you—you know how unwillingly. My address is at—London.—Adieu! —once again, adieu!"

Saying this, as by a convulsive effort of despairing energy, he darted from the apartment, and, mounting a horse which stood at the gate, swiftly sped away. Fitzeustace well knew the impossibility of his longer stay; he did not seem surprised, but sighed.

"Ah! well I know," said Eloise, violently agitated, "I well

know myself to be the occasion of these misfortunes. Nempere sought for me; the generous Mountfort would not give me up, and now is he compelled to fly—perhaps may not even escape with life. Ah! I fear it is destined that every friend must suffer in the fatality which environs me.* Fitzeustace!" she uttered this with such tenderness, that, almost involuntarily, he clasped her hand, and pressed it to his bosom, in the silent, yet expressive enthusiasm of love. "Fitzeustace! you will not likewise desert the poor isolated Eloise?"

"Say not isolated, dearest love. Can, can you fear my love, whilst your Fitzeustace exists? Say, adored Eloise, shall we *now* be united, *never*, *never* to part again? Say, will you consent to our immediate union?"

"Know you not," exclaimed Eloise, in a low, faltering voice, "know you not that I *have been* another's?"

"Oh! suppose me not," interrupted the impassioned Fitzeustace, "the slave of such vulgar and narrow-minded prejudice. Does the frightful vice and ingratitude of Nempere sully the spotless excellence of my Eloise's soul?—No, no,—that must ever continue uncontaminated by the frailty of the body in which it is enshrined. It must rise superior to the earth: 'tis that which I adore, Eloise. Say, say, was *that* Nempere's?"

"Oh! no, never!" cried Eloise, with energy. "Nothing but *fear* was Nempere's."

"Then why say you that ever you were *his?*" said Fitzeustace, reproachfully. "You never *could* have been his, destined as you were for mine, from the first instant the particles composing the soul which I adore, were assimilated by the God whom I worship."

"Indeed, believe me, dearest Fitzeustace, I love you, far beyond anything existing—indeed, existence were valueless, unless enjoyed with you!"

Eloise, though a *something* prevented her from avowing them, *felt* the enthusiastic and sanguine ideas of Fitzeustace to be true: her soul, susceptible of the most exalted virtue and expansion, though cruelly nipped in its growth, thrilled with delight unexperienced before, when she found a being who could understand and perceive the truth of her feelings, and indeed *anticipate* them, as did Fitzeustace; and *he*, while gazing on the index of that soul, which associated with his, and animated the body of Eloise, but for him, felt delight, which, glowing and enthusiastic as had been his picture of happiness, he never expected to know. His dark and beautiful eye gleamed with tenfold lustre; his every nerve, his every pulse, confessed the awakened consciousness, that *she*, on whom his soul had doted, ever since he acknowledged the existence of his intellectuality, was present before him.

A short space of time passed, and Eloise gave birth to the son of Nempere. Fitzeustace cherished it with the affection of a father; and, when occasionally he necessarily must be absent from the apartment of his beloved Eloise, his whole delight was to gaze on the child, and trace in its innocent countenance the features of the mother who was so beloved by him.

Time no longer dragged heavily to Eloise and Fitzeustace: happy in the society of each other, they wished nor wanted other joys; united by the laws of their God, and assimilated by congeniality of sentiment, they supposed that each succeeding month must be like this, must pass like this, in the full satiety of every innocent union of mental enjoyment. While thus the time sped in rapturous succession of delight, autumn advanced.

The evening was late, when, at the usual hour, Eloise and Fitzeustace took the way to their beloved pavilion. Fitzeustace was unusually desponding, and his ideas for futurity were marked by the melancholy of his mind. Eloise in vain attempted to soothe him; the contention of his mind was but too visible. She led him to the pavilion. They entered it. The autumnal moon had risen; her dimly-gleaming orb, scarcely now visible, was shrouded in the darkness of the atmosphere: like the spirit of the spotless ether, which shrinks from the obtrusive gaze of man, she hung behind a leaden-coloured cloud. The wind in low and melancholy whispering sighed among the branches of the towering trees; the melody of the nightingale, which floated upon its dying cadences, alone broke on the solemnity of the scene. Lives there, whose soul experiences no degree of delight, is susceptible of no gradations of feelings, at change of scenery? Lives there, who can listen to the cadence of the evening zephyr, and not acknowledge, in his mind, the sensations of celestial melancholy which it awakens? for, if he does, his life were valueless, his death were undeplored. Ambition, avarice, ten thousand mean, ignoble passions, had extinguished within him that soft, but indefinable sensorium of unallayed delight, with which his soul, whose susceptibility is not destroyed by the demands of selfish appetite, thrills exultingly, and wants but the union of another, of whom the feelings are in unison with his own, to constitute almost insupportable delight.

Let Epicureans argue, and say, "There is no pleasure but in the gratification of the senses." Let them enjoy their own opinion; I want not *pleasure*, when I can enjoy *happiness*. Let Stoics say, "Every idea that there are fine feelings, is weak; he who yields to them is even weaker." Let those too, wise in their own conceit, indulge themselves in sordid and degrading hypotheses; let them suppose human nature capable of no influence from anything but materiality; so long as I enjoy the innocent and *congenial* delight, which it were needless to define to those who are strangers to it, I am satisfied.

"Dear Fitzeustace," said Eloise, "tell me what afflicts you; why are you so melancholy?—Do not we mutually love, and have we not the unrestrained enjoyment of each other's society?"

Fitzeustace sighed deeply; he pressed Eloise's hand. "Why does my dearest Eloise suppose that I am unhappy?" The tone of his voice was tremulous, and a deadly settled paleness dwelt on his cheek.

"Are you not unhappy, then, Fitzeustace?"

"I know I ought not to be so," he replied, with a faint smile;—he paused—"Eloise," continued Fitzeustace, "I know I ought not to grieve, but you will, perhaps, pardon me when I say, that a father's curse, whether from the prejudice of education, or the innate consciousness of its horror, agitates my mind. I cannot leave you, I cannot go to England; and will you then leave your country, Eloise, to accommodate me? No, I do not, I ought not to expect it."

"Oh! with pleasure; what is country? what is everything without you? Come, my love, dismiss these fears, we yet may be happy."

"But before we go to England, before my father will see us, it is necessary that we should be married—nay, do not start, Eloise; I view it in the light that you do: I consider it an human institution, and incapable of furnishing that bond of union by which alone can intellect be conjoined; I regard it as but a chain, which, although it keeps the body bound, still leaves the soul unfettered: it is not so with love. But still, Eloise, to those who think like us, it is at all events harmless; it is but yielding to the prejudices of the world wherein we live, and procuring moral expediency, at a slight sacrifice of what we conceive to be right."

"Well, well, it shall be done, Fitzeustace," resumed Eloise; "but take the assurance of *my* promise that I cannot love you more."

They soon agreed on a point of, in their eyes, so trifling importance, and arriving in England, tasted that happiness, which love and innocence alone can give. Prejudice may triumph for awhile, but virtue will be eventually the conqueror.

CONCLUSION

It was night—all was still: not a breeze dared to move, not a sound to break the stillness of horror. Wolfstein has arrived at the village near which St. Irvyne stood; he has sped him to the château, and has entered the edifice; the garden door was open, and he entered the vaults.

For a time, the novelty of his situation, and the painful recurrence of past events, which, independently of his own energies, would gleam upon his soul, rendered him too much confused to investigate minutely the recesses of the cavern. Arousing himself, at last, however, from this momentary suspension of faculty, he paced the vaults in eager desire for the arrival of midnight. How inexpressible was his horror when he fell on a body which appeared motionless and without life! He raised it in his arms, and, taking it to the light, beheld, pallid in death, the features of Megalena. The laugh of anguish which had convulsed her expiring frame, still played around her mouth, as a smile of horror and despair; her hair was loose and wild, seemingly gathered in knots by the convulsive grasp of dissolution. She moved not; his soul was nerved by almost superhuman powers; yet the ice of despair chilled his burning brain Curiosity, resistless curiosity, even in a moment such as this, reigned in his bosom. The body of Megalena was breathless, and yet no visible cause could be assigned for her death. Wolfstein dashed the body convulsively on the earth, and, wildered by the suscitated energies of his soul almost to madness, rushed into the vaults.

Not yet had the bell announced the hour of midnight. Wolfstein sate on a projecting mass of stone; his frame trembled with a burning anticipation of what was about to occur; a thirst of knowledge scorched his soul to madness; yet he stilled his wild energies,—yet he awaited in silence the coming of Ginotti. At last the bell struck; Ginotti came; his step was rapid, and his manner wild; his figure was wasted almost to a skeleton, yet it retained its loftiness and grandeur; still from his eye emanated that indefinable expression which ever made Wolfstein shrink appalled. His cheek was sunken and hollow, yet was it flushed by the hectic of despairing exertion. "Wolfstein," he said, "Wolfstein, part is past—the hour of agonizing horror is past; yet the dark and icy gloom of desperation braces this soul to fortitude;—but come, let us to business." He spoke, and threw his mantle on the ground. "I am blasted to endless torment," muttered the mysterious. "Wolfstein, dost thou deny thy Creator?"—"Never, never."—"Wilt thou not?"—"No, no,—anything but that."

Deeper grew the gloom of the cavern. Darkness almost visible seemed to press around them; yet did the scintillations which flashed from Ginotti's burning gaze, dance on its bosom. Suddenly a flash of lightning hissed through the lengthened vaults: a burst of frightful thunder seemed to convulse the universal fabric of nature; and, borne on the pinions of hell's sulphurous whirlwind, he himself, the frightful prince of terror, stood before them. "Yes," howled a voice superior to the bursting thunder-peal; "yes, thou shalt have eternal life, Ginotti." On a sudden Ginotti's frame mouldered to a gigantic skeleton, yet two pale and ghastly flames glared in his eyeless sockets. Blackened in terrible convulsions, Wolfstein expired; over him had the power of hell no influence. Yes, endless existence is thine, Ginotti—a dateless and hopeless eternity of horror.

* * * * * * *

Ginotti is Nempere. Eloise is the sister of Wolfstein. Let then the memory of these victims to hell and malice live in the remembrance of those who can pity the wanderings of error; let remorse and repentance expiate the offences which arise from the delusion of the passions, and let endless life be sought from Him who alone can give an eternity of happiness.

EXPLANATORY NOTES

A NOTE ON NAMES

SOME of the names and attributes of characters in *Zastrozzi* and *St Irvyne* reveal the extent of Shelley's debt to previous Gothic fiction. Perhaps the most obvious example involves Megalena Strozzi, the sinister temptress from Charlotte Dacre's *Zofloya, or, The Moor* (1806) who engineers the stabbing of her rivals and who eventually joins a robber band before committing suicide with her lover. Megalena Strozzi lends a variant of her surname to the title of *Zastrozzi* and her general character to its figure of *Matilda*, as well as to her namesake (Megalena de Metastasio) in *St Irvyne*.

Matilda (La Contessa di Laurentini) is a name from the first Gothic novel, Horace Walpole's *The Castle of Otranto* (1764), where Matilda is the virtuous daughter of the villainous father who eventually stabs her, mortally, when he mistakes her for another. Matilda is also the name of the duplicitous demon who assumes several disguises in Matthew G. Lewis's *The Monk* (1796). In Dacre's *Zofloya* there is a Laurina, wife of the Marchese de Loridani, whose names seem to anticipate Matilda's 'Laurentini'. In this same novel, Loridani's vicious daughter Victoria loves none but herself and fears only the Inquisition, a point that might be made about Shelley's Matilda.

Shelley's *Julia* (La Marchesa de Strobazzo) has several possible antecedents. In Ann Radcliffe's *A Sicilian Romance* (1790) Julia, daughter of Ferdinand, Marquis of Mazzini, falls in love with Count Vereza (*Verezzi*?), to the consternation of her step-mother, who has her own eye on the Count. John Palmer's *The Mystery of the Black Tower* (1796) contains a virtuous Julia, a vicious Lord Edmund Fitzallan, and a lecherous baroness. Helen Maria Williams's *Julia* (1790) is thematically related to Shelley's novels, though its plot differs. Williams's preface declares her novel's purpose to be 'to trace the danger arising from the uncontrouled [sic] indulgence of strong affections', a point clearly relevant to both Shelley's novels. Moreover, like Shelley's Julia and, initially, Verezzi, and like Eloise and Fitzeustace in *St Irvyne*, Williams's Julia and her lover Frederick Seymour both excel at suppressing their passions. Finally, there is almost certainly a link with Rousseau's *Julie, ou la nouvelle Heloise* (1761), which sets out to argue that virtue and married bliss can triumph over immorality and promiscuity, and which enjoyed a considerable vogue in England.

Cavigni may be related to the anonymous *Fatal Vows, or The False Monk* (1810), in which a Count Savini has two sons (as in Schiller's *The Robbers*), one of whom leaves home and forms a relationship with a man who has saved him from a band of robbers, a situation not unlike that with which *St Irvyne* opens.

Eloise de St Irvyne's name is curiously like that of Emily St Aubert, the sensitivity-laden daughter who is orphaned in Ann Radcliffe's *The Mysteries of Udolpho* (1794). There is also an echo, both in the name and in the thematic element of the elixir of life, with William Godwin's *St Leon* (1799).

Finally, *Fitzeustace*, the very Shelleyan character in *St Irvyne*, is made the more Shelleyan by his name; Shelley and Thomas Jefferson Hogg had in 1810 published a volume of poems entitled *Posthumous Fragments of Margaret Nicholson*, supposedly edited by a fictitious 'John Fitzvictor'.

ZASTROZZI

3 *That their God . . . revenge*: the epigraph is from *Paradise Lost*, II, 368–71. Spoken to the assembly of fallen angels at the council in Hell, it is part of Beelzebub's proposal for obtaining revenge upon God. The notion of attacking God by sabotaging what is presumably dear to Him is an example of the sort of guerrilla warfare that will recur in the Creature's practice in Mary Shelley's *Frankenstein*.

7 *twined*: *turned* in the original.

11 *'Who ordered me then . . .'*: *then* is not in the original.

16 *Passau*: a Lower Bavarian river port city situated on the Austrian-German border, at the point where the Danube is joined by its tributary the Inn River, some 140km ENE. of Munich. Passau is historically associated with the Niebelungen legend and is still frequently known as the 'Niebelungen Town'.

18 *Rosenheim*: a Bavarian town on the Inn River some 120km upstream (SW.) of Passau and 40km SE. of Munich. Rosenheim was already an important trade centre in the Middle Ages.

20 *Schaffhausen*: a northern Swiss city on the right bank of the Rhine some 30km north of Zurich and 30km west of the Bodensee.

25 *the horses which Bernado brought*: this is an extreme—though not an

extraordinary—example of the tendency in Gothic fiction to telescope events and incidents. Zastrozzi mounts horses which *in the previous sentence* he was still waiting for and which are never reported to have arrived.

31 *wily*: this is the word typically associated with the Serpent of Eden, both in traditional biblical commentary and in *Paradise Lost*. There is an additional overtone here of the Circe myth, particular when on p. 32 Matilda is reported to 'practise new arts, employ new blandishments, to detain under her roof the fascinated Verezzi'. The notion of spells and deceit involved in both myths are present as well in Milton's *Comus*. The temptation through physical or sensual appetite is, of course, directly related to the myth of the Fall.

37 *VIII*: in the original edition it is Chapter IX (not Chapter VII) which appears to be omitted; that is, the sequence is chapters VI, VII, VIII, X . . ., rather than VI, VIII, IX . . . as represented by the edition reproduced here.

40 *fleeted*: this is most likely a grammatically clumsy version of 'fled'.

45 *composing*: *temporary* in the original.

52 *the memory of Julia*: *my Julia* in the original.

55 *gigantic and misshapen forms*: here and elsewhere in *Zastrozzi* and (especially) *St Irvyne*, Shelley's landscape echoes *The Wandering Jew*, the poem he had composed with Thomas Medwin. That juvenile work exhibits Shelley's strong preference for the adjective 'scathed', as in the following passage:

> The Elements respect their Maker's seal!
> Still like the scathed pine tree's height,
> Braving the tempests of the night
> Have I 'scaped the flickering flame.
> Like the scathed pine, which a monument stands
> Of faded grandeur, which the brands
> Of the tempest-shaken air
> Have riven on the desolate heath;
> Yet it stands majestic even in death,
> And rears its wild form there.
>
> [*Works*, 882–3)

59 *the feelings of his soul . . . unknown to her*: there is an interesting anticipation here of Shelley's 1816 poem *Alastor*, both in the general scene and, more importantly, in Verezzi's isolationistic devotion to

his 'idolised' (or idealized) Julia. In *Alastor* the young poet searches for an impossibly ideal female counterpart; his self-destructive pursuit leads him to abandon human society and eventually to die on a remote mountain crag. Matilda's tendency in this passage to 'affect' and 'feign' postures and responses underscores the satanic duplicity already hinted at when she is earlier described as 'wily'.

79 *il consiglio di dieci*: the Council of Ten, presumably an advisory council to the Inquisition.

81 *the Brenta*: the Brenta river flows south from the Alps to the Adriatic Sea. During Shelley's lifetime the river entered the Lagoon of Venice, but in 1896 its mouth shifted to its present location, just south-east of Chioggia, a port and fishing centre some 10km south of Venice.

the Rialto: the famous bridge over the Grand Canal in Venice. The bridge (1588–91) consists of a single marble arch. The Rialto is also the name of the oldest quarter of Venice.

83 *Julia*: this is actually our first sight of Julia.

84 *frigorific*: a deliberately archaic word meaning 'producing cold, freezing', first known as an adjective *c.*1667 (*OED*).

91 *scarcely yet cold*: even given the Italian climate, it seems unlikely the body would still be warm, considering the lapse of a night's time.

ST IRVYNE, OR, THE ROSICRUCIAN

109 *St Irvyne*: the original first page has the full title.

110 *the victims . . . inflicted on me*: note how Wolfstein's sentiments here echo the discussion between Matilda and Zastrozzi in *Zastrozzi* (pp. 47–8).

115 *'Twas dead of night . . . bear me*: this poem had already appeared, with slight variations, as a fragment in *Original Poetry by Victor and Cazire*. See *Works*, p. 856.

123 *Rise on . . . the blast*: the original contains the following footnote: 'Taken almost word for word from the poem of Lachin y Gair in Byron's *Hours of Idleness*. Newark, 1807, p. 130.—Ed.'

131 *Placenza*: this is Piacenza, occasionally still known by its ancient name of Placentia, a village in north central Italy some 50km SE. of Milan.

132 *Breno*: a village in the Italian Alps, situated on the Oglio River, in the Lombardy province of Brescia.

135 *Whence . . . athwart my way*: these are the opening lines of Satan's first speech to Death, his own child by Sin, when the two first meet at the Gates of Hell (*Paradise Lost*, II, 681–3).

143 *sensibility*: a venerable term in later eighteenth-century literature, where it denotes an extraordinary susceptibility to impression and emotion. Characters like that which Megalena *used to be*, who exhibit 'sensibility', are characterized by their powerful emotions; they tend to be less concerned with incidents and events themselves than with how they *feel* about those incidents and events. The powerful *negative* emotions and passions of characters like Megalena are, of course, directly related to the whole notion of 'sensibility', as is indeed all of Gothic fiction.

146 *whose only crime . . . adoration of you*: ironically, Megalena's professions of attachment here echo those which Wolfstein had conveyed to her earlier as Cavigni's emissary.

151 *witht*: this is simply a misprint.

155 *Chapter VII*: Shelley's chapter headings skip from Chapter IV to Chapter VII, apparently omitting Chapters V and VI. This *may* be the result of careless preparation of his manuscript, but it is equally possible that the 'gap' was created deliberately. See the Introduction.

156 *leafless from the season*: Shelley may have been thinking about Wordsworth's 'Tintern Abbey' here; Wordsworth's poem also records the return to a familiar and loved scene after an absence of five years. Shelley's early work was much influenced by Wordsworth, as is particularly apparent in a poem like *Alastor* (1816).

159 *Ah! why do . . . cease to be*: the original contains the following footnote: 'These two lines are taken *verbatim* from Byron's *Hours of Idleness.* —Ed.'

165 *Why then . . . skeleton hand*: Shelley quotes the poem he and Thomas Medwin had written.

172 *If Satan . . . for thee*: these lines are from Edward Young's tragedy, *The Revenge* (1721).

181 *Salamanca*: city in western Spain, some 190km WNW. of Madrid. The university, founded in the early thirteenth century by Alfonso

IX of Leon, soon became one of the greatest in Europe. In the later Middle Ages and the Renaissance the university was the centre of cultural and religious life in Spain. It reached its zenith in the sixteenth century, after which it declined along with the city.

194 *I fear it is destined . . . environs me*: there is a touching irony in Eloise's line, for it anticipates one Shelley would use about his own situation some ten years later. Commenting upon the death of his 'Neopolitan charge', the mysterious child Elena Adelaide [Shelley], Shelley wrote to his friends John and Maria Gisborne in July of 1820: 'It seems as if the destruction that is consuming me were as an atmosphere which wrapt & infected everything connected with me' (*Letters*, II, 211).

199 Shelley did not 'finish' his novel in the usual sense of providing a fully worked out conclusion. The haste with which he fashioned the ending is clear from the final lines. When the publisher, Stockdale, evidently objected, Shelley advised him on 14 November 1810 that

> Ginotti, as you will see did *not* die by Wolfstein's hand, but by the influence of that natural magic which when the secret was imparted to the latter, destroyed him.—Moun[t]fort, being a character of inferior import, I did not think it necessary to state the catastrophe of *him*, as at best it could be but uninteresting.—Eloise and Fitzeustace, are married and happy I suppose, and Megalena dies by the same means as Wolfstein.—I do not myself see any other explanation that is required.
>
> [*Letters*, I, 20]

Some five days later he did, however, add one other cryptic comment: 'on a re-examination you will perceive that Mountfort physically did kill Ginotti, which must appear from the latter's paleness' [*Letters*, I, 21].

THE WORLD'S CLASSICS

A Select List

SERGEI AKSAKOV: A Russian Gentleman
Translated by J. D. Duff
Edited by Edward Crankshaw

A Russian Schoolboy
Translated by J. D. Duff
With an introduction by John Bayley

Years of Childhood
Translated by J. D. Duff
With an introduction by Lord David Cecil

ROBERT BAGE: Hermsprong
Edited with an introduction by Peter Faulkner

WILLIAM BECKFORD: Vathek
Edited by Roger Lonsdale

JAMES BOSWELL: Life of Johnson
The Hill/Powell edition, revised by David Fleeman
With an introduction by Pat Rogers

JOHN CLELAND: Memoirs of a Woman of Pleasure (Fanny Hill)
Edited with an introduction by Peter Sabor

THOMAS DE QUINCEY:
The Confessions of an English Opium-Eater
Edited with an introduction by Grevel Lindop

MARIA EDGEWORTH: Castle Rackrent
Edited by George Watson

JOHN GALT: The Entail
Edited with an introduction by Ian A. Gordon

The Provost
Edited by Ian A. Gordon

WILLIAM GODWIN: Caleb Williams
Edited by David McCracken

JAMES HOGG: The Private Memoirs and
Confessions of a Justified Sinner
Edited by John Carey

MATTHEW LEWIS: The Monk
Edited by Howard Anderson

ANN RADCLIFFE:
The Italian
Edited by Frederick Garber

The Mysteries of Udolpho
Edited by Bonamy Dobrée

SIR WALTER SCOTT: The Heart of Midlothian
Edited by Clare Lamont

Redgauntlet
Edited by Kathryn Sutherland

Waverley
Edited by Claire Lamont

MARY SHELLEY: Frankenstein
Edited by M. K. Joseph

SIDNEY SMITH: Selected Letters
Edited by Nowell C. Smith
With an introduction by Auberon Waugh

HORACE WALPOLE: The Castle of Otranto
Edited by W. S. Lewis

MARY WOLLSTONECRAFT:
Mary *and* The Wrongs of Woman
Edited by Gary Kelly